Living Snakes of the World

in Color

Living
Snakes of
the World
in Color

John M. Mehrtens

Sterling Publishing Co., Inc. New York
Blandford Press Dorset, England

(Frontispiece)
Northern Central
American Dwarf Boa,
Ungaliophis
continentalis

J. Mehrtens

Library of Congress Cataloging-in-Publication Data

Mehrtens, John M.
    Living snakes of the world in color.

    Includes indexes.
    1. Snakes.   I. Title.
QL666.06M45 1987   597.96   87-9932
ISBN 0-8069-6460-X
ISBN 0-8069-6461-8 (lib. bdg.)

1   3   5   7   9   10   8   6   4   2

Copyright © 1987 by John M. Mehrtens
Published by Sterling Publishing Co., Inc.
Two Park Avenue, New York, N.Y. 10016
Distributed in Canada by Oak Tree Press Ltd.
c/o Canadian Manda Group, P.O. Box 920, Station U
Toronto, Ontario, Canada M8Z 5P9
Distributed in the United Kingdom by Blandford Press
Link House, West Street, Poole, Dorset BH15 1LL, England
Distributed in Australia by Capricorn Ltd.
P.O. Box 665, Lane Cove, NSW 2066
Manufactured in Italy
Printed in Italy

TABLE OF CONTENTS

For Doris R.

INTRODUCTION

It has been said that introductions to books are often written, but seldom read. With that in mind this introduction to *Living Snakes of the World* will be brief.

The book is intended to present an overview of the some three thousand species of snakes living today. The selection of the representative species has presented any number of difficulties, for *all* snakes are of both scientific and general interest. Nevertheless, the final selection has emphasized those that are most often seen in public reptile exhibits and private collections, or kept as "pets." It is hoped that the combination demonstrates the overall diversity of the snakes, and makes the book of value to herpetologists, both amateur and professional, reptile hobbyists, and the general reader.

The format is essentially standardized, a means of presenting a mass of generalized information in a concise manner while not neglecting details pertinent to the species discussed.

Although this book in no way purports to be a manual on captive care, brief notes on captive care have been included. These are included primarily on behalf of snakes already captive, and for those individuals whose only source of information is often overly simplified or obsolete literature. The inclusion of captive care notes is not to be construed as encouragement to keep any snake, harmless or venomous, captive, but rather to underscore the responsibility that any living thing, including the food animals, imposes upon its captor.

Those readers familiar with the technicalities, current interpretive techniques, and variables in taxonomy (the science of classification) will understand the problems of remaining abreast of valid changes in technical names. The taxonomy used here is current at the time of writing. In those cases where technical names remain in flux, e.g., *Bothrops,* both the proposed current name and the more familiar one have been used.

The conservation of snakes requires mention. Snakes are just as important to the closed ecosystem called Earth as are other animals, as well as plants. Unfortunately, they lack the emotional appeal of tigers and seal pups. However, both seal pups and snakes would benefit more from the actual control and preservation of habitat than the proliferation of regulations specifically addressed to individual species. Unfortunately, in a synthetic environment where many people view a city park as a "wild place," many conservation regulations and programs do little to salvage the remnants of the natural world.

ACKNOWLEDGMENTS

This book would have been impossible to write without drawing heavily on the accomplishments of those zoologists, past and present, whose work and dedication have contributed so greatly to the store of knowledge available to those who follow them. Far too numerous to list, their efforts are appreciated and herewith recognized.

I am indebted to a number of people, some of whom it has been my pleasure to have known for many years and others whom I have met during the compilation of this book. All have been of invaluable assistance, and their interest and support is most gratefully acknowledged.

Photographs were provided by F. Alvey, Atlanta Zoo, Atlanta, Georgia; D. Bakken, Chinook Ridge Herpetological Research Center, Alberta, Canada; D. Barker, Dallas Texas; R. D. Bartlett, Reptilian Breeding & Research Institute, Ft. Myers, Florida; W. Bazemore, Southhampton, New York; J. Behler, New York Zoological Society, New York; J. Bridges/B. Prince (DPI, Inc.), Miami, Florida; T. Buchanan, Abilene Zoological Society, Abilene, Texas; E. Chapman, Sr., Florida Reptile Importers, Miami, Florida; Dr. W. Dunson, Pennsylvania State University, Pennsylvania; Dr. H. Fischer, Los Angeles Zoo, Los Angeles, California; Dr. R. S. Funk, Wilmington, North Carolina; T. Granes, Tyler, Texas; Dr. R. Goris, Sugao, Japan; E. Harris, Binder Park Zoo, Battle Creek, Michigan; D. Hamper/F. Bolin, Columbus, Ohio; W. Lamar, University of Texas, Tyler, Texas; E. Maruska, Cincinnati Zoo, Cincinnati, Ohio; B. Mealey, Miami, Florida; L. Moor, Port Coquitlam, Canada; R. Pawley, Chicago Zoological Society, Chicago, Illinois; S. Reichling, Memphis Zoo, Memphis, Tennessee; P. Tolson/A. Weber, Toledo Zoo, Toledo, Ohio; L. Trutnau, Wittlich, West Germany; G. Van Horn, Reptile World Serpentarium, St. Cloud, Florida; E. Wagner, Seattle, Washington; J. Wahlstrom, Skansen Akvariet, Stockholm, Sweden; R. Whittall/P. Dow, Vancouver Aquarium, Vancouver, Canada.

Literature and reference material as well as specimens for photographic use were provided from the personal and/or commercial collections of M. Block, World Wide Primates, Inc.; E. Chapman, Sr. and E. Chapman, Jr., Florida Reptile Importers; Bill Chase, Charles P. Chase Co.; B. Levine (and staff), Pet Farm, Inc.; J. Waselewski, Natural Selections; and B. Brazaitis, all of Miami, Florida. D. Wong, Hong Kong, provided literature and translations relative to Chinese species. Father A. Bogadek, Hong Kong, provided copies of technical papers. T. Buchanan, General Curator, Abilene Zoological Gardens, provided both the photographs and data on *Trimerusurus wiroti*; and David E. Spiteri, Alta Loma, California, provided a pre-publication copy of his taxonomic revision of the Rosy Boas, *Lichaneura*.

For support and assistance in several ways, Gertie and Irwin Block, Miami, Florida; F. Gibbons, Torquay, England; T. Jones, Waco, Texas; and L. Van Sertima, Georgetown, Guyana are hereby acknowledged.

In addition to providing photographs, W. Lamar, Tyler, Texas, offered important taxonomic data; R. D. Bartlett reviewed several portions of the manuscript; and B. Mealey, Curator, Animal Exploratorium, Museum of Science, Miami, Florida, reviewed the entire manuscript, offering significant commentary and suggestions.

Any book requires the professional guidance of an interested and sensitive editor. Sheila Anne Barry of Sterling Publishing Company has admirably fullfilled that role as editor of *Living Snakes of the World*.

John M. Mehrtens
Miami, Florida

PRIMITIVE SNAKES

New Mexico Thread Snake, *Leptotyphlops dulcis dissectus*

R. D. Bartlett

The zoological order (group) to which all snakes (and their close relatives, the lizards) belong is the *Squamata*. Lizard-like creatures clearly belonging to this order appear as fossils in upper Permian and lower Triassic geological strata, deposited 250 million years ago. Fossils of true snakes are rare, the fragile nature of snake skeletons probably accounting for the sparsity of fossils. Nevertheless, 150 million year old (lower Cretaceous) specimens have been uncovered in South America, Africa, and elsewhere. Although readily definable as snakes (sub-order Serpentes), lizard-like skeletal structures are present.

Several major families and subfamilies of modern snakes retain anatomical remnants of their lizard-like ancestors in the form of vestigial pelvic girdles and hind limbs. Snakes possessing such vestigial structures are considered to be primitive.

All of the living species of primitive snakes with the exception of the Boas and Pythons are small animals, seldom seen as a result of their burrowing and/or subterranean (fossorial) habits.

The *Uropeltids* or Shield-tailed snakes of Asia have truncated tails larger and thicker than the rest of the body. Often covered with spines, the armored tail probably serves to protect these burrowing animals from predators.

The *Xenopeltids* also range throughout southeastern Asia. Their smooth, iridescent, metallic-appearing scales are the physical feature to which their common name, Sunbeam Snake, alludes.

An elaborate defense display is characteristic of the Asian Pipe snakes, members of another family of primitives, the *Aniliidae*. When threatened, Pipe snakes rear and flatten the posterior body, displaying the usually brightly colored ventral surface. The tail tip, projecting from the flattened body, completes the cobra-like effect. A single species of *Aniliid* occurs in South America as do some two dozen species of *Anomalepidid* snakes. These latter closely resemble the most primitive of living snakes, the Thread snakes, *Leptotyphlopids,* and Blind snakes, *Typhlopids*. Both are characterized by undifferentiated body scalations, blunt heads, diminutive eyes, and a smooth, shiny appearance—all of which are adaptations to a burrowing, underground existence.

Thread snakes are found throughout the world, in Africa, South America, and parts of Asia. Two species barely enter the United States, occurring in southern Texas and other southwestern states. They prefer a dry, sandy habitat and feed upon soft bodied insects, especially termites and ants, usually consuming only the soft abdomens of these insects. Thread snakes are oviparous, the tiny hatchlings emerging from rice grain-sized eggs.

Africa (both the continent and nearby islands), Central and South America, and the Australian region constitute the range of some 200 species of Blind snakes. Considered by some taxonomists to be degenerate blind lizards rather than snakes, most are under a foot in length, although an African species, *Typhlops schleglii,* attains nearly three feet in length.

Blind snakes feed upon termites, ants, and other small invertebrates. Most Blind snakes are oviparous, often depositing their eggs in termite nests, although several species are ovoviviparous, retaining their eggs internally and giving birth to living young. A seven-inch Australian species, *Typhlina bramina,* is known only from female specimens and is thought to be parthenogenetic, capable of reproducing without males. *Typhlina bramina* is unique among snakes in this respect, although several *Teiid* lizards, e.g., *Cnemidophorous,* reproduce in this manner.

R. D. Bartlett, R. Sayers

Australian Blind Snake, *Typhlops sp.* This blind snake photographed in New South Wales, Australia, is typical of the genus Typhlops throughout its range.

"TWO HEADED" SNAKE; FALSE CORAL SNAKE
(Anilius scytale scytale)

Habitat. Areas of loose, sandy soil

Geographic Range. The nominate race occurs from the Guianas and southeastern Venezuela, west to Ecuador and Peru.

Natural History. A red or orange snake, banded with black. The red scales of some populations are edged in black, giving a speckled effect. The color and pattern resemble that of typical Coral Snakes, *Micrurus.*

Anilius is a burrowing species, usually emerging only at night, especially during or after rains. They feed primarily upon burrowing amphibians *(Caecilians)*, lizards *(Amphisbaenids)*, and small snakes.

The sole New World representative of the *Aniliidae,* they bear living young and reach an adult length of about thirty inches. A harmless and innocuous snake, *Anilius* defends itself rather passively by hiding the head and presenting the blunt tail to the molester as a substitute; thus its popular name of "two-headed" snake.

A subspecies, *A. s. phelpsorum,* occurs in eastern and southern Venezuela.

Care. The specialized diet of *Anilius* almost precludes successful captive maintenance. If a proper food source is available, caging requirements for their Asian relatives, the Pipe Snakes, would be adequate.

PIPE SNAKE *(Cylindrophis rufus)*

Habitat. Mud flats, river deltas, rice paddies, swamps with soft, moist soil; common in cultivated areas

Geographic Range. Southeastern Asia; East Indies

Natural History. These primitive snakes, members of the family *Anilidae,* present a smooth, shiny, and slick appearance. They are black in color except for the ventral surface, which is a staggered mix of black and white squares. The underside of the tail is banded with white and sometimes red, the tip of the tail always being red or reddish-orange.

Pipe Snakes are burrowers, tunnelling through soft soil with auger-like movements of the head. A constrictor, it feeds on small snakes and eels. They are viviparous; up to twelve seven-inch-long young are born, the neonates burrowing from birth and feeding upon the same prey as the adults. Adults seldom exceed three feet in length.

An elaborate defensive procedure is used when the animal is uncovered or otherwise threatened. The body is flattened close to the ground with the head concealed beneath it. The tail and posterior portion of the body is flattened, arched and raised from the ground, the red tail tip appearing as a head. The effect is that of an angry, brightly marked cobra rearing in defense of itself.

A number of additional species of *Cylindrophis* and the closely allied genus *Anomochilus* range

from Sri Lanka westward, through Burma, Thailand, Vietnam, Malaysia, Sumatra, and other islands of Indonesia.

Care. Pipe Snakes, if received in good condition, fare well as captives. Several inches of shredded garden mulch suffice as a burrowing medium. The snakes will sometimes utilize a glass plate laid atop the substrate as part of the burrow, thus remaining visible to the keeper. Only dim lighting should be used. Temperatures of 76-80° F (24-27° C) are satisfactory. Captives accept small snakes as food as well as small, pre-killed mice.

Cylindrophis maculatus, another form of Pipe Snake from southeastern Asia. Like all Pipe Snakes, they are "cobra mimics."

SUNBEAM SNAKE
(Xenopeltis unicolor)

Habitat. Lowland river valleys, rice paddies, and similar areas with damp soil, near water

Geographic Range. Southern People's Republic of China (Guangdong and Yunnan provinces), Burma, the Malay Peninsula and Indonesia, east to the Celebes Islands

Natural History. A reddish brown, brown, or blackish, unicolored snake with an unpatterned whitish-grey venter. The popular name derives from the iridescence of its smooth, shiny scales.

Sunbeam Snakes are secretive burrowers, although they spend much time hidden beneath various shelters, emerging at dusk to forage for their prey of frogs, other snakes, and small mammals such as rodents and shrews. As do many other snakes, they apparently also feed on carrion; recorded incidents of birds included in their diet are probably based on this habit.

They are oviparous, up to eighteen eggs forming a clutch. Little is know of the hatchlings, which are identical to the adults in color and habits. Large adults may be four feet in length; the average size somewhat less.

Other than the probable future inclusion of the New World "python," *Loxocemus,* Sunbeam Snakes are now the sole representatives of the family *Xenopeltidae.* A southern People's Republic of China species, *Xenopeltis hainanensis,* found in Hainan, Zhejiang and Guangxi provinces, has been named.

Care. Sunbeam Snakes must be provided with a proper burrowing medium, which may be shredded bark garden mulch or slightly moistened sphagnum moss. They will remain hidden away most of the time; however, they will be visible to the keeper if a glass plate is placed atop the burrowing material. They require temperatures of 78-80° F (25-27° C), and will readily accept pre-killed mice from forceps.

Typical of the Shieldtails, *U. phillipsi* occurs in India. Note the similarity between head and tail.

R. S. Funk

Boa Constrictors and Anacondas

R. S. Funk

Boa Constrictor, *Boa constrictor subsp.*

Seldom if ever zoologically accurate, innumerable "jungle" movies, adventure stories and similar fictional escapades have portrayed the boa constrictor as an arch-villain sliding through the trees, and posing a threat to all and sundry, especially the heroine.

In reality, these usually docile animals do not drop out of trees, or for that matter even live in them. They most certainly do not devour people (including heroines), horses, or other large animals, simply because they do not reach the size that such gustatory feats would require. Even if they could, the ingestion of such a large-sized meal would render the boa helpless and unable to defend itself or escape from predators during such a mammoth digestive process. They do kill their prey by constriction, but do not "crush" the food animal—be it the imagined horse or the actual rat. The intense pressure of the constricting coils prevents both heart and lungs from functioning, causing almost instantaneous unconsciousness and death of the prey.

Boa constrictors and anacondas, or "water boas" as they are sometimes called, are placed within the zoological family *Boidae* and the specific subfamily *Boinae*. Both are primitive snakes, with vestigial pelvic girdles and hind limbs present. The latter terminate externally as a pair of claws or "spurs" as they are more accurately called, located on either side of the vent. Larger in males, the spurs probably are used in courtship and copulation. All of the *Boids* are ovoviviparous, giving birth to living young. Although no true placental connection between female and young exists as it does in mammals, there is undoubtedly a mechanism present that allows for the exchange of oxygen and other elements. Such a "basic" placenta has been demonstrated in a number of more advanced snakes such as rattlesnakes. Boa constrictors and anacondas are prolific animals, large specimens having litters of several dozen young, twelve to twenty-four inches or more in length, according to the size of the female.

Widespread throughout the neotropics, boa constrictors range from central Mexico through Central and South America as far south as Argentina. The vernacular, *Boa constrictor,* is identical to the technical name of this snake. Eleven subspecies have been defined.

Boa constrictor mexicana occurs in central and southern Mexico. Along with the Central American, *B. c. imperator,* it is a small, dull-colored animal, seldom exceeding four to five feet in length, although females may reach eight feet. The "Red-tailed boas" of South America are larger, heavier-bodied animals with vividly colored skin patterns, particularly in juveniles and young animals.

B. c. ortonii of Peru and western South America, the Black-bellied boa, *B. c. melanogaster* of Ecuador, and Amaral's boa, *B. c. amarali,* found in Brazil, Bolivia and Paraguay, are such subspecies. The boas occurring in northeastern South America, e.g., Venezuela, Surinam, Guyana, etc., are "red-tails" but have not yet been defined subspecifically.

The Argentine Boa, *B. c. occidentalis,* is confined to southeastern Bolivia and Argentina. Several insular races are known, which are the attractive Clouded boa, *B. c. nebulosa,* of Dominica, the Saboga boa, *B. c. sabogae,* of Saboga Island (Panama), the St. Lucia boa, *B. c. orophias* of St. Lucia in the Caribbean, and *B. c. sigma,* which occurs on the Tres Marias Islands off the coast of Mexico.

Anacondas are semi-aquatic, and thus have a more restricted geographic range than the boa constrictors that occur in a wide variety of habitats. Anacondas occur throughout most of the northern half of South America, but are confined to river valleys, swamps, marshes, and similar aquatic environments.

The Common Anaconda, *Eunectes murinus,* occurs throughout most of the geographic range. Although significant morphological variation occurs among the various populations, anacondas are poorly defined taxonomically and no reasonably valid subspecies are recognized.

The largest snake found in the neo-tropics, the Common Anaconda can reach a length of thirty-three feet and probably attains a length greater than this in rare instances.

The smaller Yellow (or Paraguayan) Anaconda, *Eunectes notaeus,* occurs in Paraguay and adjacent areas wherever suitable habitat occurs.

PERUVIAN BOA CONSTRICTOR; RED-TAILED BOA
(Boa constrictor ortonii)

Habitat. Dry, semi-arid llanos and savannahs
Geographic Range. Northwestern Peru
Natural History. For anyone unfamiliar with snakes, "boa constrictor" and "jungle" are almost synonomous. This association does not always hold true, however, and although some forms of the boa constrictor are found in what might be called "jungle," these snakes are very adaptable and occur in a very wide range of habitats. The Peruvian Boa, for example, occurs in the sparsely wooded, rocky semi-desert plains of Peru. As do all boas, they seek shelter in mammal burrows, hollow logs, and similar retreats.

The known maximum lengths of boas vary as greatly as the snakes themselves. The Central American forms rarely reach eight feet in length. The record length is based on a field measurement of the form found in Trinidad, and is eighteen and one-half feet. A captive female *B. c. ortonii* has

been taped at thirteen feet and seven inches. Two specimens of the form occurring in Surinam were thirteen feet and six inches and slightly over fourteen feet in length. All of these measurements relate to "Red-tails," and it would appear that the various subspecies found in northern South America attain the greatest lengths. Nevertheless, a really huge boa is a rarity, and a ten foot specimen may be considered an average large adult.

Boas, large and small, prey on a wide variety of mammals and birds. Young are born alive, an average fifteen to twenty inches in length. Small boas may forage in shrubs and trees, but as they grow larger and heavier they become primarily terrestrial.

As with any animal of wide geographic range and variability, boas are of considerable taxonomic interest. The Black-bellied Boa Constrictor, *B. c.*

A well-colored and patterned Surinamese *Boa constrictor*

T. Granes

melanogaster, was described and named in 1983. The same study relegated several forms, including *B. c. ortonii,* to the synonymy of *B. c. imperator.*

Care. Thousands of boas, usually juveniles, are kept as pets throughout the world. Larger specimens are a standard exhibit in zoological parks. Kept in simply furnished, clean and draft-free quarters at a substrate temperature of 78-82° F (25-28° C), and provided with adequate food in the form of pre-killed laboratory rodents and/or chicks, boas may live for more than twenty years. Properly maintained pairs reproduce readily.

Unfortunately, juvenile specimens are often sold with incorrect instructions for care that almost guarantee failure. They should not be kept on cedar shavings (odor and oils of this material irritate mucous membranes), or aquarium gravel (causes irritation and infections of the mouth), and they should not be given live food. A live mouse is an intruder in the small, caged world of the snake; its presence will trigger defense measures instead of the more important feeding response. The mouse, in addition, may seriously injure or even kill the snake!

J. Mehrtens

The Clouded Boa, *B. c. nebulosa,* is confined to the island of Dominica, and not particularly noted for having a placid disposition.

Despite their brilliant colors, *Boa constrictors* quickly vanish in the debris of the forest floor. The illustration is of a ten-foot specimen, photographed in the wild in Surinam.

F.R.I., Inc.

T. Granes

Boas are extremely variable in color and pattern as this aberrant specimen from Surinam demonstrates.

MALAGASY GROUND BOA
(Acrantophis madagascariensis)

Habitat. Sparse, open woodland
Geographic Range. Madagascar (formerly Malagasy Republic)
Natural History. This close relative of the tropical American boa constrictor occurs in suitable habitat throughout central and northern Madagascar. Pale reddish-brown in color mixed with grey, they are patterned with dorsal rhombs outlined with black or brown, occasionally creating a vague zig-zag effect. A series of black ovoid markings with reddish blotches below pattern the sides; lateral markings are often bordered or centered with white.

Similar to the neotropical boas in habits, these snakes shelter in mammal burrows, fallen logs, piles of debris, and other protected sites. They hibernate during the dry, cool months, normally May through July. *Acrantophis,* as do all boas, constricts its prey, primarily small mammals and birds.

These snakes mate after emergence from hibernation, and several males may court and copulate with the same female. After a lengthy gestation period of four to six months, small litters of four to six large young are born. Neonates are nineteen inches to two feet in length, and feed on small rodents and birds. While adults may reach ten feet in length, eight feet is considered average.

A second species, *Acrantophis dumerili,* occurs in the humid rain forests of Madagascar and the Mascarene Islands. *Dumeril's Boa* is a smaller

Dumeril's Boa,
Acrantophis dumerili

D. Hamper

animal, large adults seldom exceeding six or seven feet in length. Darker in color and not as heavy-bodied as *A. madagascariensis,* their habits are similar.

As with much of the Madagascan fauna, both forms of *Acrantophis* are threatened by deforestation, human population growth, and agricultural and industrial development; both forms have been considered endangered since 1977.

Care. Captive conditions given for other boa constrictors and/or pythons are suitable. Captive reproduction requires a brief hibernation period, which in Europe is usually effected from late May to early July, the snakes being maintained at temperatures of 60-65° F (15-18° C). Both forms have been captive bred in the United States and in Europe. Captives feed readily on pre-killed laboratory rodents, small rabbits, and chicks.

R. S. Funk

The attractively colored and patterned Dumeril's Boa relies on its cryptic coloration to remain inconspicuous.

ANACONDA; WATER BOA
(Eunectes murinus)

Habitat. Sluggish streams, rivers and adjacent swamps and marshes

Geographic Range. Trinidad and tropical South America, east of the Andes, south to Bolivia, northern Paraguay

Natural History. A heavy-bodied snake normally some shade of brownish-green, olive or greyish-green and patterned with ovoid black spots. The yellow or grey venter is speckled with small spots of brown or black.

Anacondas are confined to aquatic habitats within their range. Excellent swimmers, they utilize the shallow waters of streams and rivers for rapidly escaping predators, and as effective concealment when stalking prey. A wide variety of mammals and aquatic birds are included in their diet. Caiman and crocodiles are also eaten. Large adult specimens are capable of consuming fairly large creatures, such as subadult tapirs *(Tapirus)*.

Anacondas are the largest snakes found in the western hemisphere, vying with the Asian Reticulated Python in being the world's largest snake. Heavier bodied than the python, anacondas of comparable length normally outweigh pythons significantly.

Anacondas, like all snakes, have an "average" adult length as well as the maximum length known. Thus, adults of eighteen to twenty feet in length may be considered average; twenty-five foot animals are rare and unusual; thirty-three feet is the tentative maximum. Published estimates of thirty-five to forty feet are based on vague data and while intriguing, should be viewed with caution.

Anacondas are viviparous, with both the size of the litter and neonates varying with the size of the female. A nine foot, captive-raised specimen bore eleven young averaging twenty inches in length; a twenty-foot female produced over fifty young with an average length of three feet.

Care. Anacondas will not survive long in quarters that are perpetually damp. Dry cages supplied with a hiding place, climbing branch, and water bowl are well suited to captive maintenance of this species and easily maintained. If a "natural habitat" approach is preferred, the caging requires ample ventilation, basking areas that allow for complete drying of the skin, and stable temperatures of air, substrate, and water. Ultraviolet and infrared exposure are beneficial. Pre-killed rodents and chicks are suitable for small and medium-sized specimens; large specimens accept rabbits, chickens, and ducks. Captive reproduction is common. Anacondas are irascible creatures; they should be approached or handled with caution.

YELLOW ANACONDA
(Eunectes notaeus)

Habitat. Swamps, marshes, brush-covered banks of sluggish rivers and streams
Geographic Range. Northern Argentina, Paraguay, southeastern Bolivia, and Brazil

Natural History. A pattern of blotches, saddles, spots and streaks, usually black or dark brown, against a ground color of yellow, golden tan or greenish-yellow distinguishes this species immediately from its larger and more somberly colored relative, the Common Anaconda. They are sizable, nevertheless, reaching an average adult length of ten to twelve feet, and undoubtedly exceed this length.

A wide variety of prey species is included in the diet. Mammals such as Paca *(Cuniculus),* Agouti *(Dasyprocta),* sundry other rodents, birds, and reptiles, e.g., Caiman *(Caiman),* have been reported, although individual specimens probably confine their diet to prey species most abundant in their area. Juveniles apparently feed on fish.

Viviparous, Yellow Anacondas produce litters of up to several dozen young, eighteen inches in length.

Care. Unless very large caging is available, Yellow Anacondas are best housed in airy cages floored with shredded garden mulch, and provided with a simple water bowl rather than large basins or pools. A heavy branch for climbing is often used. Pre-killed rodents and/or chicks are readily accepted. A substrate temperature of 80° F (27° C) is required, slightly lower at night. Imported specimens should be checked for parasites. The keeper should note that this snake has an unpredictable temperament.

SPECIALIZED BOAS

Brazilian Rainbow Boa, *Epicrates cenchria cenchria*

R. D. Bartlett

In addition to the familiar boa constrictors and anacondas, the subfamily *Boinae* also includes a diverse number of species that have exploited and adapted to a wide variety of habitat niches. There are boas that do live in trees, as well as on islands, in deserts, and in temperate coniferous forests, as well as boas that burrow beneath the ground. To distinguish collectively these varied forms, they are referred to here as "specialized boas."

The neotropical Tree Boas, *Corallus,* and their close relative from Madagascar, *Sanzinia,* and the Rainbow Boas, *Epicrates,* found through South America and the Caribbean Islands—all possess thermoreceptive labial pits that aid in locating and securing prey.

Rosy Boas, *Lichanura,* range throughout the dry scrub land of the American southwest. The Rubber Boa, *Charina,* occurs in the temperate forests of western North America as far north as southern Canada. Both of these are burrowing snakes and sufficiently distinctive to be placed in a subfamily of their own, the *Erycinae.* The dozen or so species of Sand Boas, *Eryx,* that occur in southeastern Europe, Africa, Asia Minor, Pakistan, and India are also included in this group.

Another subfamily, the *Tropidophinae,* consists of four genera of dwarf boas from southern Mexico, Central and South America, and the Caribbean Islands. The several species and subspecies of the Wood Snakes, *Tropidophis,* are the best known of this group. The rough-scaled *Trachyboa* may one day be removed from this group and placed in a subfamily of its own. The arboreal *Ungaliophis* of Mexico and Central America is unusual in that females lack vestiges of the hind limbs, present in all other *Boids* except those of the subfamily, *Bolyeriinae.* The recently discovered *Exiliboa placata* is a shiny black, burrowing boa from southern Mexico and has been tentatively assigned to this subfamily.

Round Island, a small island near Mauritius, one of the Mascarene Islands in the Indian Ocean, is the home of the sole members of the subfamily *Bolyeriinae.* The Round Island Boas, *Casarea dussumieri* and *Bolyeria multicarinata,* are highly endangered species.

The genus, *Candoia,* occurs in the Fiji and Solomon Islands and parts of New Guinea in the south Pacific. Three species of these "true" boas *(Boinae)* are recognized.

B. Mealey

EMERALD TREE BOA *(Corallus canina)*

Habitat. Trees and bushes adjacent to water courses, swamps and marshes in rainforests
Geographic Range. The Amazon Basin, e.g., Peru and Ecuador, east through Brazil and Bolivia to the Guianas
Natural History. An arboreal snake, brilliant green in color, patterned with bands and flecks of white. The venter varies from dull white to bright yellow. Nocturnal, they spend the day draped in symmetrical coils over branches, the prehensile tail assuring a firm grip. The long, flat head rests atop the body coils. The position and coloration of the snake render it almost invisible.

All species of *Corallus* have well developed labial thermoreceptors, clearly defined in the illustrations. Sensitive to minute temperature gradients, these thermoreceptors aid the snake in locating its prey and aiming its strike. Huge, fang-like teeth assure rapid penetration and a secure grip through the feathers and/or fur of the birds

and small mammals upon which they prey. Prey is constricted and often ingested while the boa is suspended from a branch, which is gripped by the tail and posterior body.

Emerald Tree Boas give birth to living young, the size of the litter and neonates varying with the size of the female. Neonates are terra cotta, reddish-orange, or occasionally bluish-green in color, patterned with white. As they grow, green flecks appear over the body increasing in size and number until the emerald green of the adult appears. A remarkable ontogenetic change, the two colors are equally procryptic, the juvenile occupying small shrubs while the adults inhabit trees, often ascending to considerable heights.
Care. Not an "easy" snake to maintain, Emerald Tree Boas require high cages equipped with sturdy branches, with live or artificial foliage. Some of the branches should form right angles to each other, as these "nooks" provide the snake with

A juvenile Emerald Tree Boa beginning to develop adult coloration. Note green areas scattered over the body.

B. Mealey

necessary contact security. Optimum daytime temperatures in the low 80's (27° C), dropping to 73-75° F (22-24° C) at night are required. A warm (78° F—26° C) water misting with a spray bottle is often conducive to feeding. Food animal acceptance may be ultra-specific and specimens may refuse all but the preferred food item. If possible, determine what a newly acquired animal has previously been fed, and continue with that diet.

Pre-killed chicks, light or dark colored mice, rats, hamsters, and gerbils may be accepted. Captive-born juveniles feeding on pre-killed mice are simplest to maintain. Emerald Tree Boas are lethargic, and often develop intestinal impactions in captivity. If regular defecation does not occur, forcing the animal to swim in a large tub or tank of warm, shallow water usually solves this problem.

B. Mealey, courtesy E. Chapman

The highly sensitive thermoreceptors are clearly visible between the labial scales around the mouth of this adult Emerald Tree Boa.

B. Mealey

TREE BOA; GARDEN BOA *(Corallus enydris enydris)*

Habitat. Rainforest and broad-leaf jungle, banana plantations; usually inhabit areas in the vicinity of rivers, streams, and swamps

Geographic Range. Extreme southern Central America, south throughout northern South America, e.g., Peru, northern Brazil, Surinam, Guyana

Natural History. An arboreal boa, exorbitant in its variability. Body colors may range from muddy brown to soft orange and lemon yellow. A pattern may or may not be present. The body is somewhat compressed laterally, the tail prehensile, and the head large and distinct. The common name given this snake by the Germans is more descriptively accurate than the English "Tree Boa"—the German "Hundskopfboa" translates as "Dog-headed Boa," alluding to the chunky head and impressive array of long, recurved teeth.

Nocturnal, Tree Boas prey upon birds, bats, and small mammals. Well-developed labial thermoreceptive pits aid in locating prey.

Viviparous, they produce miniatures of themselves. Juveniles feed on small lizards and frogs, gradually changing to the adult diet as they grow. About twelve inches in length at birth, they attain an adult length of six, occasionally seven feet in length.

Many attempts to bring taxonomic order to this group of snakes have been made with little success. One form, Cook's Tree Boa, *Corallus enydris*

An orange-colored morph of the Garden Boa

cooki, has remained valid. Somewhat heavier-bodied than the nominate race, it is a brown snake patterned with indistinct tan and yellowish cross bands. Cook's Tree Boa is confined to Trinidad, Grenada, St. Vincent, Union, and Carriacou Islands.

Other poorly defined forms, variously viewed as full species or subspecies, are the grey and black Garden Tree Boa, *C. e. hortulana* and the Ringed Tree Boa, *C. e. annulata,* a brownish-red animal patterned with blackish rings or netlike reticulations.

Care. Tree Boas require much the same type of caging and care as their close relative, the Emerald Tree Boa. Misting with warm water helps prevent any problems with ecdysis. Pre-killed rodents and chicks are accepted readily, at air temperatures of 75-80° F (24-27° C). Newly acquired, wild-caught adults should be checked for internal parasites and treated accordingly.

Tree Boas are often irritable snakes and prone to strike at the source of annoyance, inflicting severe bites. It behooves the keeper to avoid such incidents by staying out of range.

This vividly patterned morph of the Garden Boa is probably *C. e. hortulana.*

MALAGASY TREE BOA *(Sanzinia madagascariensis)*

Habitat. Trees and shrubbery adjacent to streams, rivers, ponds, and swamps.

Geographic Range. Madagascar (formerly Malagasy Republic)

Natural History. Found only on the island of Madagascar, southeast of Africa in the Indian Ocean, the Malagasy Tree Boa is most closely related to species that occur in South America. They resemble morphologically the rare Brazilian boid, *Xenoboa cropanii,* and share various anatomical charateristics with the Tree Boas, *Corallus.* The specimen illustrated is typical of color and pattern.

Arboreal and usually nocturnal in habits, the Malagasy Tree Boa feeds on bats and birds, aided in locating its prey by thermoreceptive pits located between the labial scales. Small mammals other than bats are also eaten, the snake leaving the trees and actively foraging for them on the ground.

Malagasy Tree Boas bear living young, up to a dozen babies comprising a litter, each fifteen inches in length. Adults average four to five feet, although six and seven foot specimens are not uncommon.

Deforestation for agricultural development poses a serious threat to the continued existence of this species. It is protected by the Madagascan government and designated by CITES as a "threatened" species; permits are required for international shipment.

Care. Wild-caught specimens are illegal, but the species breeds readily as a captive, and juveniles are available to collectors and professional institutions. Captive conditions suitable for the Emerald Tree Boa, *Corallus canina,* satisfy requirements for the captive maintenance of *Sanzinia.*

BRAZILIAN RAINBOW BOA *(Epicrates cenchria cenchria)*

Habitat. Forests, woodlands and plains, and savannahs adjacent to them

Geographic Range. This subspecies occurs in southern Venezuela, Guyana, and Surinam, south through the Amazon Basin.

Natural History. Sometimes called the Red Rainbow Boa, the Brazilian is one of nine subspecies. All are noted for the dazzling iridescence of the skin, especially when the animal has recently shed. Close-set, microscopic epidermal ridges, akin to a prism, refract sunlight into a spectrum of color. Epidermal iridescence is common to all boas and pythons, but it is never as pronounced as in Rainbow Boas and some species of the python genus *Liasis.*

All of the Rainbow Boas are some shade of red, reddish brown, or brown, patterned with lateral rings (ocelli) and spots, normally dark in color.

The spots and ocelli are more pronounced in juveniles.

These snakes inhabit a wide variety of habitats, as described above. They also occur in or near agricultural projects such as plantations of various kinds. Powerful constrictors, they feed on a variety of small mammals and birds. They bear rather large, living young which may be fifteen to twenty inches in length at birth. A seven foot adult is considered exceptionally large.

Rainbow Boas have a wide range throughout South America. The somewhat dull-colored *E. c. maurus* occurs from Costa Rica to northern South America, Trinidad, and Tobago. *E. c. alvarezi* is found in Argentina, as is *E. c. crassus,* which also occurs in Brazil and Paraguay. *E. c. barbouri* is known only from Marajo Island off the coast of Brazil. *E. c. gaigei* occurs in Bolivia and Peru. The

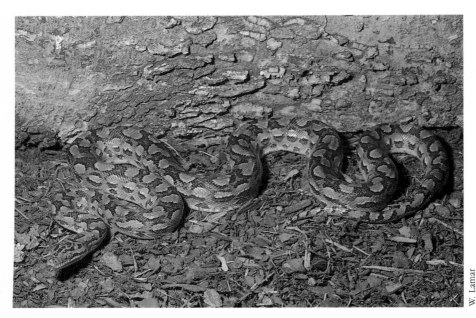

E. c. alvarezi, the subspecies of Rainbow Boa which occurs in Argentina

W. Lamar

remaining three subspecies, *polylepsis, hygrophilus,* and *assisi* are all inhabitants of Brazil.

Care. With gentle handling, Rainbow Boas soon lose any aggressive tendencies and become stable, long-lived captives. Other than a hiding place and branches for climbing, Rainbow Boas have no special requirements. They feed well on pre-killed rodents and chicks. Captive reproduction occurs frequently. (See Boa Constrictor care suggestions).

CUBAN BOA; MAJÁ *(Epicrates angulifer)*

Habitat. Wooded, grassy plains; woodland, and cane fields

Geographic Range. Cuba, Isle of Pines, and Cayo Cantiles

Natural History. Largest of the many species and subspecies of *Epicratine* boas that inhabit the numerous Caribbean islands. The establishment of large-scale sugar-cane plantations at the beginning of this century destroyed much of the Cuban Boa's habitat. This, along with frequent (and usually fatal) contact with cane field workers, severely decimated their numbers. Some effort, apparently, is now made to protect the species; it has been pictured on Cuban postage stamps as part of a public awareness program.

Cuban Boas are silver-grey in color, patterned with saddles, blotches, and spots of reddish-brown to black. Diurnal, they become crepuscular in the warm summer months. They feed on small mammals, especially rodents such as the Hutia *(Capromys),* and birds. Like all boas, they bear living young. The fifteen-inch long neonates tend to be more arboreal than the adults. They attain an adult length of ten to twelve feet.

Southeast of Cuba, the Jamaican Boa, *Epicrates subflavus,* represents the genus on this island. A grey to silver-grey in color with black crossbars, this attractive snake is severely threatened by habitat destruction and resort development on the island. It is considered an endangered species.

Jamaican Boa,
Epicrates subflavus

T. Granes

Equally endangered, the Puerto Rican Boa, *Epicrates inornatus*, is confined to this heavily populated island. Large specimens of both species may be seven to eight feet in length.

Care. Cuban, Jamaican, and Puerto Rican Boas fare quite well as captives. Cuban Boas have attained a captive longevity of over twenty-two years. All of these boas are active snakes, and caging should be at least two-thirds the length of the specimen, preferably longer. Garden bark mulch is perhaps more attractive as a substrate than paper, although either is acceptable. Hiding places and climbing branches should be provided. Substrate temperatures of 78-82° F (25-28° C) are satisfactory. A warmer basking spot is desirable, especially for the Cuban Boa. All three species reproduce readily, mating being induced by photo-period manipulation.

R. D. Bartlett

© J. Bridges

(Left) Ford's Boa, *E. f. fordi,* one of the many Caribbean insular forms of *Epicrates*, occurs on the island of Hispaniola. *(Right) E. exsul,* a small boa confined to the Bahama Islands.

The Haitian Boa, *E. striatus,* is known from eight subspecies occurring on several Caribbean islands.

R. S. Funk

The attractively patterned *E. c. chrysogaster* occurs in the Turks and Caicos Islands.

© J. Bridges

R. D. Bartlett

E. relicquus occurs on Bahama and Great Inagua Islands.

PACIFIC BOA *(Candoia carinata)*

Habitat. Rainforests, marshes and swamps, adjacent to streams and rivers; arboreal in some areas
Geographic Range. New Guinea (West Irian and Papua), adjacent islands, the Bismarck Archipelago, the Moluccan and Solomon Islands
Natural History. One of three species of boa inhabiting the islands of the south Pacific. Their ground color and pattern vary considerably. They are usually dark beige, greenish-tan, or pale reddish in color. A variety of patterns occur including blotches, blotches forming "ringed" patterns, vertebral stripes either alone or connecting blotches, or a zig-zag pattern as in the female specimen illustrated. Males have rather large anal spurs, which are usually absent in females. The scales are both keeled and smooth.

Pacific Boas are sympatric (coexist) with the various pythons and other species of *Candoia* without conflict by exploiting different habitats, e.g., terrestrial in some areas, arboreal in others.

Accordingly, a wide variety of prey species are utilized, such as frogs, large and small lizards, birds and small mammals, including bats. They will on occasion eat fish.

Candoia carinata bears living young, as do all the boas. Litters of up to fourteen young have been recorded. Adults reach a length of approximately three feet.

A subspecies, *C. c. paulsoni,* often called the "Solomon Island Boa," is no longer generally recognized. The characters defining this form apparently are not consistent with the population described, thus invalidating the subspecific rank.

Pacific Boas are "viper mimics," defending themselves by coiling in viper fashion, hissing and striking at the intruder.

Candoia bibroni, popularly called the "Fiji Boa," inhabits the Fiji Islands, Western and American Samoa, the New Hebrides, and the Solomon and Loyalty Islands. Also a variable species, it may be pale brown, tan or reddish brown, with a pattern of stripes, blotches or spots, or a combination of these, or no pattern at all. It forages both on the ground and in trees, feeding on mammals (including bats), birds, and lizards. The boa is itself included in the diet of human populations on several of the Fiji Islands. These are the largest of the Pacific boas, reaching lengths in excess of four feet.

The Samoan subspecies, *C. b. australis,* is not generally accepted inasmuch as the defining characteristics most probably represent a clinal variation rather than the consistent and confined characters that would represent a true subspecies.

The New Guinean Boa, *Candoia aspera,* is a terrestrial-aquatic form, and again, is variable in color and pattern. In areas where the Death Adder, *Acanthophis,* occurs, these boas "mimic" the pattern, colors, and actions of the formidable Elapid. They also coil into a ball with the head hidden when molested. New Guinean Boas feed on frogs, lizards, and small mammals. They occur in New Guinea (West Irian and Papua), on some of the adjacent islands, and the Bismarck Archipelago. Adults attain approximately forty inches in length.

The three Pacific boas are unique in their relationship with South American *Boids,* and are probably most closely related to the Caribbean and Rainbow Boas of the genus *Epicrates.*

Care. Caging suitable for most boas and pythons is adequate for *Candoia.* All three species feed readily on pre-killed laboratory rodents. *C. carinata* and *C. bibroni* have reproduced in captivity.

T. Granes

C. bibroni is the largest of the Pacific boas.

R. D. Bartlett

COASTAL ROSY BOA *(Lichanura trivirgata [roseofusca] myriolepis)*

Habitat. Desert and semi-desert scrub, rocky hillsides, often occurs in or near irrigated, agricultural areas

Geographic Range. The subspecies illustrated occurs in southwestern California and Arizona.

Natural History. A smooth-scaled, burrowing boa that is bluish-grey in color and patterned with reddish-brown, pink, or rose stripes. Flecks of the stripe color may be scattered over the body.

Rosy Boas are secretive creatures, spending the day hidden in burrows, under stones and debris, or simply buried in the sand. They emerge at dusk to forage for their prey of small mammals and birds, often climbing into low-growing bushes in search of the latter. Rosy Boas are powerful constrictors, but inoffensive in manner and when molested they coil into a ball, protecting the head within the body coils.

Rosy Boas mate in late spring. Young are born in early fall, ten to twelve inches long. Most adults reach a length of two to two and one-half feet.

The Mexican form, *L. t. trivirgata,* occurs in Sonora, southern Arizona and southern Baja. Two additional subspecies, *L. t. roseofusca* and *L. t. saslowi,* also occur in Baja.

Care. Rosy Boas adjust well to dry, well ventilated caging that is provided with secure hiding places. A length of plastic pipe is often preferred to the usual box or curved bark. Temperatures of 78-80° F (25-27° C) are suitable. Small, pre-killed mice are readily accepted as food. Rosy Boas have lived in excess of eighteen years as captives.

E. Wagner, D. Paulson

RUBBER BOA *(Charina bottae)*

Habitat. Fallen logs, rock crevices, and burrows in damp meadows and woodlands

Geographic Range. In suitable habitat from south central California north to southern Canada; east to Utah, Wyoming, Nevada and Montana

Natural History. One of the two species of boas that occur in the United States, this shiny, smooth-scaled snake has no pattern and varies in color from dark brown to tan or olive green. Juveniles may be pinkish in color, but they soon darken to adult colors.

The popular name alludes to the "rubbery" look and feel of this snake. The tail is blunt and resembles the head. When threatened, the snake rolls into a loose ball, hides the head, and presents the tail towards its antagonist.

Competent burrowers, they search for food in damp woodland debris, sandy soil or decaying logs. Although the tail is blunt, it is prehensile, aiding the snake in climbing shrubs and small trees to forage for nestling birds. Small litters of young, usually four or five, are born in late summer or early fall. Neonates are six to nine inches long, attaining a maximum adult length of thirty inches.

Several subspecies have been named, definition being based on scale count variations. These are *C. b utahensis* and *C. b. umbratica,* the latter known only from southern California. The validity of these forms is questionable.

Care. The drab colors and secretive nature of Rubber Boas are not conducive to their captive maintenance as "pets." They are usually maintained only in study collections or public exhibits. A substrate of shredded bark garden mulch strewn with tree bark retreats is suitable. At temperatures of 72-76° F (22-24° C), they will accept small, pre-killed mice as food. Rubber Boas have attained more than ten years longevity as captives.

EGYPTIAN SAND BOA *(Eryx colubrinus colubrinus)*

Habitat. Sandy, friable soil or sand in dry, semi-desert scrub savannahs; rock outcroppings

Geographic Range. Egypt, west to Niger, south to Kenya and Yemen

Natural History. A yellowish-white, heavy bodied boa, patterned with blotches and saddles of varying shades of brown, reddish-brown or mahogany. The head is wedge-shaped and contributes to the snake's efficiency as a burrower. The scales are smooth and glossy.

As do other members of the genus, the Egyptian Sand Boa spends most of its time in shallow burrows with only the head exposed. Prey species are quickly seized should they pass within striking range, and are killed by constriction.

During the hotter months, or at other times when the surface grows too warm, these Sand Boas seek refuge beneath stones, in the burrows of small mammals, or beneath clumps of vegetation.

Egyptian Sand Boas bear living young. The eight- to ten-inch young are usually born in early fall. Adults, which seldom exceed two feet in length, feed on rodents; the juveniles take nestling rodents and lizards.

A subspecies, *Eryx colubrinus loveridgei,* occurs in the southern portion of the geographic range.

Care. These attractive and gentle snakes are excellent subjects for captive maintenance and study. The suggestions for the captive care of John's Sand Boa, *E. j. johnii,* apply equally well to this species. They readily accept small, pre-killed mice as food.

The eyes and nostrils of the burrowing boas, *Eryx,* are placed so that they remain free of debris when the snake's body is hidden beneath the sand.

J. Mehrtens

INDIAN SAND BOA *(Eryx johnii johnii)*

Habitat. Dry, semi-desert scrub plains and rocky, dry foothills; in loose sand or friable, sandy soil

Geographic Range. Central and western India, Pakistan and Afghanistan

Natural History. A cylindrical snake with small, polished scales varying in color from reddish-brown to dull yellow-tan. The blunt, rounded tail is not distinct from the body and stump-like in appearance. The head, adapted to burrowing, is wedge-like with narrow nostrils and tiny eyes.

Indian Sand Boas are typical of the group, and like all boas they are primitive snakes, with vestigial pelvic girdles and hind limbs. They are, however, sufficiently distinct to warrant a sub-family of their own, the *Erycinae.*

Although competent burrowers, they most frequently spend their time in shallow depressions, lightly covered with soil or sand, the head partially exposed. Should suitable prey appear it is quickly seized by the Sand Boa, its body erupting from the sand covering, quickly enveloping the prey within the constricting coils.

When threatened these snakes can defend themselves with rapid, sweeping bites but prefer to form a ball with the head hidden, and the tail presented as a substitute.

Indian Sand Boas are viviparous, the young being eight to ten inches long at birth. Adults occasionally reach three feet in length, although the average specimen is seldom over two feet.

Rodents are the preferred diet of both adults and young; juveniles will prey upon lizards if suitably sized mammals are not available.

A subspecies, the Iranian (Persian) Sand Boa, *Eryx johnii persicus,* occurs throughout Iran.

Care. If kept in dry quarters, Indian Sand Boas are quite amenable to captivity. To avoid dampness, water should not be kept in the cage but offered perhaps twice per week; then removed. A shallow layer of burrowing medium, such as aquarium gravel, should be provided. Body contact with the substrate is important for the animal's security. These snakes will usually accept a piece of plate glass (with polished edges) placed atop the gravel as part of the substrate, tunnelling beneath it. This provides a double advantage in that the animal feels secure and also remains visible to the keeper. Pre-killed laboratory rodents are accepted as food, and best offered by forceps. Captive reproduction has frequently occurred.

S. Reichling, Memphis Zoo

Gongylophis conicus, the Rough-scaled Sand Boa, is the exception among the Sand Boas in having keeled rather than smooth scales. Occurs throughout India.

BIMINI DWARF BOA; WOOD SNAKE
(Tropidophis canus curtus)

Habitat. Wooded, rocky hillsides; forest edges; rocky fields adjacent or close to water

Geographic Range. Occurs on South Bimini Island, Elbow Cay, and Double-Headed Shot Cay, in the Bahamas

Natural History. Some fifteen species of these secretive dwarf boas occur throughout the West Indies, Brazil, and western South America. Many subspecies have been named, most being insular forms. Together with *Trachyboa, Ungaliophis,* and the fossorial *Exiliboa,* they comprise the subfamily *Tropidophiinae.*

Essentially nocturnal, Wood Snakes spend the day hidden beneath stones, fallen logs, or other debris. They prey upon frogs, lizards, and sometimes small birds and rodents. Adults attain a length of about three feet. They bear living young, with up to two dozen six-inch long babies forming a litter.

When threatened, Wood Snakes resort to a startling and unusual defensive behavior. Rapidly coiling into a ball, they simultaneously discharge the noxious contents of the anal glands. Further molestation results in the eyes turning red with blood, while oral veins rupture and blood trickles from the mouth. This action is similar to some species of Horned Lizards *(Phrynosoma)* that spurt blood from the eyes when threatened.

Care. Wood Snakes require hiding places into which they can literally "cram" themselves. Without the security such places provide, the snakes will refuse to feed and soon expire. Some specimens are "light shy," but for those that are not, a piece of plate glass atop the substrate will be accepted as part of the hiding spot, allowing for observation by the keeper. Shredded bark garden mulch is a suitable substrate, at a temperature of 80-85° F (26-29° C). Most specimens will feed only on lizards and small frogs; some will accept nestling mice. Captive reproduction has been recorded.

T. pardalis, a Wood
Snake confined to
Cuba.

R. S. Funk

T. greenwayi occurs
in at least two
subspecific forms in
the Turks and Caicos
Islands.

R. S. Funk

R. S. Funk

T. h. haetianus,
one of the five
subspecies occurring
in Hispaniola, Cuba
and Jamaica.

ROUGH-SCALED BOA *(Trachyboa boulengeri)*

Habitat. Rain forests
Geographic Range. Panama, Colombia, and western Ecuador
Natural History. A small snake of unusual appearance, it is currently included in the *Boid* subfamily *Tropidophiinae* which includes the dwarf boas or wood snakes, *Tropiodophis,* of the West Indies and South America, and *Ungaliophis* of Mexico and Central America.

Trachyboa, as the name implies, has heavily keeled scales, those of the top of the head and area above the nose forming "horns." The ground color is brown, becoming reddish brown ventrally. Two rows of blackish flecks pattern the sides of the animals.

Specimens have been collected on the forest floor near streams as well as in arboreal situations, but little is known about their habits. Adults reach a length of eighteen inches and feed on frogs and other amphibians as well as small fish. Viviparous, they produce small litters of young, five to six inches long.

A second species, *Trachyboa gularis,* occurs in the dry coastal areas of western Ecuador. It differs from the rainforest form in lacking cranial "horns."

Trachyboa possesses many anatomical features of the more advanced snakes, e.g., Colubrids, and may be a relict of an early form diverging from the primitive *Boids.* The genus is under study at

A specimen of *Trachyboa* from Panama. Note the rugose scalation; the splotched pattern is somewhat atypical.

R. S. Funk

this time and when its relationships are more clearly understood it will probably be reclassified and more accurately defined.

Care. *Trachyboa* does not often appear in collections, but thrives as a captive when available. Shredded garden mulch is a satisfactory substrate. Hiding places, a water supply, dim lighting, and climbing branches should be provided. Temperatures of 70-75° F (21-24° C) are suitable, with perhaps a somewhat warmer basking spot. Captives have accepted frogs, toads, and fish as food. Newly imported specimens should be checked for intestinal parasites.

CENTRAL AMERICAN DWARF BOA
(Ungaliophis panamensis)

Habitat. Rain forests

Geographic Range. Suitable habitat in Panama, Nicaragua, and Colombia

Natural History. A rare dwarf boa, pale chocolate brown in color, overlaid with greyish and rust tones. A black or blackish-brown square blotch on the head bifurcates into short cervical stripes. The body is patterned with a series of black or blackish-brown, roughly triangular, dorso-lateral blotches, ringed in white or pale rust hues.

Of the four genera of boas placed in the subfamily *Tropidophiinae, Ungaliophis* is the only form known to be at least semi-arboreal. Although the external spurs typical of boas are present, there are no internal vestiges of hind limbs.

Little is known of the habits of this snake in the wild. Juveniles probably prey upon lizards and frogs, adding small rodents and birds to the diet as they mature. Adult dwarf boas are approximately thirty inches in length.

A second species, *Ungaliophis continentalis,* occurs in extreme southern Mexico, Guatemala, and Honduras. This species differs in scalation and is patterned with widely spaced, ovoid blotches.

Ungaliophis was first described in 1882, the specimen collected in Guatemala. Until the mid 1960's, perhaps no more than six or seven specimens appeared. The first one exhibited was probably the specimen donated to an American zoological park in 1956, after its discovery in a shipment of bananas. Currently, *Ungaliophis* is represented in the collections of two American zoological parks. A specimen of *Ungaliophis continentalis* was maintained by a well known private collector for over seventeen years.

Care. *Ungaliophis* is rare in collections. Facilities suitable to *Trachyboa* should be acceptable. A specimen may be prey-specific, but most should accept small, pre-killed mice.

J. Mehrtens

A sub-adult specimen of the infrequently seen *Ungaliophis continentalis,* collected in Honduras.

T. Granes

The rare *Exiliboa placata,* a recently discovered dwarf boa which is fossorial in habit; occurs in western Mexico.

The Pythons

Boelen's Python, *Liasis boeleni*

D. Barker, Dallas Zoo

Pythons, a group of snakes that includes both giants and dwarfs, are grouped in yet another subfamily of the *Boids*—the *Pythoninae*. With but one possible exception they are confined to the tropics of Africa, Asia, and Australasia.

Pythons, like their cousins the Boas, are primitive snakes, with vestigial pelvic girdles and hind limbs terminating externally as a pair of cloacal spurs. Located immediately adjacent to the vent and usually more developed in males, the spurs are utilized during courtship and copulation.

Unlike the boas, all of which produce living young, pythons are oviparous (egg layers). The females of virtually all python species coil about their eggs for varying lengths of time. Several of the larger species are known to remain with their eggs for the full incubation period, in many cases actually incubating them by raising their own body temperatures. This is accomplished by the brooding female through muscular contractions, and in species tested temperature increases of up to 40° F (7° C) have been demonstrated—a truly remarkable feat for an *ectothermic* animal.

The survival advantage gained by pythons due to this incubation process is of great significance. All snake eggs are deposited fully supplied with sufficient nutritional elements to allow development of the embryo to the point of hatching, as well as for a short post-hatching period. After deposition, the only additional requirements of the egg and its enclosed embryo are oxygen and water (which transpire through the shell) and a temperature high enough to allow embryonic development. The critical factor is temperature, as too high or too low a temperature can present problems. Incubation temperatures may also play a role in sex determination, as has been demonstrated in turtles and tortoises (high temperatures tend to produce males; medium to low temperatures tend to produce females). The female python, coiling and uncoiling about the eggs, supplies a more reliable and consistent temperature than can earthen or decomposed plant material nests, in addition to providing protection against predators. Once hatching occurs, no further parental concern is demonstrated, and the hatchlings are left on their own.

Pythons, especially the "giant" species, have experienced a long, if not always positive, association with man. Intricate, brilliantly colored skin patterns, their great size, and a generally tractable disposition have assured their popularity in zoological park and private reptile exhibits, carnivals, and in circuses—including those staged by the ancient Romans. Hatchlings are popular as pets. These same attractive physical characteristics have, however, caused the annual slaughter of thousands of pythons to supply the leather trade. The Asian Reticulated and Burmese pythons are particularly at risk. Such exploitation of wild populations not only threatens the snakes, but has a far-reaching negative ecological impact as well.

Africa is the home of several species, only one of which, *Python sebae*, reaches an impressive length in excess of twenty feet. A small, burrowing species, *Calabaria*, also occurs in West Africa. An aberrant form, it is placed in a subfamily of its own.

Four species occur throughout India, southeast Asia (including the People's Republic of China), and the Philippines. The Reticulated, largest of all pythons, occurs throughout these areas. The attractive and endangered Indian python occurs within the sub-continent, being replaced by the Burmese subspecies elsewhere. Related forms occur on the islands of Sri Lanka and Timor. The rather unique Blood python is limited to Malaysia, Sumatra, and adjacent territory. Australia and New Guinea have the greatest number of python species, four genera and nine (perhaps more) species inhabiting Australia alone. One of these, the Green Tree python, is a remarkable example of parallel evolution, demonstrating a great similarity in habits, habitat, and general appearance and colors to the South American Emerald Tree boa.

A taxonomic debate of long standing centers on the "New World" python, *Loxocemus*, which occurs in parts of Mexico. Perhaps more properly classified with the Asian Sunbeam Snakes, *Xenopeltids*, most reference works include it with the pythons, as is done here.

Liasis, the genus to which many Australasian pythons are assigned, is also subject to frequent research and revision. A current revision, placing these pythons into the genus *Bothrochilus*, is generally considered to be invalid and the generic *Liasis* has been used here.

CALABAR PYTHON; BURROWING PYTHON
(Calabaria reinhardtii)

Habitat. Loose soil, thick leaf litter of rain forests
Geographic Range. West Africa, from Liberia eastward throughout the rain forest areas, e.g., Ivory Coast, Ghana, Nigeria
Natural History. Morphologically, this unpython-like python appears to be closely related to the boas. A few minor anatomical features have placed this species with the pythons, but in a sub-family of its own, *Calabariinae*.

The cylindrical, dark brown or black body is sprinkled with red, yellow, and/or greyish spots. The blunt head and equally blunt tail reflect its burrowing habits. Unlike the burrowing Sand Boas, *Eryx, Calabaria* tunnels about in the loose soil and forest floor litter of rain forests. It also prowls through small mammal burrows in search of prey.

It shares with a number of unrelated and inoffensive snakes the habit of substituting tail for head when threatened. *Calabaria* presses the head to the ground, often covering it with a body coil. The tail is elevated, perhaps arched slightly, and set in motion. The ruse is so effective, local natives are sometimes convinced the snake is "two-headed" and fear its presence. If further threatened, the body is coiled into a tight ball with the head in the center, much the same as the Ball Python, *P. regius*.

Biologically, this snake is poorly understood. Like all pythons it is oviparous.
Care. Seldom seen in collections, Calabar Pythons do well if given proper cage conditions. A thick layer of loose organic material as a burrowing medium is required. Several different types of shredded tree bark products used as garden mulch are available. These products, often sterilized during processing, are superior to other choices. Temperatures in the high 70's to low 80's F (25-29° C) are suitable. Pre-killed laboratory mice should be offered weekly.

ANGOLAN PYTHON *(Python anchietae)*

Habitat. Rock outcroppings, rocky areas in grasslands and open, brushy plains

Geographic Range. Southwestern Africa, e.g., southern Angola and northern Namibia

Natural History. Also commonly known as Anchieta's Dwarf Python, these rare snakes are not well known either as wild or captive specimens. They are brown to reddish-brown in color, the ground color often dark enough to appear blackish. They are patterned with irregular white or cream-colored bands and spots, bordered with dark brown or black. The venter is yellowish. The specimen illustrated is typical.

Unlike their close relative, the Ball Python, the Angolan Python is apparently always associated with rocky areas, utilizing crevices and small caves and overhangs as shelter. They are diurnal and prey upon small mammals and birds.

Data derived from captive specimens indicates that females deposit small clutches of four or five eggs. It is not known whether or not the female "incubates" and/or guards the eggs as do most pythons. The eggs hatch after approximately seventy days of incubation; hatchlings are seventeen to eighteen inches in length. Adults may attain lengths of six feet.

Care. As for the Ball Python, *P. regius,* and African Rock Python, *P. sebae.* Angolan Pythons require temperatures of about 85° F (29° C). Most captive specimens have fed readily on pre-killed rodents. Care should be taken to avoid overfeeding and obesity.

BLOOD PYTHON; SHORT PYTHON *(Python curtus)*

Habitat. Marshes, swamps, river banks and streams in rainforests

Geographic Range. Central and southern Malay Peninsula, Sarawak, Sabah, Brunei, Kalimantan (Borneo), and Sumatra

Natural History. Brick to blood-red blotches on a ground color of beige, greyish-brown, or tan suggest the common name of "blood" python. "Short" python refers to the animal's tail, extremely short in relation to its size. The head is usually dark brown or black. The colors and pattern are disruptive and help to conceal this heavy-bodied snake from both predator and prey.

Although captive adults feed almost exclusively on rats, they undoubtedly prey on a wider variety of small mammals and probably birds in the wild.

Females deposit small clutches of large eggs, seldom more than twelve. Incubation and protection is undertaken by the female in typical python fashion. Hatching takes place after two and one-half to three months incubation. Hatchlings, approximately twelve inches long, are more brightly colored than adults. The average adult length is five to six feet.

As with other snakes of wide geographic range, especially those with insular populations, attempts have been made to define subspecies. *Python curtus breitensteini* is rather tenuous and is mentioned here only because it is sometimes used to define light-colored individuals by both professional and amateur collectors.

Care. Juveniles, especially captive-bred specimens, adjust easily to caged conditions, readily accepting pre-killed laboratory mice. A substrate of sterlized, shredded garden mulch material helps to provide the humidity required without potentially lethal dampness. A substrate, air and water temperature of 80° to 85° F (26 to 29° C), cooling slightly at night, is required. A number of private collectors regularly breed Blood Pythons, and their surplus is available through dealers.

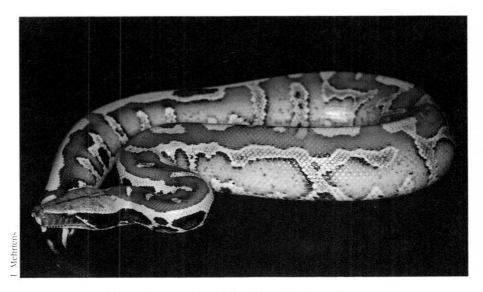

Two color morphs of the Blood Python, *P. curtus*

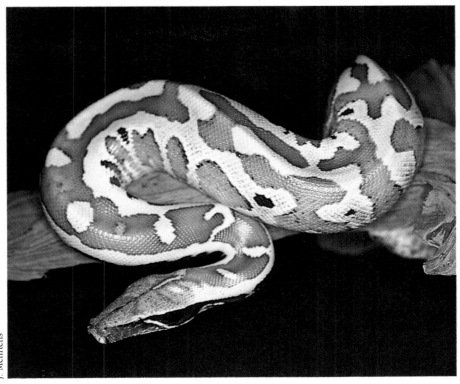

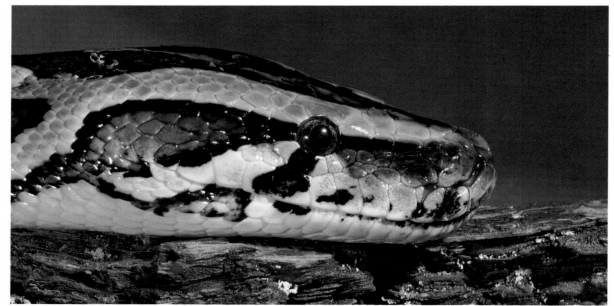

L. Moor

BURMESE PYTHON *(Python molurus bivittatus)*

Habitat. Adaptable to a wide variety of habitats, such as grasslands, swamps, marshes, rocky foothills, woodlands, "open" jungle, and river valleys. Populations are dependent upon a permanent source of water.

Geographic Range. The *subspecies* illustrated ranges from northeastern India east through southern People's Republic of China and south through the Malay Peninsula and East Indies. It is absent from the Philippines.

Natural History. Largest of the three subspecies of the Indian Python, the Burmese Python is a heavy bodied and colorful animal. A pattern of large, reddish brown blotches outlined in cream or gold overlay a ground color of pale tan, yellowish-brown or grey.

Burmese Pythons prey upon mammals, birds, and reptiles of appropriate size. The presence of domestic fowl and pigs sometimes attracts larger specimens to agricultural developments.

A prolific species, up to one hundred eggs are deposited, incubated, and protected by the female. The eighteen to twenty-four inch hatchlings leave the nest area soon after hatching, and given an abundant food supply they grow quickly. Adults may attain lengths of twenty five feet, but specimens over eighteen or twenty feet in length are rarities.

The nominate race, the Indian Python, *P. m. molurus,* is paler in color and smaller than the Burmese. It was for many years erroneously referred to as the "light phase" Indian python as opposed to the "dark phase" Burmese. Indian pythons are an endangered species, protected by both Indian and international laws. Once a common species, habitat destruction and wholesale slaughter for their skins have reduced the species to its present state. Living specimens seen in western collections are derived from reproducing captive animals.

The Ceylonese Python, *P. m. pimbura,* confined to Sri Lanka, is quite similar to the Burmese in color and pattern, but is smaller in size, usually averaging and seldom exceeding ten or twelve feet in length. It is something of a rarity and infrequently seen.

The hatchlings of Burmese Pythons are popular as pets, and sizable numbers are exported from southeast Asia annually. Wild populations are also heavily exploited by the exotic leather trade. Such exploitation could be significantly reduced or perhaps even eliminated by the development of captive breeding projects.

A small python isolated in the southern Pacific was formerly considered a fourth subspecies of *Python molurus*. Currently classified as a separate species, the Timor Python, *Python timoriensis*, occurs on Timor, a large island off the northwest coast of Australia. Rarely exceeding six feet in length, they inhabit grasslands and open forests. Birds and small mammals constitute the diet, at least in captivity.

Care. Provided with proper housing and a pre-killed food supply suitable to the size of the specimen, these pythons are hardy, long-lived captives, reproducing readily. Most are gentle and submit to handling, but as with all large snakes, adults should be manipulated with caution.

The Ceylonese subspecies, *P. m. pimbura,* closely resembles the Burmese subspecies in color and pattern.

J. Mehrtens

B. Mealey, courtesy E. Chapman

R. S. Funk

(Left) An albino Burmese Python. *(Right)* The Timor Python, *Python timoriensis,* formerly considered a subspecies of the Indian Python, is now considered a distinct species; it is rare in collections.

BALL PYTHON; ROYAL PYTHON *(Python regius)*

Habitat. Grasslands, e.g., savannahs and sparsely wooded plains

Geographic Range. West Africa, e.g., Sierra Leone, Togo, Senegal

Natural History. Ball Pythons, the smallest of the African pythons, are stocky, boldly patterned animals. The pattern of ovoid blotches on a brown or bluish-brown ground color varies considerably, but almost always includes some shade of yellow. Xanthic (yellow) color morphs frequently occur.

Seldom more than three or four feet in length, the popular name of "Ball Python" derives from the habit of coiling into a tight ball when threatened, with the head and neck tucked between the coils. In this position the snake can literally be rolled or tossed about. This passive defense posture is used by many other species, but few have refined it to this degree.

Mammal burrows and similar subterranean retreats are favored for aestivation during the dry season, as well as for deposition and incubation of eggs. Females coil about the eggs in standard python fashion, remaining with them for the three months of incubation usually required for hatching. The eggs are unusually large, and clutches small, typically consisting of six or seven eggs.

Ball Pythons are a favored food animal of various tribal groups within their range. They are also slaughtered for their skins, although not to the extent of the Indian Python. It is considered a threatened species and permits are required for its legal export, living or dead.

Care. Popular as pets, and frequently maintained by zoological parks and private collectors, Ball Pythons are often difficult to adjust to captive conditions. Captive bred and/or hatched juveniles present few problems, but are usually in short supply. Most specimens available commercially are wild-caught imports. These should be carefully checked for ticks and internal parasites, and treated accordingly. Pre-killed rodents of various kinds and colors should be offered until feeding begins, after which the food animal accepted should be continued. A temperature of approximately 80° F (27° C) is suitable. A hiding box is essential.

L. Moor

RETICULATED PYTHON *(Python reticulatus)*

Habitat. Rain forest, woodland and adjacent fringes of grassland. They frequent rivers, and areas with nearby streams and lakes.

Geographic Range. Southeastern Asia and nearby Pacific islands. Found throughout the Malay Peninsula, Borneo, Java, Sumatra, Timor, Ceram, and the Philippines.

Natural History. A strikingly colored and patterned python, best described photographically. As with many snakes whose colors and patterns appear garish when viewed in a zoo exhibit, the color pattern allows the animal to virtually vanish among the fallen leaves, debris, and lights and shadows of its environment. Termed *disruptive coloration,* it protects against enemies and assists in catching prey.

Relatively slim in relation to its length, the Reticulated Python is the largest Old World snake, reaching lengths in excess of thirty-two feet. It vies with the Anaconda *(Eunectes)* of South America for the distinction of being the largest living snake.

Excellent swimmers, they have been reported in open ocean. As a result, they can be found on many small islands within their range. Rivers are also frequented and perhaps this explains why they sometimes take up residence around wharves and docks in urban areas.

Reticulated Pythons feed on a wide variety of mammals and birds. Large lizards, such as monitors *(Varanus),* and occasionally snakes are eaten. There are several reasonably authenticated reports of predation upon humans, usually involving a small-sized individual seized along a river bank. Such incidents reflect aberrant behavior on the part of the snake and are rare occurrences.

Care. The large size and uncertain dispositions of these snakes would appear to preclude their suitability as "pets" or terrarium subjects. Large specimens are best maintained by zoological parks or specialized private collectors.

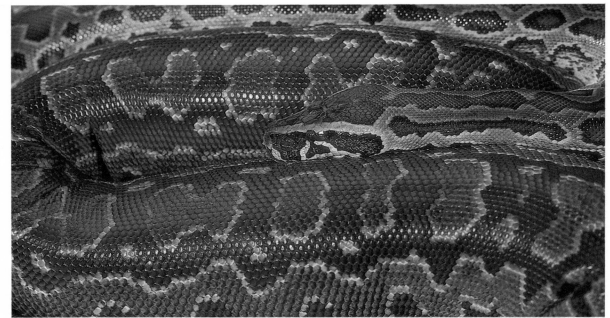

AFRICAN PYTHON; ROCK PYTHON *(Python sebae)*

Habitat. Grasslands and savannahs in the vicinity of rivers, streams and marshes, or other bodies of water. They occasionally enter the edges of forests. They are common in or around cane fields.

Geographic Range. Africa, south of the Sahara to central South Africa. Their range formerly extended farther south, but urban and agricultural development have exterminated the snake from this area, e.g., South African Cape.

Natural History. Named in honor of the eighteenth century naturalist, Albert Seba, the African Python is one of the world's largest snakes, recorded in excess of twenty feet in length. Geographically variable in pattern and color, the illustration is a typical specimen. Dependent on water, they aestivate during the dry season. Up to one hundred eggs, incubated and aggressively defended by the female, are deposited. Hatchlings emerge after approximately ninety days of incubation, and measure from eighteen to twenty-four inches.

A wide variety of mammals and birds are utilized as food. Hatchlings consume small rodents, nestlings of other mammals, and birds. Large adults frequently consume small and/or young of antelopes, wart hogs, dogs, monkeys, and waterfowl. A thirteen-foot specimen contained a small leopard! Occasional reports of man-eating, usually involving children, are possible but improbable.

As with any animal inhabiting a large geographical area, various subspecies have been described. Usually based on limited material and thus poorly defined, they are not generally recognized as valid. The exception to this is perhaps the southwest African population, described as *Python sebae nataliensis*. Acceptance of this subspecies would, of course, render the African Python as the nominate race and the trinomial, *Python s. sebae*, would apply.

Care. Hardy, long-lived captives, with up to thirty years longevity being noted. African Pythons readily accept pre-killed laboratory rodents, rabbits, and chicks. Properly cared for, captive reproduction is easily achieved. Access to water is important, but consistent dampness often results in skin disorders that may become fatally infectious. Large specimens should be handled cautiously, even if considered "tame."

BLACK-HEADED PYTHON *(Aspidites melanocephalus)*

Habitat. Adaptable to varied habitats, e.g., open woodland, grasslands, marshes, swamps, and semi-desert areas

Geographic Range. Northern Australia

Natural History. Like most of Australia's snakes, this attractive python is endemic to the island. The light brown to reddish-brown body, heavily cross-banded with red-brown or black, becomes shiny jet black on the neck and head. Both technical and common name allude to this unusual coloration. *Aspidites* is further unusual in that it lacks labial thermoreceptive pits.

Black-Headed Pythons are oviparous, the eggs incubated and protected by the female. As with most pythons properly cared for, they reproduce well in captivity. One such pair produced a clutch of eleven eggs, deposited in early fall and incubated for approximately three months. The hatchlings shed their neonatal skins approximately ten days later and fed readily on small lizards, graduating to small rodents. This pair reproduced regularly, always depositing the eggs during early fall.

Average sized adults are four to five feet long, although some may attain a length of nine feet.

Venomous snakes and other reptiles are included in the diet, as are small mammals and birds.

A slightly larger species, the Woma, *Aspidites ramseyi,* lacks the black head. It inhabits much of the arid regions adjacent to and south of the range of the Black-Headed Python. Both species are nocturnal.

Care. Black-Headed Pythons are seldom seen in collections. Australia's confusing wildlife regulations preclude exports, and captive bred hatchlings are limited. As with most pythons, these snakes are hardy captives, feeding readily on pre-killed laboratory rodents.

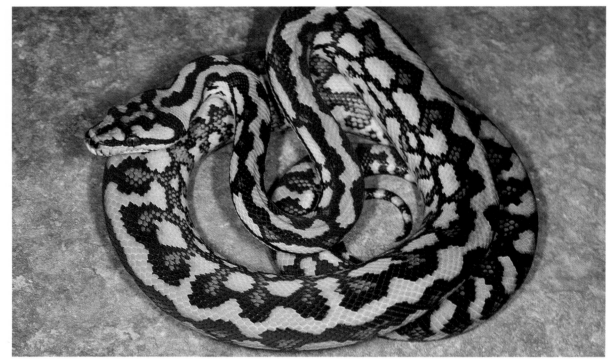

CARPET PYTHON *(Morelia spilotes variegata)*

Habitat. Adaptable to a wide variety of habitats, from humid rainforests to dry, semi-desert plains. It shelters in mammal burrows, rock piles, and trees.

Geographic Range. Australia (absent from western and extreme southeastern Australia); New Guinea (West Irian and Papua)

Natural History. A small- to medium-sized python, subject to extensive variation in pattern and color. Typically the body is some shade of beige or brown. The blackish or grey pattern may consist of blotches, cross-bands, stripes, or indistinct combinations of the three. The common name alludes to the "oriental carpet" effect. Regional color phases exist and may include bright yellow, gold, rust, and clear greys in the pattern.

Carpet Pythons feed on a wide variety of mammals and birds. Populations in forested areas are usually arboreal and feed frequently on Brush-tailed possums, *Trichosurus,* despite the strong odor of the copious secretions from this marsupial's anal glands.

Eggs are deposited in hollow logs, tree boles, and other secluded places, incubated and pro-

A dark color morph of the variable Carpet Python

The Diamond Python,
M. s. spilotes

R. S. Funk

tected by the female. Captive specimens have deposited up to eighteen eggs that hatched after an average of forty days incubation by the female. The hatchlings are approximately twelve inches long. Adults of average size are eight feet in length, exceptional specimens reaching twelve feet.

The Carpet Python is subspecific to the Diamond Python, *Morelia spilotes spilotes,* a glossy-black snake patterned with yellow spots that form rhombs (diamonds); hence the common name. Sympatric with the Carpet Python, the two forms intergrade in some areas, but not in others. Similar to the Carpet Python in habits and habitat, mature specimens are eight to ten feet in length.

Both snakes are subject to taxonomic changes that are often confusing to a non-specialist. Thus, *Morelia argus* is the same snake as *Morelia spilotes,* with the trinomial remaining constant. There is also evidence indicating that these snakes are not sufficiently distinctive to warrant placement in a genus distinct from *Python*.

Care. Popular as zoological park exhibits and with private collectors, both Diamond and Carpet Pythons are easily cared for as captives. Snug hiding places, climbing branches and a diet of pre-killed rodents or chicks are adequate to their basic needs. Temperatures of 78-85° F (25-29° C) are suitable. A misting of water of the same temperature assures normal ecdysis (skin shedding). Both forms reproduce regularly and captive-bred hatchlings are available from time to time.

R. S. Funk

The Diamond Python's vernacular name alludes to the somewhat diamond-shaped markings.

D'ALBERT'S WATER PYTHON *(Liasis albertisii)*

Habitat. Rain forests, cutover clearings, swamps
Geographic Range. Southern New Guinea and adjacent islands of the Torres Straits
Natural History. A unicolored, medium-sized python, with no pattern other than light labial markings. They occur in a wide variety of habitats, usually in the vicinity of water, into which they rapidly disappear when disturbed or threatened.

Water Pythons feed on a variety of small- to medium-sized mammals and birds. Oviparous, they deposit about a dozen adherent eggs in a compact pile about which the female coils. The fifteen-inch long hatchlings emerge after two months of incubation. Adults are an average of seven feet in length.

The relationships of Australian and southern Pacific species of Liasis are poorly understood. D'Albert's Water Python had long been considered a subspecific form of the Brown Water Python, *Liasis fuscus,* that occurs in northern Australia, islands of the Torres Straits, New Guinea, and

Timor. A 1975 revision of New Guinean pythons voided this and assigns *Liasis fuscus* to another species, Macklot's Python, *Liasis mackloti,* a seven foot, blackish-brown snake patterned with scattered, small, yellowish spots. The labials are light in color and this snake is sometimes referred to as the White-lipped Python.

Yet another poorly understood python, the rare Boelen's Python, *Liasis (Python) boeleni,* is restricted to a limited range in the mountain jungles of north central New Guinea (West Irian). This is a bluish-black snake wih a creamy white venter. The white extends in the form of streaks onto the sides of the animal. The labials are also white. Boelen's Pythons occur at heights of ten thousand feet in their mountain habitat. They feed on mammals and birds.

Care. As for the Amethystine Python, *Liasis amethystinus.* D'Albert's Water Python, the Brown Water Python, and Macklot's Python have all reproduced in captivity.

(Left) The iridescence often seen on the skin of healthy pythons is particularly evident on this freshly shed D'Albert's water python. *(Right)* Macklot's Python coils about and incubates its eggs, as demonstrated by this captive female.

Boelen's Python, a rare species from the mountains of New Guinea.

AMETHYSTINE PYTHON *(Liasis amethystinus)*

Habitat. Rain forests, mangrove swamps, woodland, and scrub land, usually along streams and rivers. Occasionally they are found on small coral islands.

Geographic Range. Widely distributed from the southern Philippine Islands eastward through the Moluccan Islands, Timor, the Bismarck Archipelago, the islands of Torres Strait, New Guinea (West Irian and Papua), and northeastern Australia (Queensland)

Natural History. A dull-colored snake, normally some shade of olive brown or greenish-yellow. A series of blackish cross bands fuse on the sides to form a netlike pattern. The common name refers to the overall bluish-purple iridescence of the scales that produce a shimmering effect, especially in sunlight.

Amethystine Pythons are good swimmers (as their geographic range suggests) and usually occur near water. Juveniles and young adults may lead an arboreal life, but large adults tend to be terrestrial in habit. They feed on a wide variety of mammals and birds, occasionally on large lizards such as monitors *(Varanus)*.

Small clutches of a dozen or more eggs are laid, incubated in standard python fashion by the female. Under captive conditions eggs hatch in less than two months, the hatchlings feeding on small mice.

Although large snakes, Amethystine Pythons are slim-bodied and do not reach the weights attained by some Asian pythons of comparable length. Average-sized adults measure twelve feet in length although they can reach greater lengths, one specimen of twenty-four feet being recorded.

Some older literature dealing with Australian pythons refer to Kinghorn's Python, *Liasis amethystinus kinghorni,* a subspecies confined to drier, more open habitat in Queensland. Now considered simply as a variant population, the subspecies is no longer recognized. Further taxonomic study may remove the Amethystine Python from the genus *Liasis,* placing it among the "true" pythons of the genus *Python.*

Care. Long-lived as a captive, they require large cages with climbing facilities and an ample water supply. Pre-killed rodents and chicks are readily accepted. Substrate temperatures of 78-85° F (25-29° C) are suitable; if the higher temperature is used, night time cooling is advised. Adults intended for breeding are best maintained separately, and brought together at the proper time.

J. Mehrtens

J. Mehrtens

Children's Python, *Liasis childreni,* a small species occurring in a wide range of habitats over much of Australia. It is sometimes confused with the no longer recognized *Liasis kinghorni.*

BISMARCK RINGED PYTHON *(Liasis [Bothrochilus] boa)*

Habitat. Open and/or cultivated areas in rain forests

Geographic Range. The Bismarck Archipelago, northeastern Papua (New Guinea)

Natural History. Despite its remote habitat this snake has been known since 1837. Its relationships have always been poorly understood, however, and it has been assigned a variety of generic names reflecting its unique nature. Only recently has it been reclassified and is now considered a form of *Liasis,* a genus of pythons widespread throughout the southern Pacific and Australia.

The pattern of brilliant orange and black rings, typical of neonates and juveniles, gradually fades as the snake matures. Adults are usually some shade of brown, with black rings, or uniformly blackish-brown. There is normally a light spot behind the eye.

Ringed Pythons are nocturnal and actively forage for small rodents, their primary diet. They have been reported as entering houses and farm buildings in search of prey.

Oviparous, they deposit up to a dozen eggs that are usually, but not always, "brooded" by the female. Captive hatchlings exhibit burrowing tendencies, and it is likely that in the wild hatchlings remain hidden in the loose debris of the forest floor. Hatchlings feed on lizards as well as nestling rodents. Adults attain a length of five to six feet.

A group of hatching Bismarck Ringed Pythons. The eggs have been incubated in vermiculite.

T. Granes

Care. Ringed Pythons are rare in collections, although a number of captive pairs reproduce regularly. Juveniles are occasionally available. Shredded bark garden mulch is an excellent substrate, which should be maintained at 80-85° F (26-29° C). Hiding places, dim lighting, and an ample water supply are required. Small pre-killed laboratory rodents are readily accepted.

R. S. Funk

This brilliantly colored juvenile Bismarck Ringed Python will fade to the adult colors in about a year.

GREEN TREE PYTHON *(Chondropython viridis)*

Habitat. Rainforest trees, bushes, and shrubs

Geographic Range. New Guinea (West Irian, Papua) and extreme northeastern Australia (Cape York)

Natural History. An exceptional example of parallel evolution, the Green Tree Python virtually duplicates in form and habits those of its distant cousin, the Emerald Tree Boa, found half a world away in South America. The same comment could apply in reverse, and, of course, there are significant differences. For one, the thermoreceptive pits, so prominent in the boa, are found only on the supralabial scales (upper lip) in this python. The Emerald Tree Boa bears living young; the python is oviparous, typically incubating and protecting the eggs.

Green Tree Pythons, as both the popular and technical name describe them, are a vivid green in color, with a broken vertebral stripe of white or dull yellow. Spots of the same color may be scattered over the body. Blue spots sometimes occur, and, although rare, cyanomorphs are known. Hatchlings are normally lemon yellow, with broken stripes and spots of purple and brown. Occasional golden or orange hatchlings appear from the same clutch as yellow ones. The vivid juvenile colors soon change to the adult green.

Completely arboreal, they frequent dense growths of epiphytic plants, their disruptive coloration effecting near invisibility. Rodents, birds, and probably bats are eaten, sometimes with the snake dangling from its roost, secured by the strong, prehensile tail.

Although known to reach seven feet in length,

average adults are three to four feet and are sexually mature at that length.

Care. Tall cages, equipped with branches, some forming right-angled nooks, are required. Broad-leaved vining plants, e.g., Pothos, either living or artificial, offer security. Imported animals should be carefully checked and treated for parasites.

Green Tree Pythons feed readily on pre-killed laboratory mice and/or chicks. Temperatures in the middle to high 70's F (low to middle 20's C) are suitable. These pythons breed well as captives, with day length, light level, humidity, and temperature being the significant factors in inducing courtship and copulation.

© J. Bridges

This bright yellow new-born Green Tree Python will change to the adult green color in six to eight months.

NEW WORLD "PYTHON"; DWARF "PYTHON"
(Loxocemus bicolor)

Habitat. Leaf litter, beneath fallen logs, stones; burrows in areas of loose, sandy soil

Geographic Range. Pacific coast of central Mexico south to Costa Rica; northwestern Honduras

Natural History. The popular English name as well as the more descriptive German popular name of Spitzkopfpython (sharp-headed python) are both misnomers. *Loxocemus* is in all probability not a python but a primitive member of the *Xenopeltids* or Sunbeam Snakes. Nevertheless, it remains classified as a subfamily of the *Boidae,* the *Loxoceminae.*

The cylindrical body, smooth scales and wedge-shaped head are typical of burrowing snakes. Body color varies from dark to light brown with no pattern except perhaps a scattering of whitish spots on the flanks of some individuals. Vestigial hind limbs are present.

Little is known of the habits of this snake in the wild, other than that it is a secretive burrower, and probably nocturnal. A constrictor, it feeds on small rodents and probably ground nesting birds. They are oviparous.

Care. *Loxocemus* is rare in collections, but apparently adjusts readily to captive conditions. A deep layer of burrowing medium such as garden mulch topped with slabs of tree bark should be provided. Dampness should be avoided. A substrate temperature of 72-78° F (22-25° C) appears satisfactory. Captive specimens feed readily on pre-killed chicks and small mice.

© J. Bridges

The "New World" Python is a highly variable species as these specimens demonstrate.

W. Lamar

The Acrochordidae

The Wart Snakes are a distinct family of one genus and two species of completely aquatic snakes that exhibit characteristics of the primitive boas and pythons as well as those of the more advanced Colubrids. Although sometimes considered a sub-family of the Colubrids, they are more accurately viewed as one of the eight families of primitive snakes. Their taxonomic position could perhaps be more readily understood as a "bridge" between the primitive snakes and the Colubrids.

D. Barker, Dallas Zoo

ELEPHANT TRUNK SNAKE, WART SNAKE, KARUNG
(Acrochordus javanicus)

Habitat. Streams, rivers, and estuaries. They occur in fresh water, brackish water, and occasionally venture into salt water.

Geographic Range. Southeastern Asia, from Burma south throughout the Malay Peninsula, east to the Philippines, East Indies, New Guinea, and north-central Australia

Natural History. Completely aquatic, the Karung is blackish-grey to brown in color, marbled with darker brown or black that may give the animal a mottled or spotted effect. Dorsal scales are juxtaposed rasp-like granules that continue on the ventral surface. The lack of broad ventral scutes is an adaptation to its aquatic habits, as is an oral flap of tissue that completely seals the internal nares. A chin pad seals off the notch through which the tongue is extruded. The single lung is large and extends nearly the entire body length.

Resembling a deflated "tire tube" when removed from the water, the Karung in its environment is a strong and graceful swimmer. Despite reports of the late nineteenth century purporting that Karungs feed on aquatic insects and fruit(!), they are entirely piscivorous, catching fish with a rapid sidewise motion of the head. They also utilize the abrasive scales in catching prey. Lying quietly on the river bottom, the Karung arranges its body in closely aligned lateral curves. A curious fish, inspecting any of the several crevices formed by the curves, triggers immediate closure and is secured within by the scales. One captive specimen caught and consumed its twice-weekly ration of goldfish using this procedure exclusively.

Viviparous, Karungs are prolific animals, with litters of two to three dozen young, approximately twelve inches in length. Adults reach lengths of six to seven feet.

A second species, *Acrochordus granulatus,* was formerly ranked as a separate genus, *Chersydrus.* It occurs over the same geographic range as the Karung, but extends its range farther west to India and Sri Lanka. A smaller species, the adult length is seldom over four feet. In addition to fish it also feeds on small crabs.

Karungs are sufficiently specialized to warrant family rank, the *Acrochordidae.*

The tanned skin of these snakes makes, unfortunately, a durable and attractive leather, and thousands are slaughtered annually for this purpose.

Care. Large aquaria, securely covered, are suited to the captive maintenance of Karungs. Nontoxic rocks forming "caves" for security must be stabilized to prevent dislodging. A heavy layer of gravel is a suitable substrate. Water should be filtered and heated to 80-85° F (26-29° C). The addition of small amounts of a salt mix used to produce synthetic sea water is beneficial. As the snakes are nocturnal, bright lighting should be avoided. Common goldfish are usually accepted as food.

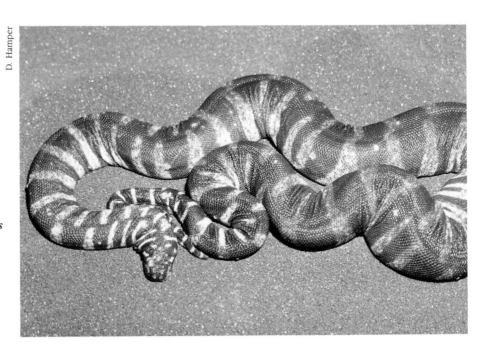

D. Hamper

File Snake, *Acrochordus granulatus*

COLUBRIDS—The "Typical" Snakes

Red Ratsnake, *Elaphe guttata guttata*

B. Mealey

Taxonomy, a word derived from Greek roots meaning "arrangement" and "law," is the science of classification. Essentially based on natural relationships, taxonomic principles and laws are standardized internationally. Indeed, there is an International Commission on Zoological Nomenclature. Although taxonomy is in a constant state of flux, it has brought order to and made possible the zoological and botanical sciences.

Initial attempts at classification were applied only to plants, due probably to their potential agricultural and medicinal importance. Over one thousand plants were systematically classified by an Italian, Andrea Cesalpino, in 1583. A Swiss, Gaspard Bauhin, spent his life devising a classification of plants, publishing the results in 1623. Bauhin was one of the first to conceptualize a system of binomial nomenclature, each organism having a generic and species name. It was this concept that was later expanded and developed by Carl Linnaeus in the early 1700's. A Swede by birth, Linnaeus is the father of modern taxonomy, in which all living things are placed first in a *class*, then further defined in an *order, sub-order, family, sub-family, genus* and *species*. In those instances in which several distinctive and constant variations of a *species* exists, a third, *subspecific* name is applied. This much abbreviated and simplified history of taxonomy serves to explain the means whereby the approximately 3,000 species of extant snakes have been classified.

Of these, most (perhaps 75 percent, plus or minus), are placed in the family *Colubridae*, the *Colubrid* snakes. The family is further sub-divided into (usually) eight sub-families. Valid, if unresolved, taxonomic arguments for seven, nine, or eleven sub-families can be made, but they are not of concern here. Suffice it to say that the *Colubrids* are the preeminent family of "typical" snakes throughout those parts of the world that provide habitats capable of supporting a snake fauna. The sole exception is Australia, where the venomous *Elapids* (cobras, coral snakes and related forms) are dominant. It is interesting that some taxonomists believe that the *Elapids* are simply proteroglyphic (fixed front-fanged) *Colubrids,* for which a separate family ranking is unwarranted.

As would be expected in such a large and diverse group of animals, *Colubrids* have exploited and adapted to virtually all imaginable habitats. They occur in temperate forests and tropical jungles. They may be arboreal, terrestrial, or aquatic. *Colubrids* are considered to be highly evolved (or "advanced") snakes, as evidenced by the total absence of any vestigial hind limb anatomy. Further, only one lung (the right) is functional, and usually elongated. The left lung is either vestigial or absent completely.

Equally diverse in feeding habits, *Colubrids,* depending on the species involved, feed on mammals, birds, reptiles (including other snakes), amphibians, fish, and invertebrates. Some are highly specialized, such as the snail eaters, *Dipsas,* that deftly extract terrestrial molluscs from their shells; and egg eaters, *Dasypeltis,* that swallow birds' eggs, neatly cutting the shell with specialized vertebral processes extending into the esophagus.

Prey may be killed by constriction or by being overpowered and swallowed. Among others, Eurasian and American ratsnakes *(Elaphe)* employ the former; water snakes *(Natrix),* the latter.

A number of *Colubrid* genera are unique within the family in the possession of enlarged, rear maxillary teeth, often but not always grooved. A venom-producing, modified salivary gland, *Duvernoy's gland,* is present. The venom injected by this inefficient apparatus is normally lethal only to the prey these *opisthoglyphous* (rear-fanged) snakes feed upon. However, some of the larger species such as the African Boomslang, *Dispholidus,* have caused human fatalities.

The sundry genera and species chosen to illustrate the *Colubrids* in the following pages are presented in purely arbitrary groupings, such as Ratsnakes, Whipsnakes, and Racers, etc. Such an arrangement should allow for a greater ease of use and understanding of this diverse family, especially for the general reader or novice herpetologist. In any event, it should be clearly understood that the groupings do not imply any taxonomic relationship between the groupings or their sequence, other than that all of the forms illustrated are *Colubrids.*

The Ratsnakes

Yellow Ratsnake, *Elaphe obsoleta quadravittata*

B. Mealey

Several genera of Colubrids are commonly called "Ratsnakes" in various parts of the world. The vernacular applies most often to the large, powerful constrictors of the genus *Elaphe,* represented by over fifty species ranging throughout Europe, Asia, and North America. They are absent in Africa and Australia.

Except for the Aesculapian snake, *Elaphe longissima,* that ranges into Germany and Poland, the several European forms occur in the more southerly countries. Several European forms are remarkably similar in appearance to North American species, e.g., the Four-lined snake, *Elaphe quatorlineata* of southeastern Europe and southwestern Asia. Multiple forms occur throughout China, Taiwan, and southeast Asia.

One form, *Elaphe climacophora,* occurs in Japan. The albino form of this species is considered an earthly form of a fertility goddess, Benzai-ten.

Five species with many subspecies occur in the United States, where they are often called Chicken snakes, alluding to their frequent consumption of chicken eggs and chicks.

Ratsnakes the world over defend themselves vigorously if attacked or threatened. The intruder is faced with the forepart of the body drawn into an impressive "S" loop, while the tail rapidly vibrates. Such actions often result in their being confused with rattlesnakes in the United States. Captive specimens soon dispense with such displays and adjust well to a caged situation.

RED RATSNAKE; CORN SNAKE *(Elaphe guttata guttata)*

Habitat. Sandy pine woods, cutover woodland, sandy scrub oak and post oak woods, especially trash piles and abandoned buildings in such areas. They are often found along abandoned railroads, utilizing the rotted ties as shelter. They have been *reputed* to be common in sewer systems of southern cities.

Geographic Range. The pine barrens of southern Jersey, south through peninsular Florida and west to Louisiana

Natural History. A pattern of blotches which may be red, grey, or brown, edged in black against a ground color that may be orange, red, tan, or grey are but a few of the more common variations of this very variable species. Some populations approach drabness, and others can be said to be among the most spectacularly colored snakes known. A secretive snake, it spends much time hidden in or prowling through rotted logs, uprooted trees, rodent and other burrows, and trash or log piles. It feeds on rodents, bats, birds,

This Rosy Ratsnake was photographed on Long Key, Florida.

and lizards, some southern Florida populations preying upon the last almost exclusively.

The Rosy Ratsnake, *Elaphe guttata rosacea,* a poorly defined subspecies, occurs in the middle and lower Florida Keys. Unlike the Red Ratsnake, the Rosy is often seen in trees and shrubs.

The Prairie, or Great Plains, Ratsnake, *Elaphe guttata emoryi,* might be described as a black and white version of the technicolored Red Ratsnake. Also secretive, this nocturnal snake is usually found near permanent water courses throughout the Great Plains states, Texas, and south to central Mexico.

Care. The Red Ratsnake's brilliant colors, docile disposition, and hardiness make it a favored reptilian "pet" both in the United States and Europe. Captive specimens reproduce well and several color morphs (or variants) are bred and prized by collectors, pink-eyed albinos being especially popular. There are also xanthic (yellow), erythritic (red), leucistic (white) and melanistic (black) morphs available. Red Ratsnakes as well as the Prairie Ratsnake adapt well to a caged environment, readily accepting pre-killed rodents or chicks.

R. S. Funk

The Great Plains or Prairie Ratsnake, *Elaphe g. emoryi.*

BLACK RATSNAKE (ALSO PILOT SNAKE, RATTLESNAKE PILOT)
(Elaphe obsoleta obsoleta)

Habitat. Usually associated with rocky areas, such as montane forests, rock outcroppings, stone walls, etc. They frequent abandoned buildings, wood piles, and trash dumps adjacent to such areas. They also spend considerable time in large trees.

Geographic Range. Northeastern United States, west to Wisconsin, Oklahoma, northern Louisiana to central Georgia (the range is discontinuous)

Natural History. A typical, large ratsnake that can reach nine feet in length, although average specimens are seldom over six. Seven sub-species of the Black Ratsnake occur in the United States, all of which freely interbreed in areas where geographic ranges overlap. Several distinctive intergrade populations are known. They feed on a wide variety of rodents and birds, as well as their eggs, and are frequently found in barnyards in search of such prey. They are diurnal; high sum-

mer temperatures may force nocturnal activity. They breed shortly after spring emergence from hibernation, with up to thirty-six eggs being deposited, usually in decomposing plant material. Hatchlings may be large (fifteen inches or more) and, like all ratsnakes, have a pattern of dark blotches on a light background.

Black Ratsnakes aggregate in numbers at preferred hibernation sites often in company with Rattlesnakes *(Crotalus)* and/or Copperheads *(Agkistrodon)*. The use of "Pilot snake" or "Rattlesnake Pilot" as their common name in sections of the northeastern United States alludes to the (erroneous) belief that the ratsnakes guide other snakes to suitable denning areas.

Care. The Black Ratsnake and its subspecies adapt to a wide variety of habitats, and most specimens readily adapt to proper captive condi-

Always a startling color variant, albinism is particularly so in the case of a normally black animal. This albino Black Ratsnake was captive bred and hatched.

R. S. Funk

tions. Hatchlings feed readily, grow normally, and in time, reproduce. All of the American ratsnakes readily reproduce in captivity. When color variants such as albinos have appeared, the genetic variations have been fixed by carefully controlled matings. Color variants are especially popular with private collectors, with the supply of captive bred hatchlings seldom meeting demand.

Although many European collectors arrange terrariums simulating natural habitats, American collectors generally keep snakes under "sterile" conditons, e.g., paper substrate, hiding box, water bowl and perhaps a climbing branch. American ratsnakes do well in either housing choice, provided dry conditions prevail. Consistent dampness and/or humidity leads to epidermal and respiratory problems. Ratsnakes feed readily on pre-killed rodents of a size appropriate to the specimen. Chick culls are also accepted. Some specimens will consume chicken eggs, but these are neither a complete nor a proper steady diet. Temperatures from the mid 70's to lower 80's F (low to mid 20's C) are suitable. The foregoing comments on captive care are applicable for all subspecies of *Elaphe obsoleta*.

TEXAS RATSNAKE *(Elaphe obsoleta lindheimeri)*

Habitat. Open woodland adjacent to swamps, marshes, and streams. Rocky arroyos and canyons are favored in central Texas. They also frequent barnyards and trash piles.

Geographic Range. Western Arkansas, most of Louisiana, east and central Texas

Natural History. Patterned much like the Gray Ratsnake, although there is usually little or no contrast between the blotched pattern and ground color. Some Texas populations have scale edges and interstitial skin of red or orange, a striking color combination. They feed on a wide variety of small mammals (mostly rodents) and birds. Hatchlings add lizards and small frogs to the diet. As do most snakes, they will gorge themselves if abundant food is present. A specimen from central Texas, well over six feet in length, disgorged seven weanling rabbits when captured. Texas Ratsnakes also prowl about barns and hen houses in search of prey, taking rodents, chicks, and eggs. Porcelain door knobs are often used as decoy nest eggs (at least in some rural Texas areas) and frequently are swallowed along with actual eggs. Almost certainly such an object would prove fatal unless regurgitated or surgically removed.

Except for the cooler spring months, this is a nocturnal species. They are most often seen on roads and highways, attracted by the radiation of residual heat. Unfortunately, this is a dangerous habit, and numbers of ratsnakes are killed by motorists each year.

An almost patternless, smaller ratsnake abuts the southern edges of the Texas Ratsnake's range. Seldom more than five feet in length, Baird's Ratsnake, *Elaphe obsoleta bairdii,* occurs in similar habitat, in south central Texas. Reasonably common in the Big Bend area, it extends its range farther south into Mexico. Its habits are similar to those of the Texas Ratsnake.

Care. As for the Black Ratsnake, *E. o. obsoleta.*

A juvenile Texas Ratsnake, which will darken considerably as it matures.

W. Lamar

E. Wagner

A group of captive Baird's Ratsnakes; note the pattern variations.

B. Mealey

YELLOW RATSNAKE *(Elaphe obsoleta quadravittata)*

Habitat. Usually near a permanent water supply, such as canals, irrigation ditches, etc. They are also found in cutover woodland adjacent to cleared fields; and commonly found around deserted farm buildings, pump houses, trash and log piles. Live oak and other thick-limbed trees are favored haunts.

Geographic Range. Central Florida, north through Georgia, South Carolina, and southeastern coastal areas of North Carolina

Natural History. By controlling populations of noxious rodents in agricultural areas, these snakes are of significant agricultural importance. Large specimens from such areas are often heavily scarred, the result of rodents objecting to becoming a dinner entree. Adroit climbers, they frequently raid bird nests for eggs and hatchlings. They are also fond of chicken eggs and chicks, and

are often referred to as "chicken snakes" in parts of their range.

Yellow Ratsnakes breed as early as late March, through May, depositing up to several dozen smooth-shelled eggs in warm, damp locations. Rotted logs and abandoned sawmills (sawdust piles) are favored nesting sites. Hatchlings, twelve inches or more in length, are heavily blotched, assuming the yellow color and stripes of the adult as they mature. Unlike adults, hatchlings often feed on small lizards and frogs.

A "greenish" color phase occurs in populations from northern portions of its range. These animals are intergrades with Black Ratsnakes. In southern Florida, the Yellow Ratsnake is replaced by the Everglades Ratsnake, *Elaphe obsoleta rossalleni.* Usually orange in color with indistinct stripes, it is less heavy-bodied than the Yellow Ratsnake.

Both subspecies may reach an adult length of seven feet or more. The Everglades Ratsnake is frequently arboreal, and its populations have benefitted from the plantings of Australian Casuarina trees along south Florida highways.

The Key Ratsnake, *Elaphe obsoleta deckerti,* occurs in the northern Florida Keys. It is unusual in that it retains much of the juvenile pattern of blotches as well as the adult stripes. Its habits are similar to both the Yellow and Everglades subspecies.

Care. As for the Black Ratsnake, *E. o. obsoleta.*

D. Hamper

The Everglades Ratsnake, *E. o. rossalleni.*

D. Hamper

GRAY RATSNAKE; OAK SNAKE *(Elaphe obsoleta spiloides)*

Habitat. Sparse woodlands, especially where soil is sandy. Areas of scrub and post oak are favored locations. They frequent barns, abandoned buildings, and trash piles in agricultural areas.

Geographic Range. Southern Illinois and adjacent Indiana, south to Mississippi and western Georgia

Natural History. Populations vary considerably in color. Its pattern consists of dark blotches against a contrasting background of pale or dark brown, or grey, to nearly white, making it one of North America's most attractive ratsnakes. An excellent climber, it is often found in oak trees; hence the localized common name, "Oak snake." The habits of the Gray Ratsnake are similar if not identical to those of the Black Ratsnake, with which it frequently intergrades in areas of range overlap. Unlike most other American ratsnakes, however, hatchlings are similar to adults in appearance. Hatchlings are about twelve inches in length and may reach an adult length in excess of seven feet, although an adult of five feet may be considered as large.

The Gray Ratsnake population of the Florida Panhandle has been considered sufficiently distinct to be assigned subspecific rank. This snake, the Gulf Hammock Ratsnake, *Elaphe obsoleta williamsi,* differs little from *E. o. spiloides* in pattern or habits. In all probability its subspecific rank is unwarranted.

Care. As for the Black Ratsnake, *E. o. obsoleta.*

The Gulf Hammock
Ratsnake, *E. o.
williamsi.*

TRANS-PECOS RATSNAKE *(Elaphe subocularis)*

Habitat. A desert species, it prefers rock slides, talus slopes and other rock-strewn areas with abundant crevices. It frequents armadillo, gopher, and rodent burrows.

Geographic Range. Suitable habitat from north central Mexico through southwest Texas and south central New Mexico, e.g., Chihuahuan desert

Natural History. Distinctive in appearance, this tan or yellowish-tan snake is patterned with two, usually unbroken, longitudinal stripes connected over the back with blotches. The very large eyes are also distinctive and unlike any other American ratsnake. Nocturnal, it spends the day hidden away in burrows and crevices. Hatchlings are approximately twelve inches in length and feed primarily on lizards, although nestling rodents are also taken. Adults include rodents, birds, and occasionally bats in the diet. The species is protected by the state of Texas.

Care. Virtually all of the *Elaphe* do well as captives, and the Trans-Pecos Ratsnake is no exception. A hiding place is important, especially for nervous specimens. They reproduce readily as captives, most specimens commercially available being captive bred. They will accept pre-killed rodents and chicks.

D. Hamper

GREEN RATSNAKE *(Elaphe triaspis intermedia)*

Habitat. Brushy, wooded, rock-strewn canyons adjacent to streams

Geographic Range. Mountain valleys of extreme southeastern Arizona, south into Mexico

Natural History. A slim, patternless snake that is partially arboreal. Little is known of its habits in the wild other than that it is crepuscular, active in the morning and evening hours. A good climber, it basks in trees and shrubs and forages for birds and their young. Small rodents are included in the diet. Prey is quickly killed by constriction.

Average sized adults are three to three and one-half feet in length, rarely exceeding four feet. Small clutches of eggs, perhaps six or so, are deposited beneath stones and similar sites. Hatchlings feed on small lizards and nestling rodents.

Two other subspecies are known. The nominate race, *Elaphe t. triaspis,* occurs from the central Yucatan peninsula south to northeastern Guatemala. *Elaphe t. mutabilis* is found in the highlands of Guatemala and Costa Rica.

Care. The Green Ratsnake can be maintained under conditions suitable to other members of the genus. They require branches for climbing and sunning. Temperatures of 78-85° F (25-29° C) are acceptable. Small pre-killed rodents are usually readily accepted as food.

The Mexican Ratsnake, *Elaphe flavirufa,* occurs as four subspecies from coastal eastern Mexico south to Guatemala and Nicaragua. They are colorful, and bear a resemblance to both the Red Ratsnake and Trans-Pecos Ratsnake of the United States.

W. Lamar

E. Harris, Binder Park Zoo

FOX SNAKE *(Elaphe vulpina)*

Habitat. Marshland, grass prairies, agricultural areas, and woodlands adjacent to streams and brooks

Geographic Range. Barely entering Canada (Ontario), south to Indiana, and west to Nebraska. They are abundant in marshes and dunes bordering the Great Lakes.

Natural History. Two subspecies are recognized: the Western, *Elaphe vulpina vulpina* and the Eastern, *E. v. gloydi*. Both races are vividly marked snakes, with a "typical" ratsnake pattern of dark blotches on a tannish yellow, yellow, tan, or orange ground color. Some specimens have red-orange heads and are mistaken for Copperheads (Agkistrodon). Quick to defend themselves in standard ratsnake fashion, e.g., S-loop, open mouth and rapidly vibrating tail, they are often confused with Timber Rattlesnakes (Crotalus). Fox snakes may gather in sizable numbers at favored hibernation sites, often abandoned rockwalled wells. They feed on rodents, birds and their eggs. Hatchlings probably include frogs in the diet.

Many snakes discharge foul-smelling anal fluids when threatened. Fox snakes are adept at this, and their common name refers to the "fox-like" odor associated with the fluid discharge.

Care. Fox snakes, especially adults, do not readily accept captivity, often refusing to feed and remaining nervous and defensive. Hatchlings and/or young specimens, carefully handled, settle down quickly, however, readily accepting pre-killed small mice. Hiding places and avoidance of dampness are essential to their well-being. Fox snakes should not be kept in a caged situation, unless the captor is willing to provide the care and attention to detail that is required.

AESCULAPIAN SNAKE *(Elaphe longissima longissima)*

Habitat. Sparsely wooded areas, e.g., hillsides, farmland and hedgerows. They favor rock fences, walls, and ruins.

Geographic Range. Northwest Iran, western Turkey, and adjacent areas of the U.S.S.R., west through central and southern Europe to France. Isolated populations are found in Germany, Switzerland, and southern Poland. Historically occurred in Denmark, but it is now extinct in that country. The range is discontinuous.

Natural History. This somber but attractive ratsnake varies in color from olive brown to black, with a greyish or yellowish venter. The dorsal scales are edged with white or yellow.

The Greek god of healing, Aesculapius, was adopted by the Romans, who built temples in his honor the length and breadth of Europe. The Aesculapian Snake was considered the earthly manifestation of the god as well as a messenger. This concept of a snake, incidentally, is not unusual. The Romans stocked their temples with these snakes, specifically imported for the purpose. The present erratic distribution of the species is directly attributed to the Roman dissemination of the animal throughout Europe. The snake's original range is rather difficult to determine for this reason, but probably was Asia Minor. The association of this snake with the healing arts continues into modern times in the form of the caduceus, the staff of Hermes (Mercury) entwined with snakes. It is the symbol of the physician. The position of the entwined snakes on the staff is suggestive of the position assumed by rival males of this species when competing for the favors of a single female. Male snakes of many species indulge in various rearing, pushing, and snapping contests, referred to as "combat dances." Aesculapian Snakes perform a series of stylized rituals almost bird-like in complexity.

Aesculapian Snakes deposit up to two dozen eggs in rotted logs or similar decaying plant material. The eight-inch hatchlings emerge after some two months of incubation. Juveniles feed on lizards, soon changing to the adult diet of rodents, birds and their eggs. Adults average four to five feet in length, rarely exceeding six feet.

Several subspecies are recognized, all similar in habits, habitat and diet. *Elaphe longissima persica* is found in northern Iran; *E. l. romana* inhabits the southern half of Italy and the island of Sicily; and *E. l. rechingeri* is confined to Amorgos Island in the Cyclades.

Care. Aesculapian Snakes are rather difficult to maintain in captivity, unusual for ratsnakes. They require large, dry cages equipped with hiding places and branches for climbing and sunning. In lieu of natural sunlight, a source of ultra-violet should be provided. Feeding idiosyncrasies must be catered to. Pre-killed small rodents, chicks, or small birds (sparrows, finches) may be accepted. Captive breeding has occurred, the snakes usually mating after emergence from hibernation.

D. Hamper

STINK SNAKE *(Elaphe carinata)*

Habitat. Montane forests, bamboo thickets, rocky valleys, highland agricultural areas
Geographic Range. People's Republic of China, from Sichuan and Yunnan provinces east to the coast and Taiwan
Natural History. Usually inhabiting thickly forested areas of high mountain sides, the snake is brownish-yellow, olive yellow, or bronze in color, with heavily keeled scales bordered in black giving a spotted or sometimes partially banded appearance. Black (melanistic) specimens frequently occur in normally colored populations.

The presence of exceptionally large anal glands and the rapid discharge of their noxious contents when threatened provides the common name.

Although rodents are frequent prey, Stink Snakes are primarily ophiophagous (snake-eating) animals, consuming harmless and venomous species, as well as their own young.

A dozen relatively large eggs are deposited in decaying vegetation, hatching after approximately two months. The twelve to fifteen-inch young are colored and patterned differently from adults, being pale with indistinct markings; occasionally striped. Six to seven foot adults are average; lengths of eight feet or more are known.

Care. As for the Russian Ratsnake, *Elaphe s. schrenckii.* Captive Stink Snakes feed readily on pre-killed laboratory rodents and chicks. Captive breeding requires a period of hibernation or at least a resting period, with cooler temperatures and dim lighting.

D. Hamper

Note the change in pattern from the anterior to posterior portions of the body.

D. Hamper

MOELLENDORFF'S RATSNAKE *(Elaphe moellendorffi)*

Habitat. Rocky, forested hillsides, meadows, and bamboo thickets

Geographic Range. Extreme southeastern People's Republic of China (Guangdong and Guangxi provinces) and northern Vietnam (Tonkin)

R. D. Bartlett

The head of the "Hundred Flower" Snake is somewhat elongated, typical of the many Asian species of *Elaphe*.

Natural History. An exceptionally attractive ratsnake, its complex patterns and colors are extremely variable. The specimen illustrated is typical, although the white area posterior to the head is an old scar. Its descriptive Chinese name translates as "Hundred-flower snake."

Initially described in 1886 and named for naturalist and explorer, O. F. von Moellendorff, the snake's habits in the wild and its geographic range are ill-defined.

Captives have deposited eggs in the fall of the year that have hatched after an incubation of two months. The behavior of the hatchlings is typical of rat snakes. Adults, known to reach a length of seven feet, feed on rodents and birds.

Care. Moellendorff's Ratsnakes are often heavily parasitized, and prompt elimination of identified forms is essential. Secure hiding places aid in reducing stress. Conditions acceptable for other rat snakes should be provided. Pre-killed laboratory rodents and/or chicks are accepted as food. Temperatures of 70-75° F (21-24° C) are satisfactory; higher temperatures should be avoided.

RUSSIAN RATSNAKE *(Elaphe schrenckii schrenckii)*

Habitat. Open montane forests, wooded valleys, and plains

Geographic Range. Eastern Asiatic U.S.S.R.

Natural History. An inhabitant of the temperate montane forests within its range (such as the Amurs), the adult ground color of indigo blue with crossbands of white or yellow superficially resembles that of the common Kingsnake, *L. g. getulus,* of the United States.

Powerful constrictors, they forage for small mammals, birds, and eggs, often frequenting agricultural areas in search of rats.

Russian Ratsnakes may retain their eggs, allowing for partial embryonic development, before deposition. Up to thirty eggs are deposited in mid-July and hatch in late August. The hatchlings are about a foot in length. Juveniles are unlike the adults in color and pattern, appearing indeed as a different snake entirely. A ground color of whitish-grey flecked with black and patterned with reddish-brown saddles gradually changes with age, however, to the adult pattern. Hatchlings and juveniles feed on nestling rodents and small birds. Adults may exceed six feet in length.

A subspecies, *Elaphe schrenckii anomala,* occurs in northeastern People's Republic of China and Korea, ranging south to Hunan province. This is a brown snake patterned with black blotches and crossbands. Juveniles are virtually identical to juveniles of the nominate race.

Care. Captive requirements suggested for American Ratsnakes apply equally well to these snakes. They should not be subjected to high temperatures, 74° F (23° C) being quite adequate. Pre-killed rodents and chicks are readily accepted as food. The species has been captive bred on numerous occasions.

The distinctive pattern
of the juvenile Russian
Ratsnake changes to
that of the adult
during its first
eighteen months.

J. Mehrtens

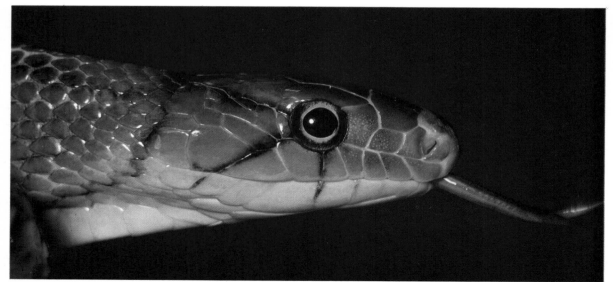

D. Hamper

RADIATED RATSNAKE; COPPERHEAD RACER (*Elaphe radiata*)

Habitat. Grassy river valleys; fields, open woodland and clearings; agricultural areas

Geographic Range. The Malay Archipelago and peninsula, north through Burma and southeastern People's Republic of China and Hong Kong

Natural History. Inhabiting open areas, the Radiated Ratsnake varies in ground color from yellowish to reddish brown, patterned with both dorsal and lateral black stripes anteriorly. A thin black band across the neck, in addition to three bands radiating from the eye, gives rise to the common name. These snakes are often found in the animal markets of southeastern Asia and are exported from Bangkok as "Copper-headed Racers."

Adults are diurnal. Young animals, however, tend to be nocturnal, a probable accommodation to the ready availability of frogs upon which they prey. Adults consume a variety of small mammals and birds, ascending shrubs in pursuit of the latter.

These ratsnakes are oviparous, with up to twelve eggs in gravid females being recorded in late spring and early summer. Hatchlings remain undescribed. Adults of five to six feet in length may be considered an average size.

As with many Asian ratsnakes, these animals compress their bodies vertically, form S-loops well above the ground and gape the mouth when threatened. The sudden appearance of white flecks produced by the vertical compression increases the effect of the display.

Care. Imported specimens should be checked and treated for parasites. Captive conditions suitable for other Asian rat snakes will suffice for this species. They accept pre-killed rodents and chicks as food.

D. Hamper

Often called the "Copper Headed" Racer

© J. Bridges

MANGROVE RATSNAKE *(Gonyosoma sp.)*

Habitat. Mangrove swamps and riverine forests
Geographic Range. Southeastern Asia and the Philippines
Natural History. The specimen illustrated was selected as a representative of the genus on the basis of its unusual color. Both subspecies of the single form of this genus, *Gonyosoma oxycephala,* are green in color.

Gonyosoma has been included in the Ratsnake genus, *Elaphe,* in the past, and is an equally powerful constrictor. Although primarily an arboreal form, they often descend to the ground to forage. They prey upon birds, their eggs and nestlings as well as small mammals.

They are oviparous; their eggs hatch after an incubation period of approximately three months.

The hatchlings measure about eighteen inches in length. They probably add frogs and lizards to the diet. Adults can exceed seven feet in length, but normally average about five.

Care. Newly imported specimens are often dehydrated and parasitized. The addition of electrolytes to water free of purification chemicals as well as treatment to eliminate intestinal parasites are necessary to stabilize and eliminate these conditions. Tall cages, fitted with branches for climbing, are required. Temperatures of about 80° F (27° C) and relatively high humidity should be provided. Captives accept pre-killed chicks and laboratory rodents. Captive longevities of six years have been attained.

S. Reichling, Memphis Zoo

D. Hamper

(Left) The Mandarin Ratsnake, *Elaphe mandarina,* a brilliantly colored and patterned species from southern China, has just recently begun to appear in western collections. It is sometimes called a ''Jade'' snake in the Orient. *(Right)* The Aodaisho or Japanese Ratsnake, *Elaphe climacophora,* occurs in Japan; an albino color morph is often associated with the goddess of love and fertility.

D. Hamper

F. Bolin, D. Hamper

(Left) Elaphe taeniurus is widely distributed throughout southern People's Republic of China, Burma, Laos and Assam; the Formosan form, *E. t. friesi,* is considered a subspecies. These colorful Ratsnakes probably owe their wide distribution to the fact that they are often kept in houses as a means of rodent control. *(Right)* The nine forms of Trinket Snakes found in India are here represented by the Common Trinket Snake, *Elaphe helena,* found throughout India. It reaches an adult length of about five feet. The lateral flattening of the neck in the specimen illustrated is a typical action of these snakes when annoyed or threatened. As do all Ratsnakes, they feed on rodents and birds.

Bullsnakes, Pine Snakes, and Gopher Snakes

Sonora Gopher Snake, *Pituophis melanoleucus affinis*

R. S. Funk

Often vividly patterned and of large size, these powerful constrictors were until several years ago considered to be of two species. The various Pine Snakes were subspecific to the species *melanoleucus*. The various Gopher Snakes and the Bullsnake were subspecific to the species *catenifer*. Intensive taxonomic study has demonstrated the species *catenifer* to be invalid. Thus, all are now subspecies of *melanoleucus*, the nominate race being the Northern Pine Snake, *Pituophis melanoleucus melanoleucus*. Ten subspecies are found in the United States and southwestern Canada. An additional five occur in Mexico, Central America, and Baja California. None are found in the northeastern states except for southern New Jersey.

Various rodents make up the bulk of the diet, and these snakes are of great benefit in farming and agricultural areas. Bullsnakes have been captured, and sometimes purchased, for release in barns, granaries, and the like. As "ratters," the snakes are far more skilful than cats.

When threatened, an elaborate defensive ritual is performed. The source of the annoyance or threat is faced with flattened head, open mouth and raised "S" loops of the body, and the tail vibrates rapidly. The snake appears larger as a result of large amounts of inhaled air. Forcibly expelled, this air produces loud hissing noises usually accompanied by strikes at the threat. When performed by a large specimen, the effect is formidable. Like most such displays, it is mostly bluster and given a chance for a safe exit, gracious or otherwise, the snake quickly takes it.

NORTHERN PINE SNAKE
(Pituophis melanoleucus melanoleucus)

Habitat. Sandy pine woods, sandhills, foothills
Geographic Range. Southern New Jersey, suitable habitat in northern Alabama, Virginia, Kentucky, and Tennessee
Natural History. This is one of North America's most dramatically colored and patterned non-venomous snakes. Some specimens, especially when freshly shed, may be enamel white with black and reddish-brown blotches. Pine Snakes are inveterate burrowers, which unfortunately soon dulls their vivid coloring.

A secretive snake, it spends much time underground, either in self-dug burrows or those made by other animals. Most often it prowls through rodent burrows in search of prey. As with other Pine, Bull, and Gopher snakes, multiple catches of rodents are frequent. This is accomplished by immobilizing mice or other prey against burrow walls, with half coils of the snake's body.

They are oviparous; up to several dozen creamy-white eggs are deposited in damp burrows or other suitable sites. Incubation, depending on temperatures, usually requires two and one-half to three months. Hatchlings, like the adults, are heavy-bodied and large, often eighteen inches in length. Adults may reach lengths of seven feet.

Equally large, often larger, the Southern Pine

D. Hamper

Southern Pine Snake, *Pituophis m. mugitus*

Snake, *Pituophis melanoleucus mugitus*, occurs from southern Florida north to southern South Carolina, and west to Alabama. Beige or tan in color, the blotch pattern is usually faded or indistinct and almost never as sharply defined as in its northern neighbor. Both subspecies are virtually identical in habits and habitat and freely intergrade over a wide area of range overlap.

Both subspecies are protected by state laws, the Northern by New Jersey and the Southern by Florida.

Care. Hatchlings and/or young animals are readily adaptable to captive care, feeding on pre-killed laboratory rodents. Wild-caught adults may prove difficult, often refusing to feed. Secure hiding places are necessary. If a "natural" substrate is used, avoid fine sand, as it causes potentially infectious abrasions of the skin between the scales.

S. Reichling, Memphis Zoo

S. Reichling, Memphis Zoo

(Left) Southern Pine Snake, *P. m. mugitus;* an unusual specimen with no pattern. *(Right)* The Louisiana Pine Snake, *P. m. ruthveni,* is an uncommon subspecies which ranges through the sandy soil of the pine woods in western Louisiana and eastern Texas.

The Black Pine Snake, *P. m. lodingi,* a melanistic Pine Snake which occurs in sandy pine woods in eastern Louisiana and southwestern Alabama.

S. Reichling, Memphis Zoo

R. Pawley

BULLSNAKE *(Pituophis melanoleucus sayi)*

Habitat. Grassy plains, prairies, sandy, semi-desert cactus "forests," agricultural areas, e.g., wheat fields

Geographic Range. Much of the central United States, east of the Rocky Mountains to western Indiana, north to southern Canada, south through central and western Texas into northeastern Mexico

Natural History. A yellowish-tan to yellow snake, thickly spotted and blotched with brown, reddish-brown, or rust. The color intensity varies more than the pattern. Specimens from semi-desert areas with light colored sand, for example, are usually very pale in color.

Although capable burrowers, they are more likely to shelter in mammal burrows or the cavities formed by the root systems of fallen trees. In southern Texas, clumps of Prickly Pear cactus *(Opuntia)* are favored.

When threatened, Bullsnakes are masters of the typical defense stance. Large specimens especially, produce sounds bordering on snorts and bovine grunts; hence, their common name.

One of the largest species found in the United States, Bullsnakes reach and probably exceed nine feet in length, although an average adult is usually about five feet long. Large eggs (three and one-half to four inches long) produce hatchlings approximately eighteen inches in length, capable of consuming fair-sized mice. Rodents form the primary diet, although other small mammals, birds, and occasionally eggs are eaten.

Care. Bullsnakes require dry, roomy caging, a secure hiding place, and a stable, rough-surfaced rock or log to assist in skin shedding. Hatchlings or young animals are most suited to a captive environment and present few if any problems. Substrate temperatures of 75-80° F (23-27° C) are suitable. Pre-killed laboratory rodents are the preferred diet.

D. Hamper

D. Hamper

(Left) The Mexican Bullsnake, *P. m. deppei,* superficially resembles in color and pattern its northern relative, the Bullsnake. *(Right)* In the western U.S. the Bullsnakes and Pine Snakes are generally referred to as "Gopher Snakes." The Great Basin Gopher Snake, *P. m. deserticola,* which ranges from southern British Columbia, Canada throughout much of the western portion of the U.S., is a typical example of these snakes.

The Baja Bullsnake, *P. m. vertebralis,* is a colorful subspecies which occurs in Baja California (Mexico).

E. Wagner

TEXAS GLOSSY SNAKE *(Arizona elegans arenicola)*

Habitat. Open woodland or plains in areas of sandy soil

Geographic Range. The *subspecies* illustrated occurs in southeastern Texas.

Natural History. A close relative of the Bullsnakes, *Pituophis,* Glossy Snakes have smooth scales, giving a polished appearance. They are pale yellow to beige in color, patterned with light to dark brown blotches and spots. The western subspecies are very pale in color and are commonly called "Faded" Snakes.

Glossy Snakes are efficient burrowers and spend much time underground. They emerge at night or in the early morning hours to forage for small mammals and lizards.

Up to two dozen eggs are deposited in early summer. Ten to twelve inches in length, the hatchlings are identical to adults, and feed primarily on lizards. Adults only occasionally attain a length of over three feet.

Arizona has an extensive range in the United States and Mexico, and a number of subspecies are recognized, although some are poorly defined. The nominate race, *A. e. elegans,* occurs from Kansas and southern Nebraska south through west Texas, into Mexico. *A. e. noctivaga* occurs in Sinaloa, Mexico, and north into Arizona. The Baja California form, *A. e. occidentalis,* also occurs in southern and central California.

Care. As for the Bullsnake, *Pituophis.*

Bullsnakes, Pine Snakes, and Gopher Snakes 113

The Kingsnakes

Florida Kingsnake, *Lampropeltis getulus floridana*

This wide-ranging group of Colubrids is confined to North, Central, and South America. As variable as the habitats they occupy, six species with more than thirty subspecies within one genus, *Lampropeltis,* are found within the United States.

The common name, Kingsnake, is usually applied to large-sized snakes that are subspecies of *Lampropeltis getulus.* These snakes occur coast to coast within the United States and well into Mexico. In addition to rodents, birds, and eggs (both bird and reptile) they also eat snakes, including venomous species. Although wholly or partially immune to the venom of North American Crotalids (rattlesnakes, copperheads, and cottonmouths), Kingsnakes do not seek them out to the exclusion of other prey species, a common belief in many rural areas. The misconception provides Kingsnakes a good reputation, however, and has saved the life of many a snake.

The Milk Snake, *Lampropeltis triangulum,* and its subspecies range from southeastern Canada over much of the United States south through Mexico, Central America and South America. The common name derives from the persistent (and ridiculous) belief that these snakes milk cows, usually while entwined about the bovine's rear leg. Oddly enough, many versions of this "milk snake" myth occur throughout the world.

A number of *Lampropeltis triangulum* subspecies have patterns of red, black, white, or yellow rings. They are often referred to as False Corals or Tri-colored Kingsnakes. These races share the pattern and common name with a number of western and Mexican species. Tricolored Kingsnakes are popular with collectors, and a number of forms are captive bred on a near commercial basis to supply this market.

J. Mehrtens

PRAIRIE KINGSNAKE *(Lampropeltis calligaster calligaster)*

Habitat. Open woodland, brushy hillsides, agricultural areas, grasslands, and pastures

Geographic Range. Western Louisiana, eastern Texas, Oklahoma, Kansas, north to Indiana and adjacent areas

Natural History. A slim Kingsnake, of attractive and variable pattern and color. The snake usually is some shade of tan or greyish-tan, with brown or reddish saddle markings. The pattern may fade and color darken with age, giving the appearance of a striped pattern. Prairie Kingsnakes are often confused with the Great Plains Ratsnake. The striped specimens superficially resemble Black and Yellow Ratsnake intergrades.

Very secretive burrowers, they are usually nocturnal, often seen on black-topped roads where they are attracted by residual warmth. Trash piles, discarded lumber, fallen logs and similar niches provide tight, secure hiding places for both the Kingsnake and its prey. Smaller snakes, mice, shrews, and lizards constitute the diet, with small birds and frogs occasionally added.

The young, ten inches in length, are hatched in early fall after an incubation period of less than

W. Lamar

A female *L. c. calligaster* collected in eastern Texas.

two months. Adults seldom exceed four feet in length.

A subspecies confined primarily to the eastern and gulf coast states, the Mole Snake, *Lampropeltis calligaster rhombomaculata,* lives up to its common name by spending most of its time in shallow, self-made burrows. Young animals may have a slight pattern of small, dark spots or blotches, but these fade with age. Adults are thus some uniform shade of brown, and its other common name, the Brown Kingsnake, is not inappropriate.

Mole snakes occur in much the same habitat as Prairie Kingsnakes. Diet and reproduction are identical and the two subspecies intergrade in range overlap areas.

Care. Plain caging, provided with a secure hiding place, is acceptable. If a "natural" substrate is used, dry leaves or shredded garden mulch is preferred to sand or gravel. A length of plastic pipe, open at both ends and buried in the leaves, makes a suitable simulated burrow. Pre-killed, small laboratory rodents are acceptable food, at a substrate temperature of 75-80° F (23-27° C).

A young specimen of the Mole Snake, *L. c. rhombomaculata*

D. Hamper

EASTERN KINGSNAKE; CHAIN KINGSNAKE
(Lampropeltis getulus getulus)

Habitat. Open woodland, especially pine or oak woods. The borders of swamps, canals, and streams are also favored.

Geographic Range. Suitable habitat from the pine barrens of southern New Jersey south to northern Florida and southern Alabama

Natural History. A large, secretive snake, its black, blue-black or dark brown body patterned with chain-like rings of white allows quick identification. Such ease of recognition and the common belief that they actively seek out and consume venomous snakes helps to protect them from immediate death, the usual fate of most snakes crossing a human's path.

They are oviparous; up to several dozen eggs usually incubate for two or two and one-half months before hatching. The brightly colored hatchlings feed on small snakes, lizards, and rodents.

Islands and banks occuring off the coast of North Carolina, e.g., Cape Hatteras, support a subspecies of a generally brown body color, with white or creamy speckles and rings. *Lampropeltis getulus sticticeps* is difficult to specifically identify without precise locality data.

Care. Kingsnakes have been favorites of collectors for years. Captive specimens have lived for twenty-five years and probably can exceed this age. Dry, clean cages, ample water, and pre-killed laboratory rodents and/or chicks meet their basic requirements. A temperature (substrate) in the middle to high 70's° F (mid 20's° C) is suitable.

R. D. Bartlett

D. Hamper

(Left) The Speckled Kingsnake, *L. g. holbrooki,* a subspecies ranging from southern Iowa and Illinois, south to eastern Texas, Mississippi and Alabama. *(Right)* The Black Kingsnake, *L. g. niger,* a glossy black subspecies occasionally patterned with a faint "chain" effect, occurs from southern Ohio and W. Virginia to northern Alabama and Georgia.

R. S. Funk

R. D. Bartlett

(Left) The Sonoran Kingsnake, *L. g. splendida,* ranges in semi-arid areas of central Texas and southeastern Arizona, south into central Mexico. *(Right)* The Yuma Kingsnake, *L. g. yumensis,* occurs in brushy, desert habitats in southeastern Arizona; this subspecies is not always recognized as a valid form.

FLORIDA KINGSNAKE *(Lampropeltis getulus floridana)*

Habitat. Varied, usually in the vicinity of canals, lakes or streams. They are commonly found in and around sugar cane fields and farmland.

Geographic Range. Central and southern Florida

Natural History. Yellow and brown scales often give this Kingsnake a "polka dot" appearance. Florida Kingsnakes naturally intergrade with Eastern Kingsnakes over the wide geographic area in which the ranges overlap. This, of course, makes precise identification difficult unless the specimen comes from an area well outside the area of intergradation. It should also be noted that a currently undescribed but apparently valid subspecies occurs in the Florida panhandle.

The very yellow Kingsnakes of extreme southern Florida, often cross-banded with reddish-brown, are sometimes referred to as Brooks's Kingsnake, *Lampropeltis g. brooksi*. This snake is probably a clinal variation of the Florida Kingsnake and not a valid subspecies.

Florida Kingsnakes breed early in the year, often during early March. Hatchlings feed on lizards, small snakes, and nestling rodents. Adults, seldom more than four feet in length, share the same

habits and diet as those of the Eastern Kingsnake.

Care. As for the Eastern Kingsnake, *L. g. getulus*.

B. Mealey

Brooks's Kingsnake, *L. g. brooksi*, a yellow Florida form whose subspecific status is controversial

CALIFORNIA KINGSNAKE *(Lampropeltis getulus californiae)*

Habitat. Varied, but usually associated with rocky outcrops, brushy semi-desert areas, and brushy hillsides. The snake also occurs in pine forests. **Geographic Range.** Baja California, north to

The striped morph of the California Kingsnake, *L. g. californiae*

Oregon and southern Utah and east to western Arizona

Natural History. Usually seen as a banded or striped snake, the California Kingsnake is so variable that the two pattern phases were once considered separate species. Pattern and color variables are seemingly endless. Black with creamy-yellow bands, brown with yellow bands, black with a white vertebral stripe (or brown with a yellow stripe!) and speckled patterns are the ones usually seen. Any combination of patterns may appear in the hatchlings of a single clutch of eggs.

Crepuscular, the California Kingsnakes become nocturnal during the hot summer months, especially in desert areas. As with other subspecies of the *getulus* group, these snakes feed upon other snakes, including venomous forms. They also feed on mice, birds, and lizards.

Up to two dozen eggs are deposited in rotted logs or similar locations. The foot long hatchlings emerge after two months (or slightly more) of incubation. Adults are usually three feet in length, rarely exceeding four.

Care. As for the Eastern Kingsnake, *L. g. getulus.* California Kingsnakes accept small, pre-killed rodents as food. They are regularly bred in captivity.

GRAY-BANDED KINGSNAKE
(Lampropeltis mexicana alterna)

Habitat. Varied; ranges from arid brushland to humid montane woodland

Geographic Range. Trans-Pecos area of Texas, south to Durango, Mexico

Natural History. Although the pattern of grey crossbands is normally present, this Kingsnake is so completely diverse in color and pattern that it almost defies verbal description. A few of the variations are illustrated.

A common snake within its range, it is so secretive that for many years it was considered rare. It emerges from its hiding place at night to forage for small mammals, snakes, lizards, and occasionally frogs.

Gray-Banded Kingsnakes breed in the spring and deposit small clutches of eggs beneath stones, logs or in other warm, damp locations. The ten-inch hatchlings emerge after some two months incubation, and do not necessarily resemble the parents or their siblings in color or pattern.

Several Mexican subspecies have been named, but they are difficult to define except perhaps by geographic location. Those most frequently referred to are Blair's Kingsnake, *L. m. blairi,* Thayer's Kingsnake, *L. m. thayeri,* and Greer's Kingsnake, *L. m. greeri.* All of the subspecies are slim snakes, averaging approximately three feet in length.

Care. These colorful snakes are popular in both public and private collections and as "pets." The majority of specimens available commercially are captive-bred. Captive conditions suited to other Kingsnakes are satisfactory.

L. m. thayeri adds to the difficulty of accurate identification of the Gray-banded Kingsnake subspecies, as it occurs in several color phases, the specimen illustrated being of the so-called "Milk Snake" phase.

E. Wagner

T. Granes

L. m. greeri occurs in various color morphs in Mexico (specimen illustrated was collected in the State of Guerrero in southwestern Mexico).

R. S. Funk

HUACHUCA MOUNTAIN KINGSNAKE
(Lampropeltis pyromelana woodini)

Habitat. Montane coniferous forest and brushland

Geographic Range. The *subspecies* illustrated ranges from southern Arizona south into northern Mexico.

Natural History. Another form of the "Tricolored" Kingsnakes so popular with collectors and pet keepers, they are ringed with red, black and white bands. The white bands may be yellowish, and the black bands are usually confined to the dorsum. The snout is usually white or yellowish.

A montane species occurring at elevations as high as 9,000 feet, they are found most often near streams in areas that are rocky or heavily littered with fallen, rotted logs, and similar cover. They may be diurnal or crepuscular, often basking in full sunlight during the cooler months. They forage for small mammals, small snakes, and lizards, and they subdue their prey by constriction.

Females deposit small clutches of up to six eggs in suitable nesting sites. After an incubation of approximately three months, the ten-inch young emerge and are identical to the adults. Although usually somewhat smaller, adults may attain up to forty inches in length.

In addition to *L. p. woodini,* three additional subspecies occur. The Arizona Mountain Kingsnake, *L. p. pyromelana,* ranges from central Arizona south into northwestern Mexico. *L. p. infralabialis* occurs in the Grand Canyon area north to Nevada, and *L. p. knoblochi* occurs in northwestern and western Chihuahua, Mexico.

Those forms found in Arizona are protected by state law.

Care. As for the various forms of the Milk Snake, *L. triangulum.* The various Mountain Kingsnakes are regularly bred in captivity and commercially available specimens are usually derived from such breedings. Captive longevities have exceeded fifteen years.

This specimen of *L. p. woodini* is a pattern variant in which the red bands are not suffused with black, the black appearing as clearly defined narrow bands.

S. Reichling, Memphis Zoo

The nominate race, *L. p. pyromelana,* occurs in northwestern Mexico extending northward to southeastern Arizona and southwestern New Mexico.

R. D. Bartlett

A. Weber, Toledo Zoo

EASTERN MILK SNAKE
(Lampropeltis triangulum triangulum)

Habitat. Varied, such as river valleys, hillsides, open mountain and lowland woodlands, fields, and agricultural areas

Geographic Range. This subspecies ranges from the northeastern United States west to Minnesota and south, at higher elevations, to northern Alabama.

Natural History. A slim Kingsnake, its ground color varies from very pale brown or tan to grey. It is patterned with several rows of black-bordered blotches that are dark red, reddish-brown, or brown. The venter is black and white, the colors arranged in a checkerboard fashion.

Called the "Milk Snake" because of a widespread and false belief that it milks cows, it does frequent barns, but in search of rodents and not milk! Milk Snakes also feed on small snakes, lizards, and occasionally small birds. It is secretive, sheltering in fallen logs, under stones or piles of debris. Favorite haunts are old stone walls, common in rural New England.

Milk Snakes are oviparous, the elliptical eggs being deposited beneath stones, in plant debris or in rotted logs. The eight-inch young are brighter in color than adults. Although four-foot specimens have been recorded, the average adult length seldom exceeds three feet.

There are over seventeen subspecies of the Milk Snake, ten of which are found in the United States. Others range through Mexico, and Central and South America. Banded or blotched with brilliant reds, white, and black, they are often mistaken for the venomous Coral Snake, *Micrurus*. The colors, shared with other species of Kingsnakes, are the basis for the collective name of "Tri-color Kings." Many of the American subspecies intergrade in areas of range overlap, the many resultant combinations of color and pattern creating confusion as to "which is what."

The Scarlet Kingsnake, *L. t. elapsoides,* is banded with red, yellow, and black, a near-perfect "mimic" of the Coral Snakes, except for the sequence of the colors. They occur in the southeastern United States. A western prairie form, *L. t. multistrata,* has orange rings instead of red. The Black-bellied Mexican Milk Snake, *L. t. annulata,* ranges into central Texas. Other Mexican subspecies such as *L. t. arcifera* and *L. t. nelsoni* are montane forms, occurring at higher elevations in the Sierras.

Tropical Milk Snakes are much larger than the northern forms. All are secretive animals, spending much time burrowing through loose forest litter. *L. t. hondurensis* occurs in several color morphs, one being tangerine. It is found in Honduras and adjacent areas. *L. t. abnorma* occurs in nearby Guatemala. *L. t. micropholis* ranges from Costa Rica south to Colombia and Ecuador. It is darker in color and attains lengths up to five feet. It is the most southerly ranging subspecies known.

Care. Milk Snakes are quite popular with collectors. Their brilliant colors, inoffensive dispositions, and captive stability insure their popularity as "pets." Considerable numbers are captive bred by professionals, and it is probably safe to say that the majority of Milk Snakes commercially traded are captive-bred specimens.

Basically, Milk Snakes can be housed in simple caging, free of drafts, and provided with a hiding place and water supply. Dampness should be avoided. Temperatures of about 78° F (26° C) are adequate for most forms, but may be slightly higher for the arid or tropical subspecies. The latter should be provided with a burrowing medium such as shredded-bark garden mulch. All of the forms will accept pre-killed mice of a size suitable to the snake. Captive longevities in excess of eighteen years have been recorded.

R. S. Funk

R. S. Funk

The central plains subspecies, *L. t. gentilis,* occurs in the panhandle region of Texas and adjacent Oklahoma and Kansas, as well as Colorado and southern Nebraska.

E. Wagner

R. D. Bartlett

The Red Milk Snake, *L. t. syspila,* occasionally attains lengths of forty inches, large for a North American Milk Snake; it occurs in northeastern Oklahoma, north to Indiana, Illinois, Iowa and southern S. Dakota.

D. Hamper

J. Mehrtens

(Left) The Mexican Milk Snake, *L. t. annulata,* occurs in rocky, brushy areas in south Texas and extends well into Mexico. *(Right)* The Sinaloan Milk Snake, *L. t. sinaloae,* a slender subspecies, occurs in western Mexico, e.g., Sinaloa.

T. Granes

R. D. Bartlett

(Left) The Pueblan Milk Snake, *L. t. campbelli,* is found in south central Mexico; the pattern and color are clear and distinct. *(Right) L. t. gaigae,* a montane form occurring in Panama and Costa Rica, is a somewhat somber-colored subspecies of a species known for its vivid coloration.

J. Mehrtens

R. S. Funk

(Left) The Honduran Milk Snake, *L. t. hondurensis,* a large subspecies from Honduras and adjacent areas; occurs in a wide variety of color morphs, e.g., red, orange, tangerine and "normal." *(Right)* Honduran Milk Snake, *L. t. hondurensis*; normal color and pattern phase

R. S. Funk

D. Barker, Dallas Zoo

(Left) The orange color morph of the Honduran Milk Snake, *L. t. hondurensis. (Right)* A tangerine color morph of the Honduran Milk Snake, *L. t. hondurensis*

R. S. Funk

The Scarlet Kingsnake, *L. t. elapsoides,* a brilliantly colored subspecies, ranges widely over the southern and southeastern United States.

SAN DIEGO MOUNTAIN KINGSNAKE; CORAL KINGSNAKE
(Lampropeltis zonata pulchra)

Habitat. Humid woodlands, pine forests, especially near brooks and streams

Geographic Range. The *subspecies* illustrated occurs in the montane areas of southern California (San Diego County).

Natural History. A tricolored Kingsnake with a black snout, patterned with black rings divided by red and separated by white rings. The specimen illustrated is typical of the subspecies.

They are secretive snakes, sheltering within and beneath fallen, rotted logs, drifted piles of leaves, or stones. They frequently bask during the cooler months, especially at higher elevations. Coral Kingsnakes forage for small rodents, lizards, and small snakes. They also climb into low-growing foliage in search of nestling birds, as well as to bask.

Up to eight eggs are deposited, the eight-inch hatchlings emerging after slightly more than two months of incubation. Adults average twenty-four to thirty inches in length, sometimes reaching forty inches.

Collectively referred to as California Mountain Kingsnakes, the seven subspecies of *Lampropeltis zonata* range along the western coast of the United States and parts of Baja California. The nominate race, *L. z. zonata,* occurs in Sonoma, Mendocino, and Lake Counties as well as Napa, California. The Sierra form, *L. z. multicincta,* is found on the western side of the Sierra Nevada. *L. z. parvirubra* is found in southern California. A rarely seen form, *L. z. agalma,* occurs in Baja California.

Care. As for the Sonoran Mountain Kingsnake, *L. pyromelana.*

A recently hatched San Diego Mountain Kingsnake.

Indigo Snakes, Cribos, Whipsnakes, and Racers

Ravergier's Racer, *Haemorrhois ravergieri*

R. D. Bartlett

This is a wide ranging and diverse group of Colubrids collectively circum-global in distribution. Their habitats are as varied as the snakes themselves and include deserts, semi-deserts, plains, savannahs, brushy hillsides, open woodlands, and agricultural areas.

Rodents and birds are dietary staples for these alert and active predators. Lizards, snakes, and insects are also eaten. One species, the Indigo Snake, includes small turtles in the diet.

None of these snakes are constrictors. Prey is quickly seized, immobilized with a body loop or coil, and rapidly swallowed.

All are oviparous, depositing their roughly-textured eggs in rotted logs, decaying plant material, under stones, or similar warm, damp locations. Hatchlings of some forms of the Racers, in which the adults are unicolored and patternless, are brightly colored and patterned, appearing to be of a different species. These juvenile patterns fade, however, as the snake matures.

Indigo Snakes, called Cribos in Latin America, are large, robust animals of a single species, *Drymarchon corais*. Its various subspecies range from the southern United States through Mexico, Central, and South America, to northern Argentina.

As the popular name implies, Whipsnakes, *Masticophis,* are long and rather slim snakes, found throughout the United States, extending south to northern South America.

The Racers, *Coluber,* range over much of the United States, adjacent Canada, and south to Central America. The closely related Speckled Racer, *Drymobius,* extends the range farther south into South America.

Various species of Racers occur in North Africa, southern Europe, the Middle East, and other parts of Asia. For many years Racers from these areas were referred to the genus *Coluber.* Relatively recent nomenclatural revisions now place them in the genus *Haemorrhois,* distinct from *Coluber.*

WESTERN YELLOW-BELLIED RACER
(Coluber constrictor mormon)

Habitat. Open grassland such as meadows, pastures, overgrown canal banks; edges of swamps and lakes. They are commonly found along highways having peripheral brushy growth.

Geographic Range. This subspecies ranges from western Wyoming, Colorado, and Montana, north to British Columbia, Canada, and south to Baja California.

Natural History. Typical of the many subspecies of racers, this is a unicolored, patternless snake that is diurnal in habit. Racers forage actively for food, feeding upon small rodents, birds, lizards, snakes, frogs, and insects such as locusts. Average adults are usually about four feet in length, although six-foot specimens are not unusual. Up to two dozen eggs are deposited in decomposing plant material such as fallen logs, sawdust piles, and leaf piles. When suitable nest sites are scarce, clutches from several females may be deposited in the same nest. Hatchlings are eight to twelve inches long, vividly patterned with red, brown, or greyish blotches on a grey ground color that fade as the animals mature.

Racers prefer rapidly vacating the area if threatened, but if captured or prevented from escaping will defend themselves vigorously, striking repeatedly and rapidly vibrating the tail.

Including the Mexican racer, *Coluber constrictor oaxaca,* which barely enters southern Texas, there are eleven subspecies that occur in the United States. The nominate race, *C. c. constrictor,* is popularly called the Black Racer and occurs in the northeastern United States. The Southern Black Racer, *C. c. priapus,* of the southeastern United States is sometimes referred to as the "White-chinned Racer." The two Yellow-bellied Racers, the eastern, *C. c. flaviventris,* and western, *C. c. mormon,* range throughout much of the central and western area of the United States. The Blue Racer, *C. c. foxi,* enters southern Canada.

Indigo Snakes, Cribos, Whipsnakes, and Racers 135

Some are slightly patterned at maturity, e.g., the Black-masked Racer, *C. c. etheridgei,* of eastern Texas, and the Buttermilk Racer, *C. c. anthicus,* a bluish-green snake speckled with creamy-white or yellow spots.

The technical name of the Racers is a misnomer, as racers are not constrictors. Their prey is seized, immobilized with a body loop if large, and summarily swallowed.

Care. There are always exceptions, but generally racers make poor captives. Nervous and irritable, they often refuse to eat. They are prone to infections and appear to be more susceptible than other species to snake mites, a dangerous ectoparasite. Cage-raised juveniles fare somewhat better. They require sizable caging, furnished with plentiful branches and twigs that increase the surface area, allowing the snake to "roam" over a greater area of varied surfaces. Water should not remain in the cage, but offered perhaps twice weekly. Exposure to ultraviolet light is beneficial. Small, pre-killed mice are acceptable food. Avoid if possible the use of lizards, frogs, or insects as food, as they are possible vectors of parasites. A substrate temperature of ± 80° F (27° C) is required.

R. S. Funk   R. S. Funk

(Left) **The Eastern Yellow-bellied Racer,** *C. c. flaviventris. (Right)* **The Blue Racer,** *C. c. foxi*

INDIGO SNAKE *(Drymarchon corais couperi)*

Habitat. Sandy-soiled, open woodland, especially areas of sabal palm, palmetto, pine and scrub oaks; near canals and other water sources; argricultural areas such as truck farms, mango and orange orchards

Geographic Range. Georgia, Florida and the Florida Keys. They have also been noted in extreme southern South Carolina and Alabama.

Natural History. A large, glossy, blue-black snake with a red, orange, or reddish-brown throat. Diurnal, they actively forage for prey, feeding on a wide variety of prey species including mice, rats, birds, frogs, lizards, and other snakes. As do the Kingsnakes, they attack and consume venomous snakes. Indigo Snakes frequently consume small turtles, an unusual food for snakes. Captive specimens have also fed on fish.

Eastern Indigo Snakes mate in late fall and early winter, depositing a dozen or so eggs in rotted logs, and mammal or gopher tortoise burrows. Hatchlings are patterned with whitish bands, and may be two feet in length. Average sized adults are five to six feet long, with exceptional specimens attaining nearly nine feet in length.

Indigo Snakes have vanished from many areas in which they were once common, primarily as a result of urban sprawl. The snakes are protected by Florida regulations that are, unfortunately, unrealistically conceived, e.g., they do not protect the habitat.

The Texas Indigo Snake, *Drymarchon corais erebennus,* occurs in the semi-arid areas of southern Texas, south to north-central Mexico. Similar in form and habit to the eastern subspecies, it differs only in the forepart of the body, which is reddish or tannish-brown in color. The sides of the head are patterned with black or brown lines, radiating from the eye. This subspecies is protected by the state of Texas.

Care. Indigo Snakes require large, dry cages, hiding places, and a water supply. Such minimal provisions are suited to their needs, and they quickly accept captive conditions, rapidly losing any aggressive tendencies towards their keepers. Substrate temperatures in the range of 80° F (27° C) are required. Captive specimens readily accept rodents and chicks. Reproduction of captive pairs is frequent and easily induced.

R. D. Bartlett   R. D. Bartlett

(Left) This hatchling Eastern Indigo Snake will lose its juvenile pattern as it matures. *(Right)* The Texas Indigo Snake, *D. c. erebennus*

R. D. Bartlett

CRIBO; YELLOW-TAILED CRIBO
(Drymarchon corais corais)

Habitat. Open woodland, savannahs, llanos, and swamps bordering forests

Geographic Range. Trinidad, Tobago, Surinam, Venezuela, south through Amazonia and Paraguay to Argentina

Natural History. These are large, robust snakes, dark brown to black in color anteriorly, fading to olive yellow, tan or pale yellow, patterned with brown posteriorly.

The tropical Cribos have habits similar to those of the northern Indigo snake, frequenting large, undeveloped areas. They are often common in the vicinity of cattle ranching operations. Diurnal, they forage for small mammals, birds, frogs, and snakes. They occasionally eat fish. They shelter in hollow logs, piles of debris, and burrows of mammals and tortoises, also using these shelters to deposit their eggs. Hatchlings may be eighteen to twenty-four inches in length. Adults average six feet, but may exceed eight feet in length.

Several other Cribos occur throughout the tropics. The Red-tailed Cribo, *D. c. rubidus,* ranges throughout western Mexico to southwestern Guatemala. *Drymarchon c. unicolor* occurs in Nicaragua, north to Chiapas in Mexico. As its subspecific name implies, it is of a uniform color, usually brown with no pattern.

The attractive Grey Cribo, *D. c. melanurus,* varies from grey to black in color with a pattern of dark slashes. It occurs from southern Mexico throughout Central America into northern South America.

Care. All of the Cribos fare well as captives when maintained under proper conditions. They soon dispense with any initial aggressive tendencies. Caging, temperatures, and diet suggested for Indigo Snakes, *D. c. couperi,* apply here as well. The Red-tailed Cribo, *D. c. rubidus,* has reproduced in captivity.

The Red-tailed Cribo,
D. c. rubidus

HORSESHOE RACER
(Haemorrhois [Coluber] hippocrepis hippocrepis)

Habitat. Brush, rocky hillsides; dry, sparsely wooded plains

Geographic Range. Spain, Portugal, Morocco, Tunisia, and northern Algeria

Natural History. A typical European Racer, these attractive snakes may be black, greyish-green, reddish-yellow, or reddish-orange in color, patterned with dark dorso-lateral blotches that may produce a ringed effect. The common name alludes to a dark horseshoe-shaped marking on the head.

Active snakes, they emerge from their hiding places as the day warms, often basking in full sun until optimum metabolic temperatures are reached. Their primary diet is lizards and small birds; small mammals and occasionally frogs are also eaten.

Mating takes place in early spring, with up to ten eggs deposited beneath stones, in fallen logs, or burrows. The slim hatchlings, perhaps ten inches in length, feed primarily on lizards. Adults can attain six feet in length, but they average about four.

A subspecies, *H. h. intermedius,* is found in Saharan Morocco and southern Algeria.

Care. Horseshoe Racers, as do most European racers and whipsnakes, usually remain nervous and aggressive as captives. They require dry, well-ventilated cages of good size, with temperatures of about 85° F (29° C), preferably dropping five degrees (three degrees C) or more at night. Branches for climbing and basking should be provided, as well as exposure to natural sunlight or ultraviolet. Adults will accept pre-killed mice and/or chicks. Small specimens will accept lizards, pre-killed small mice, and occasionally large arthropods, such as crickets or grasshoppers.

Indigo Snakes, Cribos, Whipsnakes, and Racers 141

Ravergier's Racer, *Haemorrhois ravergieri,* inhabits the dry, sandy areas of northeastern Africa (Egypt), ranging north into Israel to Turkey, Afghanistan and Pakistan. (A subspecies, *H. r. cernovi,* occurs in eastern Turkey and the U.S.S.R.)

R. D. Bartlett

RED WHIPSNAKE
(Masticophis flagellum piceus)

Habitat. Dry or semi-arid rocky areas, usually adjacent to low, brushy hills

Geographic Range. Northern Sinaloa and Sonora, Mexico; Baja California, north to southern California, Arizona, and Nevada

Natural History. A subspecies of the Coachwhip, this snake occurs in two color morphs (phases). The red phase (illustrated) varies from red to pink in color, patterned with dark crossbands on the neck. The black phase is unicolor and may be red beneath the tail. Juveniles are crossbanded or blotched with dark brown or black.

Similar in habits to other Coachwhips, the Red Whipsnake is an active, diurnal forager for rodents, small birds, and lizards. Young snakes also feed on large arthropods.

Care. As for the Western Coachwhip. Red Whipsnakes have a recorded captive longevity in excess of twelve years.

R. D. Bartlett

WESTERN COACHWHIP
(Masticophis flagellum testaceous)

Habitat. Open, brushy areas such as cedar brakes, mesquite prairie, grasslands, and pastures

Geographic Range. This subspecies ranges from northern Mexico through central Texas and Oklahoma, west to New Mexico and Nebraska.

Natural History. Quite variable in color, this snake may be unicolor black, brown, or pinkish-red; some populations may be olive, yellow-tan or pinkish, crossbanded with black or brown; or the head and anterior portion of the body may be dark.

Large, slim, and diurnal snakes, Western Coachwhips are capable of short bursts of very high speed, and can overtake the small mammals, lizards, small snakes, and occasionally birds on which they prey.

They breed in early spring after emergence from hibernation, often at sites shared with the Western

Diamondback Rattlesnake, *C. atrox*. The clutch of up to eighteen eggs produces hatchlings about fifteen inches long, which feed on the same prey as that of the adults, often including grasshoppers as well. Adults average five feet in length, but they can exceed seven feet.

The Western Coachwhip is one of eight subspecies of Coachwhips found in the United States. Additional forms occur in Mexico. All are subjects of various myths, such as excessive speed or utilizing its own body as a "whip" for flagellating enemies to death.

Care. Adults are often irritable and aggressive captives. Young adults or juveniles reared in a captive environment usually are more tractable and have attained captive longevities in excess of fifteen years. They require large, dry, and well-ventilated housing, equipped with hiding places and climbing branches. Substrate temperatures should be 80-85° F (26-29° C), and exposure to ultraviolet is beneficial. They accept pre-killed laboratory rodents and chicks as food. Captive breeding has been recorded.

The eastern Coachwhip, *M. f. flagellum,* ranges throughout the southeastern United States, west to eastern Texas.

R. S. Funk

The banded pattern morph of the eastern Coachwhip, *M. f. flagellum*

W. Lamar

Indigo Snakes, Cribos, Whipsnakes, and Racers 145

The Sonoran Whipsnake, *M. bilineatus,* occurs in northern Mexico, New Mexico and southern Arizona. Specimen illustrated is the Ajo Mountain Whipsnake, *M. b. lineolatus.*

R. D. Bartlett

Masticophis striolatus, a large Mexican species especially common in cultivated areas and grasslands, it is diurnal and terrestrial, but will sometimes climb to considerable heights in search of nestling birds. Juveniles have light bands on the neck region which gradually fade to the uniform adult color.

© J. Bridges

ORNATE WHIPSNAKE; CENTRAL TEXAS WHIPSNAKE
(*Masticophis taeniatus ornatus*)

Habitat. Rocky cedar brakes, hillsides, mesquite grasslands

Geographic Range. Western and central Texas, south to central Mexico

Natural History. Long, slim and fast-moving, these Whipsnakes vary in color from glossy black to pinkish or reddish brown. A series of white lateral markings with blurred edges may sometimes appear as indistinct crossbands. A reddish ventrolateral stripe is present; the venter of the tail is a vivid pink.

An active, diurnal species, they move about with the head raised well above the ground, watching for prey. Once sighted, the prey is quickly run down, the snake's burst of speed overtaking all but the most nimble of the lizards and small rodents that constitute the primary diet. Ornate Whipsnakes also prey upon small snakes (both harmless and venomous) as well as birds. They often climb into trees and bushes to forage for nestling birds, or to bask.

Up to twelve eggs are deposited beneath piles of leaves or other debris, or in unused mammal burrows. Hatchlings measure about fifteen inches in length. Adults average approximately five feet, and they may occasionally reach six feet in length.

Including the Ornate Whipsnake, five subspecies are recognized. The nominate form, the Desert Whipsnake, *M. t. taeniatus,* ranges from the southern part of Washington, southeast to New Mexico, western Texas and Mexico. *M. t. ruthveni,* a bluish-green snake, occurs in northeastern and central Mexico, barely entering southern Texas. The similar Schott's Whipsnake, *M. t. schotti,* occurs in southern Texas and southwestern Mexico. The southern race, *M. t. australis,* is an inhabitant of the dry grasslands of the Mexican Plateau and occurs as far south as the state of Michoacan.

Care. As for the Western Coachwhip, *M. f. testaceous.* Water should be offered several times weekly, but should not remain in the cage.

A dark specimen of the Ornate Whipsnake, *M. t. ornatus,* typical of west Texas populations

R. S. Funk

F.R.I., Inc.

SPECKLED RACER
(Drymobius margaritiferus margaritiferus)

Habitat. Thickets, brush-covered hillsides along streams or other bodies of water

Geographic Range. The *species* ranges from extreme southern Texas south along the east coast of Mexico, through Central America into northern South America. The nominate race (illustrated) occurs in the northern portion of the range.

Natural History. The yellow and blue spots on the scales of this attractive racer give the illusion of a green snake, especially when the animal is in motion.

Like all racers and whipsnakes, they feed on a wide variety of prey species. However, populations may "specialize" by concentrating on the most abundant prey species available and ignoring others. Frogs are usually considered the food of choice, but lizards, small rodents and small birds are also included in the diet.

Seldom attaining an adult length of over four feet in length, Speckled Racers deposit small clutches of four to eight eggs that incubate for usually less than two months. The hatchlings look much as the adults, although colors and pattern are not as well defined.

Throughout its extended range, *Drymobius* is represented by four species. *Drymobius margaritiferus* is represented by four subspecies, the illustration being the nominate race.

Care. Speckled Racers, despite their attractive appearance, are not often seen in captive collections. They require caging large enough to allow them to move and climb about freely. Security spots (hiding boxes) are very necessary, especially for recently captured or acquired specimens. A flattish water dish should be available. Temperatures between 80-85° F (26-29° C) are required, with a five degrees (two degrees C) nighttime reduction beneficial. Some daily exposure to ultraviolet is in the animal's best interest, but it is not critical. Frogs, small laboratory rodents (especially mice), or chicks may be accepted as food. When feeding pre-killed animals it may be necessary to attract the snake's attention to it by slight movement.

FOREST RACER *(Drymoluber dichrous)*

Habitat. Open forest
Geographic Range. Ecuador and Peru, east to southern Venezuela and northern Brazil
Natural History. A unicolored snake, varying in color from dark indigo to bluish-green. Hatchlings and juveniles are reddish-brown in color and crossbanded with black; the bands may be separated with white.

Drymoluber is a diurnal species, foraging for frogs and lizards through the forest floor litter. As with many tropical snakes, there is apparently no specific breeding season. Hatchlings have been observed in early and late spring as well as in the fall of the year. Adults attain a length of four and one-half feet.

A second species, *Drymoluber brazili,* is known from southern Brazil.
Care. It is assumed that conditions suitable for the Speckled Racer, *Drymobius,* would serve equally well for *Drymoluber.*

W. Lamar, courtesy E. Chapman

GREEN HEADED TREE SNAKE; WHIPSNAKE
(Chironius scurrulus)

Habitat. Forest edges and adjacent open areas; swamps

Geographic Range. The species illustrated ranges from eastern Peru, east through Amazonas.

Natural History. These large, slim snakes are dark brown to reddish-brown in color, with a scattering of blue and/or black scales over the body. The head may be irregularly colored with green and/or yellow. Hatchlings and juveniles are green in color, gradually darkening to the adult colors. They have very large eyes.

Chironius is a diurnal, semi-arboreal snake, and often shelters in small trees and shrubs. They actively forage for frogs and lizards, their primary prey. Oviparous, they deposit small clutches of eggs (seven or eight) in late spring. Adults attain a length of six feet or more.

Some fifteen species of *Chironius* range from Nicaragua south to Argentina and southern Brazil. They are a highly variable genus and often occur in areas of difficult access. Continued studies of these snakes will probably reduce the plethora of species, clarifying their currently somewhat confused relationships.

Care. *Chironius* is seldom included in collections, at least within the United States. Limited personal experience indicates that juveniles adjust to captive conditions far more readily than adults, which are frequently heavily parasitized. *Chironius* requires large, high cages equipped with climbing branches and a basking spot. *Chironius carinatus,* a species found in Central America and Trinidad, has accepted pre-killed mice, but most captives feed only upon frogs. Temperatures in the low 80's F (high 20's C), cooling at night, should be provided.

Chironius fuscus, ranging through central Brazil and northern South America, from French Guiana to Peru in the west, is a banded form similar in habits to the Green-headed Tree Snake.

Water Snakes and Their Allies

San Francisco Garter Snake, *Thamnophis sirtalis tetrataenia*

R. S. Funk

Worldwide in distribution, water snakes are a group of *Colubrids* sufficiently distinctive to warrant subfamily status, the *Natricinae.* A diverse lot, they bear little physical resemblance to each other. However, all share habitats associated with fresh or brackish water.

Some eighty species more or less are known, the largest number of these occurring in Asia. In the United States they are represented by several genera, perhaps ten species and many subspecies.

Several forms occur in Mexico, but with the exception of one subspecies, *Nerodia fasciata compressicauda,* which occurs in Cuba, water snakes are absent from the Caribbean Islands, Central, and South America.

Europe has several species, such as the wide-ranging Ringed Snake, *Natrix natrix,* and its many subspecies. This snake as well as two other European species also occurs in North Africa.

The Olive Marsh Snake, *Natriciteres olivacea,* represented by several subspecies, ranges from the Sudan south to Angola, Zimbabwe, and Mozambique. Another uniquely African species, *Afronatrix anoscopus,* is found in Liberia and Sierra Leone.

Asia has a seemingly endless variety of *Natricines,* usually referred to locally as "rice paddy" snakes or "keelbacks." Several forms such as *Natrix (Xenochrophis) piscator* and *Natrix macropthalmus* have elongated ribs that enable them to rear and spread a cobra-like hood when threatened. Several Asian *Natricines* have been noted as possessing salivary secretions of a toxic nature. The presence of venomous saliva in the absence of hollow fangs or grooved teeth is of considerable herpetological interest and may well result in reclassification of these forms.

Water snakes feed primarily on frogs, toads, and other amphibians, as well as small fish. A few forms add small mammals to the diet, and some are specialized such as the Queen Snake, *Regina septemvittata,* which feeds on crayfish almost exclusively.

All North American water snakes are ovoviviparous, some species giving birth to broods of nearly one hundred young. European and Asian species are oviparous, depositing up to fifty eggs in late spring and early summer.

The *Natricines* have been the subject of many taxonomic studies and interpretations, and remain in a state of taxonomic "flux." American water snakes, for many years included in the genus *Natrix,* have been placed into several different genera, e.g., *Nerodia* and *Regina.* These generic changes have been generally accepted as more accurately defining this group, and they are used here. Many current publications still use *Natrix,* however, and to minimize any confusion, *Natrix* has been inserted parenthetically in the species accounts, where applicable.

FLORIDA GREEN WATER SNAKE
(Nerodia [Natrix] cyclopion floridana)

Habitat. Swamps, marshes; sluggish streams
Geographic Range. Florida, north to South Carolina, and west to Alabama
Natural History. More often olive-brown, brown, or reddish-brown than green, the body is pattterned with brown or black crossbars and side bars. Large and heavy-bodied, they occur in considerable numbers in undisturbed areas, such as the Everglades. Size and availability of this snake encouraged several attempts, fortunately abortive, to establish a Florida snake leather industry in the 1940's.

Green Water Snakes feed primarily on small fish such as minnows. Diurnal, they frequently bask on low tree limbs and shrubbery overhanging water, into which they quickly fall if disturbed. One of the most prolific of the *Natricines,* large females may bear over one hundred young, eight inches or more in length. Adults average three to four feet, but six foot specimens are not uncommon.

The nominate race, *Nerodia (Natrix) c. cyclopion,* is virtually identical in color except for a dark colored venter speckled with cream-colored spots. It occurs from Alabama, north to Illinois, and west to Texas.

Care. Caging must be dry with adequate air circulation. Dampness quickly results in skin problems that are potentially infectious and often fatal. Exposure to ultraviolet is beneficial. A substrate temperature of 75-80° F (23-27° C) is adequate. Bait minnows and goldfish are accepted as food. Some specimens may also accept strips of fish and/or thawed, frozen fish such as smelts. Fish strips alone, however, are not nutritionally complete and should be used only if whole fish are unavailable. When feeding whole, thawed frozen fish (smelts), a brewer's yeast tablet should be inserted into each fish prior to feeding. This is a simple means of avoiding avitaminosis, which can result from the ingestion of frozen/thawed fish liver.

MANGROVE SNAKE; FLAT-TAILED WATER SNAKE
(Nerodia [Natrix] fasciata compressicauda)

Habitat. Coastal mangrove swamps

Geographic Range. Suitable habitat in the Florida Keys; southeastern and western Florida north to Tampa; northern Cuba

Natural History. One of the three subspecies of the Southern Banded Water Snake, *Nerodia (Natrix) fasciata fasciata,* that enter salt and/or brackish water habitats. Extremely variable, they may be solid black, brownish yellow or greenish in color, with or without black crossbars or bands. The specimen illustrated is typical of the red-orange phase. Identification of this subspecies is compounded by intergradation with the Florida Water Snake, *Nerodia (Natrix) fasciata pictiventris,* and the Salt Marsh Water Snake, *Nerodia (Natrix) fasciata clarki,* where ranges overlap.

Mangrove Snakes are small animals, seldom exceeding three feet in length. The tangled buttress roots of mangrove trees provide security and concealment, and these snakes are most often seen in the wild while sunning. The tail is slightly compressed laterally, and they are strong swimmers. Foraging mostly at night, they feed on small fish. In areas bordering fresh water, frogs are added to the diet.

Ovoviviparous, these snakes bear litters of a dozen or more young, eight inches in length. Secretive, the neonates spend much of their time in hiding beneath available debris, emerging in the evening to forage for small fish.

Care. Well-ventilated cages equipped with numerous branches for climbing and basking are necessary. Dampness should be avoided, and ultraviolet light is beneficial. Cool temperatures of 70-75° F (21-24° C) and a *warmer* basking spot should be provided. Bait minnows are acceptable as food.

The "normal" color morph of the Flat-tailed Water Snake

B. Mealey

B. Mealey

R. D. Bartlett

(Left) The attractive reddish-orange, patternless color morph of the Flat-tailed Water Snake. *(Right)* The Southern Banded Water Snake, *N. f. pictiventris,* often intergrades with the Flat-tailed Water Snake.

Water Snakes and Their Allies 157

W. Lamar

BROAD-BANDED WATER SNAKE
(Nerodia [Natrix] fasciata confluens)

Habitat. Marshes, swamps, lakes and streams; areas adjacent to them

Geographic Range. Eastern Texas, Louisiana, Mississippi, north through southeastern Oklahoma to southern Illinois (Mississippi Valley)

Natural History. North America's most colorful water snake, with broad black, dark brown or reddish-brown crossbands separated by irregular patches of yellow. The pattern is not usually clearly defined, and the colors may run together, often producing a "crazy quilt" effect.

Generally diurnal, Broad-banded Water Snakes become nocturnal during the hot summer months. Amphibians, especially frogs and small fish, constitute the diet. As with other American water snakes, young are born alive, usually in late summer. The eight- to ten-inch young are more vividly colored than the adults. They average about three feet at maturity.

Care. As for the Florida Green Water Snake, *N. c. floridana.*

R. D. Bartlett

The Southern Banded Water Snake, *N. f. pictiventris,* occurs within parts of the range of the Broad-banded Water Snake, with which it is sometimes confused.

LAKE ERIE WATER SNAKE
(Nerodia [Natrix] sipedon insularum)

Habitat. Marshes, swamps, ponds, and lakes
Geographic Range. Confined to the islands of Lake Erie's Put-In-Bay
Natural History. A usually patternless subspecies of the Northern Water Snake, *Nerodia (Natrix) s. sipedon,* Lake Erie Water Snakes are grey or greenish grey in color with a plain white venter.

Although isolated, the habits of this snake are essentially the same as those of the other *sipedon* subspecies. It frequently basks in shrubbery overhanging water and quickly plunges into it for safety if disturbed. Nocturnal during the warmer months, they forage for frogs and other amphibians, small fish, and crustaceans (crayfish).

Up to two dozen young are born in early fall. They feed on small frogs, tadpoles, and minnows.

Water Snakes of this species *(N. sipedon)* have an anticoagulant factor in their saliva. Bites inflicted by these snakes result in scratches and punctures that bleed freely.
Care. The care suggested for the Florida Green Water Snake *(N. c. floridana)* is suited to the Lake Erie Water Snake. Temperatures of 72-76° (22-24° C) are suitable, with a warmer spot for basking. Bait minnows are an acceptable food.

The Northern Banded Water Snake, *N. s. sipedon,* is patterned and colored quite differently from the isolated Lake Erie form.

Water Snakes and Their Allies 159

**BROWN
WATER
SNAKE
(Nerodia
[Natrix]
taxispilota)**

J. Mehrtens

Habitat. Swamps, lakes, rivers, and streams
Geographic Range. Southeastern United States, e.g., southern Florida, north to Virginia, and west to Alabama
Natural History. A large, heavy-bodied water snake, pale to dark brown in color, and patterned with a series of dorsal and lateral dark-brown blotches, somewhat square in shape. The venter is yellow.

Brown Water Snakes aare excellent climbers and are often seen basking at considerable heights in trees overhanging water. As do most water snakes, they quickly plunge into water when disturbed. They are diurnal and feed upon fish and amphibians, especially frogs.

Females produce up to fifty young, ten to twelve inches in length, during the summer months. Adults are usually four to five feet in length, and they may attain six feet.

Brown Water Snakes defend themselves vigorously, inflicting lacerating bites and voiding the contents of the anal sacs when threatened or restrained.

Care. As for other species of this genus. Captive breeding has been recorded.

R. D. Bartlett

The Diamond-backed Water Snake, *N. r. rhombifera,* ranges from southern Alabama west throughout Oklahoma and Texas and south into Mexico, where two additional subspecies occur. In the eastern edges of its range it is sometimes confused with the Brown Water Snake.

D. Hamper

RINGED SNAKE; GRASS SNAKE
(Natrix natrix natrix)

Habitat. Marshes, bogs, wet meadowland, grassy hillsides adjacent to streams or rivers; farmland
Geographic Range. Germany, Denmark north to Scandinavia, east to the U.S.S.R., south to Iran, Iraq, Syria, and Cyprus
Natural History. The most widespread of the European water snakes, the ten subspecies occur the length and breadth of the continent. A whitish-yellow, yellow, or yellow-orange band behind the head is characteristic, although this may be absent in some specimens or indistinct in others. Body color varies from a silvery grey to

olive brown, with a pattern of black flecks, bars or stripes.

Ringed Snakes are oviparous, but unlike most egg-laying snakes, retain the eggs for up to two months after mating, and then deposit them in compost heaps, hay piles, and similar sites of decomposing plant material. The embryos are thus well advanced, and external incubation time is shorter. Utilization of the same nesting site by many females is common, and aggregations of over one hundred eggs are known. The shortened incubation period has allowed the Ringed Snake to extend its range well into the sub-arctic of Scandinavia.

These snakes feed primarily on frogs, small toads, and other amphibians, as well as fish. Large specimens add small rodents to the diet.

Adult size varies from subspecies to subspecies. *Natrix n. helvetica* (England, France, Belgium, the Iberian peninsula) and *N. n. astreptophora* of northwest Africa average three to four feet in length. *Natrix n. persa* (Transcaucasia) may exceed six feet. The central European subspecies average four to five feet in length.

Ringed Snakes are inoffensive, even when threatened. If escape is impossible they void the contents of both cloaca and anal glands, writhe and contort the body, and eventually "die" with open mouth and lolling tongue. The performance of these "death throes" is similar to the technique used by the American Hognose Snakes, *Heterodon.*

Care. Ringed Snakes should not be maintained unless a long-term supply of frogs or bait minnows are available. Standard simple caging, free from dampness, is adequate. Temperatures of 75-80° F (23-27° C) (cooler at night) allow normal activity. Exposure to ultaviolet is beneficial. A hibernation period is essential to reproduction.

DICE SNAKE *(Natrix tessellata tessellata)*

Habitat. Brushy, grassy or rocky areas adjacent to sluggish streams, canals, ditches, ponds, and similar slow-moving bodies of water.

Geographic Range. Switzerland, south through Italy, east and south to the U.S.S.R., Turkey, Egypt, and Cyprus. The range extends farther eastward to Afghanistan and from Pakistan to extreme western People's Republic of China.

Natural History. The popular name alludes to the pattern of square, dark markings giving a checkerboard effect on a ground color of greyish or brownish-green. Black examples are known. Some populations are yellow or pale green, the contrasting dark pattern of squares being especially vivid in these variants.

Dice Snakes seldom stray far from water and spend much time basking in overhanging shrubs and small trees. If alarmed they quickly fall into the water to escape. Their eyes, set high in the head, allow them to remain hidden in water while safely surveying their surroundings.

Dice Snakes mate shortly after emergence from hibernation, depositing up to two dozen eggs in rotted logs, under stones or other warm, damp locations. Hatchlings, six or seven inches in length, feed on small frogs, tadpoles, and fish. Adults vary in length, the southern populations being larger, but rarely exceeding four feet in length.

Care. As for the Ringed Snake, *N. n. natrix.* The cage should be equipped with branches to allow basking at a warmer temperature than the substrate, which should be maintained at 72-78° F (22-26° C). Exposure to ultraviolet or natural sunlight is beneficial. Dice Snakes accept frogs and bait minnows as food.

J. Mehrtens

RED-NECKED KEELBACK *(Rhabdophis subminiatus)*

Habitat. Brush-covered or grassy fields adjacent to streams, ditches, paddies

Geographic Range. Eastern India, southern People's Republic of China, Hong Kong, Taiwan, the Malay Peninsula and Indonesia

Natural History. An olive, greenish-grey or greenish-brown snake patterned with indistinct flecks of black and yellow, which in some specimens may appear as netlike reticulations, or as a mid-dorsal stripe. The neck and forepart of the body are vivid red; the sides of the head are yellow, patterned with a subocular black streak.

Similar to American Garter Snakes, *Thamnophis,* in habits, they remain hidden during the day, emerging at dusk to forage. Amphibians are their primary prey, especially frogs. They also eat small fish.

Red-necked Keelback Snakes are oviparous, with up to fifteen eggs being recorded. The eight- to ten-inch young hatch in July and August, dif-fering from adults by the addition of a yellow-bordered black band or collar on the neck, which fades as the snake reaches its mature length of forty inches.

These snakes, as well as other species of *Rhabdophis,* are so-called "cobra mimics." When threatened, the snake rears the forepart of the body and spreads a hood, which in the Red-necked Keelback prominently displays its bright coloration.

There are some twelve species of *Rhabdophis* found throughout southeastern Asia. One species, *Rhabdophis tigrinus,* occurs in Japan. All are typical Colubrid natricine snakes, but they have enlarged, ungrooved rear teeth, and for many years they were included in the genus *Natrix* that included both American and European water snakes.

In 1974, a case of human envenomation from a bite delivered by *R. tigrinus* (commonly called the "Yamakagashi") in Japan was reported. Another report of severe envenomation was reported in England, from the bite of a "pet" Red-necked Keelback, and since that period of time a fatality resulting from the bite of a Yamakagashi has been reported. Not all bites from *Rhabdophis* are envenomated, and often the snakes appear reluctant to bite (the specimen illustrated required considerable provocation to spread even a minimal hood and did not threaten to bite). However, these snakes can deliver a fatal bite and should be handled with respect and caution.

Care. Newly imported specimens should be carefully checked for internal parasites and treated accordingly. Any substrate other than fine sand or gravel is suitable. This snake's requirements include a sizeable water dish, hiding box, and climbing branches. They readily accept bait minnows or strips of fortified fish (from forceps) as well as frogs. Temperatures of 75-80° F (23-27° C) are suitable. Several species of *Rhabdophis* are exported from Asia under the obsolete generic *Natrix*, mentioned here as a reminder that one unfamiliar with the lethal potential of this species may assume this to be a harmless water snake. *Rhabdophis* should not be kept as a "pet" snake.

Defensive stance of *Rhabdophis*; note the flattened neck area

J. Mehrtens

BLACK SWAMP SNAKE
(Seminatrix pygaea pygaea)

Habitat. Aquatic vegetation in sloughs, ditches, swamps

Geographic Range. Alabama east to coastal Georgia, south to central Florida

Natural History. A relative of the water snakes, Swamp Snakes are small in size, unicolor black with a red venter, and their scales are smooth with a "patent leather" sheen.

Although they may prowl about on land on warm and rainy nights, they normally occur in tangles of floating vegetation. The introduced water hyacinth, considered a plant pest throughout the southeast, is a perfect home for Swamp Snakes. They prey upon small amphibians, tadpoles, small fish, and worms.

Swamp Snakes bear living young, up to a dozen four-inch babies being born in late summer and early fall. Adults do not usually attain more than eighteen inches in length.

Two additional subspecies occur in the southeastern United States. *S. p. cyclas* is found in southern Florida and *S. p. paludis* occurs in North and South Carolina.

Care. Simple to house and maintain, *Seminatrix* is a good "classroom" snake. Its study may include such topics as food chains, ecology, the effect of introduced species (hyacinths), and other aspects of its life history and environment. They should be housed in aquaria in shallow water and provided with sundry water plants and a branch for basking. A temperature of 75-80° F (23-27° C) is suitable. Small goldfish or minnows as well as earthworms are accepted as food.

Regina septemvittata,
a close relative of the
water, swamp and
garter snakes, feeds
exclusively upon
crayfish. It is found in
the Great Lakes region,
south to the Gulf
Coast, and is
commonly known as
the Queen Snake.

R. S. Funk

SAN FRANCISCO GARTER SNAKE
(Thamnophis sirtalis tetrataenia)

Habitat. Areas adjacent to ponds, ditches, streams, e.g., meadows, farmland, open woodland, marshes

Geographic Range. San Mateo County, California

Natural History. Perhaps the most vividly colored of the many dozens of species and subspecies of garter snakes found throughout the United States, Canada, and Mexico, the San Francisco Garter Snake is patterned with red, black, and greenish-yellow stripes. The venter is blue. Primarily as a result of land reclamation and drainage projects, the San Francisco Garter Snake is an endangered species and is protected by both California and the federal government. It is one of about twelve subspecies of the Common Garter Snake, *Thamnophis sirtalis.*

Garter snakes are adaptable animals and occur in coastal areas as well as montane habitats. They occur near streams and rivers in arid areas, both in the United States and Mexico. They frequently occur in urban areas, taking up residence in empty lots, parks, and often cemeteries. Some forms gather in astonishing numbers at hibernation sites, particularly the Plains Garter Snake, *T. radix.* The spring emergence from hibernation is actually a tourist attraction in southern Canada.

As would be expected, garter snakes prey upon

a wide variety of species. While certain species may concentrate on a specific food item or two, as a genus they feed upon small mammals, birds, carrion, amphibians, especially frogs and salamanders, fish both live and dead, earthworms, and leeches. *Thamnophis couchi,* a species of western North America, includes fish eggs in the diet.

Garter snakes may be active day or night, remaining hidden away in or beneath various shelters when not actively foraging.

All garter snakes bear living young. Neonates vary in size according to the species involved, and may be from six to ten inches in length. Litter size also varies, and may be as few as six or as many as eighty-five. Adult specimens are usually twenty-four to thirty inches in length, although some, such as Butler's Garter Snake, *T. butleri,* of the north central states, are smaller (adults being fifteen to eighteen inches); and the largest, the Aquatic Garter Snake, *T. couchi,* may exceed four feet in length.

Ribbon Snakes, close relatives of the garter snakes, are similar in pattern but slimmer. They are almost always associated with water or wet meadows. The Eastern form, *Thamnophis sauritus,* occurs over the eastern third of the United States and is represented by four subspecies. The Western Ribbon Snake, *T. proximus,* is represented by six subspecies ranging throughout the central United States, south to Costa Rica.

When molested or captured most garter snakes void the cloacal contents as well as the contents of the anal glands. They can deliver lacerating bites, which may bleed freely, possibly as a result of an anti-coagulant factor in their saliva.

Care. Along with other small snakes that often occur in company with garter snakes, e.g., Brown Snakes, *Storeria,* Lined Snakes, *Tropidoclonion,* and Ring-necked Snakes, *Diadophis,* garter snakes are the snakes usually found in the pockets of schoolboys, as well as in the classroom terrarium. Many herpetologists were first introduced to snakes in this manner, and with one of these species.

With the exception of trouser pockets, garter snakes will accept a wide assortment of caging and conditions. It is critical to their well-being that cag-

D. Hamper

R. S. Funk

(Left) The Common Garter Snake, *T. s. sirtalis,* is known from twelve subspecies, widely ranging over most of the U.S. and southern Canada. *(Right)* The Blue-striped Garter Snake, *T. s. similis,* is confined to northwestern peninsular Florida.

ing be kept dry; only a water bowl for drinking is required. Damp conditions result in skin problems that are difficult to cure and often prove fatal. Most forms will accept earthworms or small minnows as food. They may also be conditioned to accept strips of fortified fish (although not as the sole diet).

R. D. Bartlett

R. D. Bartlett

R. S. Funk

(Top Left) The Two-Striped Aquatic Garter snake, *T. couchi hammondi,* a western form occurring from Monteray, California to Baja California. It is among the largest of the garter snakes. *(Top Right)* Occurring in the southwestern United States, western Texas and western Oklahoma, the Checkered Garter Snake, *T. m. marcianus,* extends into northern Mexico (the Mexican form is subspecifically distinct). It feeds on frogs, minnows and small crayfish. *(Bottom Left)* Both the western *(T. proximus)* and the eastern *(T. sauritus)* Ribbon Snakes are slender versions of the heavier bodied Garter Snakes. The Peninsula Ribbon Snake, *T. s. sackeni,* found in South Carolina, Georgia and Florida, is a typical example.

D. Hamper

Eight subspecies of the Brown Snake, *Storeria dekayi,* occur in moist woodlands, marshes and swamps as well as vacant lots, from southern Canada to northern Mexico. They seldom exceed twenty inches, and are often confused with the Eastern Garter Snake, with which they often occur. They feed upon earthworms and slugs. They are able to survive even within large urban centers. The closely related Red-Bellied Snake, *Storeria o. occipitomaculata* (illustrated) is known from three subspecies and occurs over much the same range.

Other Colubrids

Eastern Hognose Snake, *Heterodon platyrhinos*

B. Mealey

EASTERN WORM SNAKE *(Carphophis amoenus amoenus)*

Habitat. Woodland, meadows, and agricultural areas

Geographic Range. Southeastern Massachusetts south to central Georgia, west to Alabama

Natural History. Smooth and glossy, these little snakes are pale, unicolor brown with no pattern. The venter is pink.

They are secretive snakes and virtually never appear in the open, unless flooded from their subterranean tunnels. They also shelter beneath stones, trash piles, and in decaying, fallen logs. They prey upon earthworms and the soft larvae of insects.

Clutches of up to eight eggs, less than an inch in length, hatch after an incubation period of about seven weeks. Hatchlings are about four inches long, maturing to an average length of ten inches, rarely exceeding twelve inches.

The Midwestern race, *C. a. helenae,* occurs east of the Mississippi River, from Ohio to the southern gulf coast. The Western Worm Snake, *C. a. vermis,* is found west of the river from Nebraska to northern Louisiana.

Worm snakes are a frequent prey species for Kingsnakes and Milk Snakes, *Lampropeltis.*

Care. Shredded bark garden mulch as a burrowing medium allows captive Worm Snakes to remain contentedly hidden most of the time. Earthworms released into the burrowing medium will be found by the snake. This species is usually kept as a captive only for demonstration purposes.

R. D. Bartlett

(Top) The twelve subspecies of Ringneck Snakes, *Diadophis punctatus,* occur over much of the eastern and south central United States. They are secretive, sheltering under rocks or logs. They are weak constrictors and prey upon earthworms, small salamanders, lizards and occasionally hatchling snakes. They share the common characteristic of tightly coiling and elevating the tail and posterior portion of the body to display the bright red, orange or yellow venter as a defense posture. The specimen illustrated is the Northern Ringneck Snake, *D. p. edwardsi,* found from Nova Scotia south to northeastern Georgia and Alabama. *(Bottom)* The San Diego Ringneck Snake, *D. p. similis,* found in southern California and Baja California, displays its red venter in a tight curl when molested.

R. S. Funk

SCARLET SNAKE *(Cemophora coccinea coccinea)*

Habitat. Areas of friable or sandy soil, in or near open woodland

Geographic Range. The nominate race illustrated occurs in peninsular Florida.

Natural History. This snake is often confused with the Coral Snake, *Micrurus,* and ringed kingsnakes such as the Scarlet Kingsnake, *Lampropeltis,* despite the fact that the pattern is saddle-like and the venter is plain colored, usually white or cream.

Scarlet Snakes are secretive animals, sheltering in or under logs or similar debris or in self-made burrows. Although they are competent constrictors and feed on small snakes, lizards, and nestling mice, the preferred food is reptile eggs, a dietary preference shared with the Asian genus, *Oligodon.* Both snakes possess specialized, enlarged, maxillary teeth enabling them to slit the soft shells of eggs too large to be swallowed whole.

Oviparous, Scarlet Snakes deposit up to eight or ten eggs, the six-inch hatchlings emerging in late summer. Adults average two feet in length.

The northern race, *C. c. copei,* occurs in northern Florida, north to New Jersey, and west to eastern Oklahoma. The Texas subspecies, *C. c. lineri,* occurs in southern Texas.

Care. They require a shredded bark substrate for burrowing, and temperatures of 75-80° F (23-27° C) are suitable. Many specimens stubbornly refuse all food except reptile eggs. In this case, some specimens have been maintained successfully through the "ruse" of filling empty shells of snake or turtle eggs with beaten chicken egg. However, the procedure is effective only if the empty reptile egg shells retain the appropriate odor.

An unusual albino example of the Scarlet Snake, *C. c. coccinea*

B. Mealey

SHOVEL NOSED SNAKE
(Chionactis occipitalis occipitalis)

Habitat. Desert; rocky hillsides, arroyos, creosote bush and mesquite areas

Geographic Range. Deserts of the southwestern United States and adjacent Mexico

Natural History. An attractive little snake, well adapted to burrowing and "swimming" in fine, loose, desert sand. The nostrils, equipped with valves, can be closed to prevent entry of sand. The smooth scales and angular head enable it to vanish with astonishing speed beneath the sand.

Shovel Nosed Snakes, like other desert denizens, are nocturnal, foraging in the open for spiders, scorpions, and centipedes. They also eat insects and their pupae.

Oviparous, they deposit small clutches of up to four eggs. The tiny hatchlings feed upon the same prey as adults. Average sized adults are twelve inches in length.

Three additional subspecies are known, including the Nevada Shovel Nosed Snake, *C. o. talpina*, the Tucson subspecies, *C. o. klauberi*, and the Colorado desert form, *C. o. annulatus*, which ranges south into Mexico.

Care. The difficulty in securing or maintaining an adequate food supply precludes the captive maintenance in these snakes, except by specialists.

SMOOTH SNAKE; CROWNED SNAKE *(Coronella girondica)*

Habitat. Hedgerows, grassy hillsides, and rock slides, meadows and fields; rock walls

Geographic Range. Southern France, the Iberian peninsula, adjacent northwest Africa, Sicily, Italy, and southwestern Austria

Natural History. Unlike its widely ranging relative, *Coronella austriaca,* this snake is more variable in color and shows no evidence of possible sexual dichromatism. The ground color may be brown, grey, or yellowish, often suffused with shades of pink. Flecks of dark brown or black coalesce on the dorsum to form small blotches. The characteristic "crown," or horseshoe pattern, on the head gives the popular name.

Closely related to the American Kingsnakes, *Lampropeltis,* both snakes were once classified within the same genus.

Somewhat lizard-like in habits, they shelter in damp rock crevices and tunnels, emerging to sun themselves and forage. Constrictors, they feed primarily on lizards, but they also feed on small snakes, lizard and snake eggs, mice, and occasionally small birds. Juveniles may also feed on crickets, grasshoppers, and similar insects.

Mating takes place upon emergence from hibernation, and the young are born in late summer. Neonates are approximately six inches in length. Adults average two feet. Specimens larger than this are considered unusual and rare.

Coronella austriaca, similar to *C. girondica* in habits and habitat, is often but not always sexually dimorphic. Males are brown or reddish-brown with a brownish venter; females are brownish-black or grey with a grey venter. The pattern of flecks and blotches may form a dorsal zig-zag line similar to that of the European Adder, *Vipera berus,* with which it is sometimes confused.

Seldom more than two feet in length, *C. au-*

striaca is one of the few snakes ranging into far northern Europe. It occurs in Sweden, Norway and southeastern England where, incidentally, it is protected.

Two subspecies are recognized. The nominate race, *C. a. austriaca,* ranges from southern England and Scandinavia south through France and eastward to the Balkan countries, northern Turkey, and adjacent Iran. *C. a. fitzingeri* is confined to southern Italy and Sicily.

C. austriaca has virtually vanished from many parts of Great Britain; now considered a protected species by the British government.

L. Trutnau

Care. Smooth Snakes are difficult to maintain, and any attempts at captive maintenance should only be for purposes of serious research and study. Physical requirements of humidity, temperature, and food are difficult to reproduce or simulate, and in addition hibernation is a prerequisite to breeding. Smooth Snakes are best left in the wild.

AFRICAN EGG-EATING SNAKE *(Dasypeltis scabra)*

Habitat. Primarily plains, savannahs and open woodlands; utilizes many different habitats, but does not occur in deserts or rain forests.

Geographic Range. Northeastern Africa (Egypt, Somalia) southern Arabia, west to Gambia, and south to the Cape of South Africa

Natural History. Considered to be a "viper mimic," these snakes are usually some shade of brown, or reddish or pinkish brown. They can be grey, and are occasionally black. They are patterned with black rhombs or diamond shapes, often forming a chain-like effect. The dorsal scales are heavily keeled and the lower lateral scales are serrated.

Egg-Eating Snakes are partially arboreal, often utilizing birds' nests as a retreat after consuming the eggs. They also shelter beneath loose tree bark, or under stones, and sundry debris on the ground.

Adults average thirty inches in length and may attain three and one-half feet. Up to eighteen eggs are deposited singularly, over a period of a day or so, and not always at the same nesting site. The seven- to ten-inch young feed only on small bird eggs.

These snakes are completely adapted to their sole diet of hard-shelled eggs, and they are all the more unique in their ability to swallow whole eggs of a diameter far greater than that of the snakes themselves, which are seldom thicker than a small finger. Virtually toothless, the snakes have a few minute teeth embedded in their gums. A bellows-like fold of skin between the mandibles and extremely elastic gular skin enable the snake to engulf a chicken egg with ease. The ventral projections of some thirty vertebrae (Hypapophyses) are modified to complete the ingestion of the egg;

those of the twenty-second to twenty-eighth vertebrae are capped with enamel and penetrate the esophagus. Once the egg is in the throat, vertebrae twenty-nine and thirty prevent its moving, while vertebrae one through twenty-one prevent the egg's slipping out of the mouth. The pointed, enamelled hypapophyses of vertebrae twenty-two and twenty-eight pierce the egg shell, while those of vertebrae twenty-three to twenty-seven neatly crack the shell between the two punctures. The contents of the egg then drain into the stomach, and the two halves of the shell are manipulated into an elongated mass and regurgitated. Egg-eating Snakes prefer fresh eggs, and if an embryo is present, it is usually ejected along with the shell.

Egg-Eating Snakes have little or nothing with which to defend themselves. They rely on mimicry of the defensive actions of venomous snakes, duplicating the rasping, saw-like sounds of the Saw-scaled Viper, *Echis,* by rubbing the serrated, lower lateral scales over each other in rapid coiling and uncoiling motions. In areas where this viper does not occur, Egg-Eating Snakes mimic the actions of the Night Adder, *Causus,* by inflating the body with air, loudly hissing and feigning open-mouthed, aggressive strikes.

The Egg-Eating Snakes are placed in a subfamily of their own, the *Dasypeltinae,* that consists of two genera, *Dasypeltis* and *Elachistodon.* The African genus, *Dasypeltis,* is represented by five species, in addition to *D. scabra.* The Forest Egg-Eater, *D. atra,* occurs in Zaire, Uganda, and Kenya.

D. fasciata is found in western Uganda, west to Gambia. The attractive *D. m. medici* occurs in Tanzania, Mozambique, Malawi, and Zimbabwe. A subspecies, *D. m. jamuensis,* ranges from Somalia south through Kenya. *D. inornata* and *D. palmarum* are southern forms, the former is found in Natal and Swaziland. The latter is found in Angola and Zaire.

The Indian Egg-Eating Snake, *Elachistodon westermanni,* is something of an enigma, in that along with the same modifications for consuming eggs as those of *Dasypeltis,* it also has two grooved, maxillary teeth at the rear of the mouth. Venom-conducting teeth are obviously of no use in "attacking" eggs, and the reason for the presence of these teeth is unknown. *E. westermanni* is found in Bengal. It is a small snake, and adults reach about thirty inches in length. It is considered an endangered species.

Care. Although these snakes can swallow hen eggs when adult, quail or pigeon eggs are a better choice, as they are easier for the snake to deal with. Juveniles may be fed sparrow or finch eggs. Egg-Eaters usually will not accept cleaned or washed eggs. Placing the eggs in the debris of a chicken coop or active nest imparts the required odor. Substrate material should allow the snake to stabilize its body while positioning and swallowing its food. Drinking water should always be available. Provide a hiding box and branches for climbing. Temperatures of 78-85° F (25-29° C) should be maintained.

R. S. Funk

TROPICAL CHICKEN SNAKE *(Spilotes pullatus pullatus)*

Habitat. Rain forests, open brushy woodland; partially cleared areas near farms and villages
Geographic Range. Trinidad, Tobago, Surinam, Guyana, south to northern Argentina, and north to southern Central America
Natural History. This brightly colored, long-tailed, slender snake ranges vertically through all levels of tropical forests. Variable in color and pattern, individuals may be lemon yellow with blue-black stripes and blotches, or nearly solid black with a few yellow and orange markings.

An intimidating display of raised body loops, inflated throat area, and rapidly thrashing tail is performed to ward off predators and other threats.

Rarely found far from water, they actively forage for both arboreal and terrestrial prey, including small mammals, birds, frogs, lizards, and snakes. Rural livestock areas with a resident rodent population attract these snakes, which often find chicks and pullets an easier meal; thus the popular name. Prey is killed by constriction.

Spilotes are oviparous, with egg deposition and incubation procedures typical of Colubrids. Hatchlings feed primarily on frogs and lizards. Adults average six to seven feet in length, ten feet is not unusual, and twelve feet has been recorded.

Including the nominate race, five subspecies are known. One of these, *S. p. mexicanus,* ranges as far north as Tamaulipas, Mexico.

A bizarre version of the "milk snake" myth revolves around these snakes in many rural areas of the tropics. The snake is reputed to seek out sleeping, nursing mothers, who are placed into a deeper sleep with breath from the snake's inflated throat. The snake then proceeds to replace the infant at the mother's breast, assuring itself of an uninterrupted meal by allowing the evicted infant the use of its tail as a pacifier!
Care. Specimens available to collectors are almost always wild-caught and should be carefully checked and treated for parasites. Caging should be of generous proportions, provided with ample opportunities for climbing. Right-angled branches partially covered with foliage are preferred hiding places. Temperatures of 78-85° F (26-29° C) are suitable. Misting with water of the same temperature assures proper skin shedding. Pre-killed rodents and chicks are accepted food. Captive reproduction has occured.

SNAIL-EATING SNAKE; THIRST SNAKE
(Dipsas variegata variegata)

Habitat. Bushes, shrubbery, and trees in humid forests

Geographic Range. French Guiana, west to Ecuador and Peru

Natural History. These snakes, anatomically specialized for efficiently extracting snails from their shells, are placed in a subfamily of their own, the *Dispsadinae.* They are represented by several genera occurring in Central and South America, of which *Dipsas* is the most widespread and most well known. The specimen ilustrated is typical of the arboreal forms and was collected in southern Surinam.

The arboreal forms have rather wide, short heads and long, thin tails that function as balancing poles as the snake moves from branch to branch. Unlike that of many other arboreal species, the tail of *Dipsas* is not truly prehensile. They are most active at night or in the early morning, when their molluscan prey is also active. Their specialized skull structure allows the lower jaw (mandible) to move forward and backward independently of the upper jaw (maxilla). When extracting a snail from its shell, the snail is grasped and securely held in place by the sharp, recurved teeth located at the front of the maxilla.

The mandible is then pushed into the shell and engages the mandibular teeth into the body of the snail, after which the mandible is withdrawn, bringing the snail with it, neatly extracted from the shell.

Thirst Snakes are oviparous, but few facts are

known of their eggs or young. Adults of most forms are usually no longer than thirty inches.

Two additional races of *Dipsas variegata* are known. *D. v. trinitatis* is confined to Trinidad; *D. v. nicholsi* occurs along the eastern coast of Panama, south to northwestern Ecuador. Although subject to considerable taxonomic revision, *Dispas* is known from some thirty species. Additional genera in the subfamily are *Sibynomorphus*, *Sibon*, and *Tropidodipsas*, the latter a terrestrial form, which occasionally climbs into low-growing shrubs. It is considered by some taxonomists to be synonymous with *Sibon*.

Snail-eaters are represented in Asia by several genera such as *Pareas*, but they are placed in a subfamily of their own, the *Pareinae*. They are much like the neotropical species in habits and habitat.

The African Slug-eating Snake, *Duberria*, is not related to either of the foregoing subfamilies, other than that it is a Colubrid. Feeding primarily on slugs, it also preys upon shelled molluscs. It deals with the problem of the hard shell by simply grasping the exposed portion of the snail's body and smashing the shell against a convenient rock or other hard object!

Care. Caging suitable for other tropical, arboreal snakes will suffice for Snail-eaters. Temperatures of 76-78° F (24-26° C) are adequate. These snakes will usually accept edible snails *(Helix sp., Octala sp.)*, which are available in specialized, ethnic markets in the larger cities.

© J. Bridges

T. sartori, a terrestrial snail-eating species which occurs as three subspecies, ranging on both the Atlantic and Pacific coasts of southern Mexico, south to Guatemala

MUD SNAKE; HORN SNAKE
(Farancia abacura abacura)

Habitat. Muddy ditches, streams, sloughs, swamps, marshes, and flood plains

Geographic Range. Florida, north to southern Virginia, and west to Alabama, usually in coastal areas

Natural History. A cylindrical, smooth-scaled, bluish-black snake patterned with red or pinkish-red on the venter and sides. The tip of the tail terminates in a sharp, conical scale that becomes blunted as the snake matures. The terminal scale has a two-fold function. It aids the snake in manipulating its slippery prey of salamanders and fish into an alignment allowing for ease of swallowing. It is also used as a somewhat feeble deterrent to capture by a predator in being repeatedly pressed against the skin of the aggressor. Its popular name of "Horn Snake" (or "Stinging Snake") derives from this defensive action.

Mud Snakes are avid burrowers in soft soil and mud as well as being good swimmers, foraging for food in shallow water. Although small fish and amphibians, especially tapoles, are eaten, their primary prey are the eel-shaped salamanders, *Amphiuma* and *Siren*.

Up to one hundred eggs are deposited in cavities in the drier soil of stream banks or in hollow, rotted logs. The female will often coil about the eggs and remain with them until they hatch, usually a two-month period. The eight- or nine-inch hatchlings feed on tadpoles as well as other small amphibians. Adults are usually about four feet in length, but specimens in excess of six feet have been recorded.

A western subspecies, *Farancia abacura reinwardti,* ranges through eastern Texas and western Alabama, north to southern Illinois.

Care. The specialized diet of Mud Snakes would be difficult to provide on a long-term captive basis. However, these snakes respond well to odor-manipulated food. A living specimen of *Siren* or *Amphiuma* can be maintained for this purpose.

Strips of vitamin fortified fish, or beef of a size and shape simulating a salamander is placed in a container with the live salamander for an hour or two. Once thoroughly scented, the food may be presented to the Mud Snake, which in most cases is readily accepted.

An aquarium with several inches of wet garden mulch strewn with bark slabs provides adequate housing. Provision of a suitable, *dry* basking area is essential, and temperatures of 75-80° F (23-27° C) are suitable. Captive specimens have achieved longevities of twenty years.

Both subspecies of the Mud Snake coil about their eggs which are deposited in an underground chamber. The female illustrated is the western form, *F. a. reinwardti.*

R. S. Funk

This juvenile *F. a. reinwardti* has reared the posterior body and tail, a defensive stance used by many snakes, including the Pipe Snakes and Coral Snakes.

R. S. Funk

RAINBOW SNAKE
(Farancia erytrogramma erytrogramma)

Habitat. Cypress swamps, marshes, and sandy fields near water

Geographic Range. Lowlands of the eastern United States, from Maryland south to central Florida and west to the Mississippi Valley

Natural History. A secretive, smooth-scaled burrower that is seldom seen. Bluish-black or black in color, they are patterned with three vivid red stripes the length of the body. A yellow stripe appears along the side, normally just above the red ventral scales.

When not hidden in burrows or beneath logs or other debris, they swim about in search of eels, their principal and often only prey.

Females deposit up to fifty eggs in a cavity formed in damp soil or beneath fallen logs. The eight-inch young feed on tadpoles, small frogs and salamanders. The average adult length is four feet. Occasionally they attain, but rarely exceed, five-and-one-half feet.

The terminal scale of the tail is pointed and sharp, and the snake is reputed to "sting" to death its prey or molester. Actually, Rainbow Snakes are timid and innocuous animals, and of course, the sharp terminal scale is harmless.

A subspecies, *F. e. seminola,* with a black venter as opposed to the red venter of the nominate race, occurs in the vicinity of Lake Okeechobee in southern Florida.

Care. Adults should not be maintained as captives unless a consistent supply of eels can be assured by local fish markets or other sources. Housing suitable for the Mud Snake, *F. abacura,* will suffice for this species.

EASTERN HOGNOSE SNAKE *(Heterodon platyrhinos)*

Habitat. Areas of sandy or friable soil in meadows, fields, open woodland

Geographic Range. A large part of the eastern half of the United States. Central Minnesota, western Kansas, and eastern Texas are the western boundaries of the range.

Natural History. Variable in color, this stocky snake may be brownish, grey, yellow, red, or tan, patterned with dark blotches on the back and sides. Local populations of completely black specimens are common.

Diurnal snakes, they are competent burrowers and when foraging for their primary prey of frogs and toads will root out toads burrowed beneath several inches of soil. The generic name, *Heterodon,* means "different tooth," a reference to enlarged rear teeth that serve to introduce a mild venom into prey.

Eastern Hognose Snakes are oviparous, and they place up to sixty eggs in cavities dug in loose soil. The hatchlings may vary from six to ten inches in length. The average adult size is three feet.

These snakes perform an elaborate defensive ritual when molested. Flattening the neck somewhat in the manner of a cobra, they hiss like a leaky radiator, inflate the body, and strike at the intruder with apparent determination, but usually with a closed mouth. Should this defense appear ineffective, the snake suddenly collapses, voids the cloacal contents, writhes about and gapes the mouth; after which it rolls convulsively on its back, and with a final shudder or two becomes totally limp. Apparently convinced that a dead snake must be "belly up," it promptly rolls on its back if turned right side up. After a brief interval, the snake observes the area, and, if the coast is clear, flips over and leaves.

Hognose Snakes of the genus *Heterodon* occur only in the United States, Canada, and northern Mexico. However, a small group of South American snakes were included in this genus during the nineteenth century. Today these snakes are known as *Lystrophis,* the three species occurring in Brazil, Argentina, Paraguay, and Bolivia. *Lystrophis* performs much the same defense procedures as those of *Heterodon.*

Care. Unless an adequate supply of frogs or toads is available, Eastern Hognose Snakes should not be maintained. If a food supply is available, however, proper housing would include a substrate of shredded-bark garden mulch, a hiding place and a water dish. Temperatures of 75-80° F (23-27° C) are adequate. Captive Hognose Snakes quickly lose interest in performing "death throes" theatrics.

The finale of the complex defense display of the Hognose Snake; when the threat has passed, the animal will cautiously peer about, right itself and move quickly away

R. S. Funk

Lystrophis semicinctus, a brightly colored South American species, performs much the same defense procedures as the North American Hognose Snakes.

W. Lamar

WESTERN HOGNOSE SNAKE *(Heterodon nasicus nasicus)*

Habitat. Prairies, abandoned farmland, sparsely wooded flood plains, especially in areas of sandy or friable soil

Geographic Range. The nominate race occurs in New Mexico, the Texas Panhandle, and western Oklahoma, north to southern Canada

Natural History. A short and stocky snake, lighter in color than its eastern relatives. A ground color of tan, brownish-yellow or greyish-yellow is patterned with dark blotches on the back and sides. The venter is usually blackish with white or yellow-white markings.

Unlike their eastern relatives, Western Hognose Snakes usually do not perform the elaborate defense procedures of spreading a hood and demonstrating "death throes." The usual procedure is spreading a slight hood, hissing softly, and if at all possible, quickly leaving the area. Competent burrowers, they escape mid-day heat and night-time chill underground. Essentially crepuscular, they forage for small rodents, nestling birds, lizards, and amphibians. They will on occasion also eat small snakes and reptile eggs.

Up to two dozen eggs are deposited, the seven-inch hatchlings emerging after about a two-month incubation period. Adults rarely exceed two feet in length.

Several subspecies are recognized. The nominate race (illustrated) is often called the Plains Hognose. Others are *H. n. gloydi,* found in Texas and Kansas, and *H. n. kennerlyi,* which occurs in southern Texas, southern Arizona, and Mexico.

Care. A substrate of dry, shredded-bark garden mulch is superior to abrasive gravel or sand. Avoid wood shavings. Provide a hiding place and water bowl, and a temperature of 75-80° F (23-27° C). Most specimens readily accept small, pre-killed mice as food.

The burrowing
Southern Hognose
Snake, *Heterodon
simus,* ranges from
extreme southeastern
North Carolina, south
to central Florida and
west to eastern
Mississippi. It inhabits
dry, sandy open areas
and feeds upon
amphibians and
occasionally small
rodents.

© J. Bridges

*Xenodon r.
rabdocephalus,* a
South American
relative of the
Hognose Snake, is
often called the "False
Fer de Lance." Several
species of *Xenodon*
occur throughout
central and South
America. They
feed primarily upon
amphibians.

© J. Bridges

R. S. Funk

SPECKLED SNAKE *(Leimadophis poecilogyrus reticulatus)*

Habitat. Open forests, fields adjacent to swamps and streams

Geographic Range. The *subspecies* illustrated occurs in Bolivia, Paraguay, northern Argentina, and southern Brazil.

Natural History. The twelve subspecies vary greatly in color and pattern, ranging from pinkish-brown to bottle green and patterned with stripes, spots, or zig-zag dorsal stripes. The specimen illustrated is typical of the subspecies *reticulatus.*

This species occurs in habitats similar to those of the Northern American water snakes, *Nerodia,* and some of the Garter Snakes, *Thamnophis.* Although not aquatic, they are good swimmers and forage in marshes and swamps for their primary prey of amphibians and small fish. Some of the subspecies inhabiting drier habitats prey upon lizards and small rodents.

While a relatively common snake, details of reproduction in wild populations are meager. Captive females have deposited small clutches of six or seven eggs that hatch after about forty days of incubation at 80° F (27° C). The eight- to ten-inch young prey upon small frogs. The adult size of *L. p. reticulatus* is about forty to forty-eight inches.

The genus *Leimadophis* encompasses some forty species, which range collectively from southern Central America and several of the Caribbean islands (Trinidad, Tobago, Curaçao, and Grenada) south over much of South America. The various species and subspecies occupy a wide variety of habitats. A species occupying the forest floor, *Leimadophis typhlus,* occurs in South America, east of the Andes.

Care. As for American water snakes, *Nerodia.* *Leimadophis* usually refuses small, dead rodents, but has accepted small, whole fish, e.g., minnows and goldfish, offered from forceps.

Leimadophis typhlus, a terrestrial species, occurs in South America

R. S. Funk

Placed by some taxonomists in the genus *Liophis, Leimadophis reginae* occurs as two subspecies in northern South America, east of the Andes.

W. Lamar

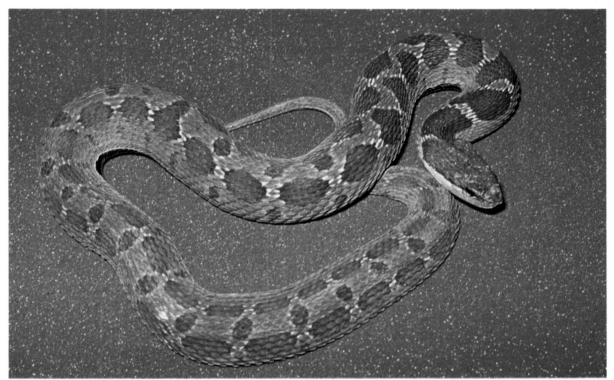

FALSE HABU *(Macropisthodon rudis)*

Habitat. Montane meadows, forests, and wooded hillsides

Geographic Range. South central and southeastern People's Republic of China; Taiwan

Natural History. A grey, brown or reddish-brown snake patterned with darker blotches, spots and triangles. A light-colored band defines the head. The scales are strongly keeled and rasp-like in appearance.

Habu is the commonly used vernacular for a group of Asian Crotalids, *Trimeresurus,* that occur on many islands in the western Pacific and the China Sea. *Macropisthodon,* when annoyed or otherwise threatened, flattens its body and coils in a manner similar to that of venomous snakes.

The head is flattened into a roughly triangular shape and drawn back as if to strike. The ruse is effective, and the snake is considered venomous by many people living within its range. It is, of course, harmless.

False Habus are relatively rare snakes and little is known of their habits. Seldom exceeding three feet in length, they are oviparous. Hatchlings are patterned and colored like the adults. Frogs, other amphibians, and small snakes are preyed upon.

Care. Rarely seen in collections. Captive specimens have accepted frogs as food. A substrate temperature of 72-76° F (22-24° C) with some exposure to natural sunlight or ultraviolet appears necessary.

ROUGH GREEN SNAKE *(Opheodrys aestivus)*

Habitat. Low trees, shrubbery and bushes, usually near streams, canals, lakes, and ponds

Geographic Range. Eastern United States, from New Jersey to Florida, west to Texas, Kansas and northeastern Mexico

Natural History. One of several species of semi-arboreal green snakes that occur in the United States and eastern Asia

Rough Green Snakes are diurnal, foraging in shrubbery and bushes for grasshoppers, spiders, and other insects and arachnids, their primary prey. Occasionally small frogs and lizards are eaten.

Rough Green Snakes deposit up to a dozen eggs, the eight-inch hatchlings being duller in color than the thirty- to forty-inch, bright-green adults.

The small Smooth Green Snake, *Opheodrys vernalis,* is found throughout southern Canada, the northeastern and north central United States, south through Texas and northern Mexico. Two forms are known, the Eastern Smooth Green Snake, *Opheodrys v. vernalis* and the Western, *Opheodrys v. blanchardi.* Seldom more than twenty inches in length, they feed on insects and spiders.

Several species occur in Asia. The large, forty-inch long *Opheodrys major* is found on Taiwan, the southeastern provinces of the People's Republic of China, Hong Kong and south into Vietnam. It frequents hillsides and bamboo thickets, usually in mountainous regions. It feeds largely on earthworms. The Japanese Green Snake,

Opheodrys herminae, occurs in southern Japan and the Ryu Kyu Islands.

Care. Green Snakes are gentle creatures and adjust well to proper captive conditions. The Rough Green Snake should be provided with caging offering vertical climbing space, equipped with a sturdy, well branched plant. The Smooth Green Snake of the United States does not require the height for climbing; a cage floored with shredded garden mulch and a branch or two suffices. Temperatures of 75-78° F (23-24° C) are suitable, and exposure to ultraviolet is beneficial. American species may be fed bait crickets. The Asian forms, housed in the same manner as the Smooth Green Snake, accept earthworms.

The arboreal Rough Green Snake, *O. aestivus,* is an accomplished climber, and difficult to detect in heavy foliage

R. S. Funk

R. D. Bartlett

D. Hamper

(Left) Although primarily a terrestrial snake, the Smooth Green Snake, *O. vernalis,* frequently forages in shrubs and bushes. *(Right)* The large oriental species, *O. major,* occurs in mountainous areas; this specimen was collected on Taiwan.

MOLE SNAKE *(Pseudaspis cana cana)*

Habitat. Grasslands, savannahs, sandy open woodlands, adjacent rocky foothills

Geographic Range. Suitable habitat from Kenya south through South Africa, west to Angola

Natural History. A large, stocky constrictor whose popular name of "mole snake" derives from its hearty appetite for the many and varied species of moles that inhabit the plains and savannahs of Africa.

A unicolored species that varies from pale grey or tan to black. Lighter-colored specimens occasionally have darker tones on the edges of the scales, which produce a spotted effect.

Mole Snakes spend much time searching through rodent burrows for prey. Often common in agricultural areas, they are sometimes kept in barns and granaries for rodent control, much like the American Bullsnake. Birds, as well as their eggs, are also eaten, usually if typical prey is in short supply.

Viviparity in Colubrids is somewhat unusual. The Mole Snake is viviparous, bearing young that show no resemblance to the adults. Juveniles are tan, pale brown, yellowish, pale dusty red, or pink in color, with four rows of spots, usually dark brown or black that may appear as spots, blotches, stripes, or zig-zag lines. It is not at all surprising that adults and young are often thought of as two different species of snakes. The juvenile pattern fades rapidly, however, with little trace showing in a specimen of two feet in length.

Litters are large, and three to six dozen are average. A specimen in the collection of Regents Park Zoo (London) is recorded as producing a litter of 95! Neonates are eight to ten inches in length, and adults may reach six feet.

A subspecies, *Pseudaspis cana anchietae*, occurs in Burundi, Rwanda, Zaire, and Angola.

Care. Mole Snakes readily accept pre-killed rodents and are quick to adjust to captive conditions. Secure hiding places, fresh water and a substrate temperature of 80-85° F (26-29° C) are required.

MAHOGANY RAT SNAKE; PUFFING SNAKE
(Pseutes poecilonotus polylepis)

Habitat. Trees and shrubs in open forest; savannahs

Geographic Range. The illustrated subspecies ranges from Trinidad and the Guianas west to Ecuador and Peru, south to Brazil and Bolivia.

Natural History. A large, light to dark brown snake with a greyish-white venter. Subadults are greyish brown and patterned with indistinct grey crossbands. The scales are keeled and may give the appearance of thin, longitudinal stripes.

Mahogany Rat Snakes are excellent climbers and forage at considerable heights. They are not truly arboreal, however, frequenting terrestrial habitats as well. Their prey includes small mammals, birds and their eggs, and probably large lizards. Hatchlings add frogs to the diet.

When threatened, *Pseutes* flattens the body laterally, and inflating the throat and neck, hisses loudly. Large specimens can strike out at intruders from a considerable distance, especially from an elevated position in high shrubbery. Average adults are five feet in length, although some specimens may exceed this.

Three additional subspecies are known. *P. p. argus* and *P. p. poecilonotus* occur in Mexico, Honduras, and Guatemala. *P. p. chrysobronchus*, an attractive black and grey snake, is found in Costa Rica and Nicaragua.

Care. As for the tropical Chicken Snake, *Spilotes*. Newly imported specimens should be carefully checked and treated for parasites.

Two subspecies of the Yellow-throated Puffing Snake, *P. sulphureus,* occur in South America, from central Brazil north to Trinidad. The specimen shown is the nominate race, collected in Surinam. They can attain lengths of eight to nine feet.

W. Lamar, courtesy E. Chapman

MEXICAN LONG-NOSED SNAKE *(Rhinocheilus lecontei antonii)*

Habitat. Lowland thorn scrub, and dry woodlands

Geographic Range. Western Mexico, e. g., Sinaloa, Sonora

Natural History. A common snake in the dry and semi-arid habitats of its range, the Mexican Long-Nosed Snake has a more clearly defined pattern than that of the subspecies found farther north. The specimen illustrated is typical in color and pattern. The snout is pointed and projects past the lower jaw, an aid to burrowing.

During the day they remain hidden in self-dug burrows, rock crevices or other shelters, emerging at night in search of prey, which includes small mammals and snakes, lizards, and reptile eggs.

Long-Nosed Snakes are oviparous, depositing their eggs in underground cavities. The hatchlings are about ten inches long and feed primarily on lizards. They average about three feet as adults.

These snakes quickly hide their heads under the body when molested, simultaneously raising the tail and lashing it about while voiding the contents of anal glands and cloaca, mixed with a bloody fluid.

Paler in color and speckled in appearance, the Texas Long-Nosed Snake, *R. l. tessellatus,* is found from San Luis Potosi and Chihuahua, north through Texas and New Mexico. The nominate race, *R. l. lecontei,* occurs in Arizona, Utah, Nevada, California, and Baja.

Care. Dry, draft-free caging should be equipped with a substrate suitable for burrowing, or with tight, flat hiding places. Small branches should be provided for climbing as well as an aid to skin shedding. Temperatures of 80-85 ° F (26-29 ° C) are required for normal activity. Small, pre-killed laboratory mice are accepted as food. Captive longevity has exceeded sixteen years.

The Texas Long-nosed Snake, *R. l. tessellatus*; the specimen illustrated was collected in Valverde County, north of Del Rio, Texas.

W. Lamar

© J. Bridges

NECK-BANDED SNAKE
(Scaphiodontophis annulatus hondurensis)

Habitat. Rocky areas in humid forests; borders of swamps and streams

Geographic Range. The *subspecies* illustrated occurs in northern Honduras.

Natural History. A rare and unusual Colubrid, the forepart of the body is red, banded with black; the black bands are separated by grey. With the exception of several black dorsal blotches following the banded area, the rest of the body is unicolor light brown and patterned with three, dark brown, longitudinal stripes.

These are secretive snakes, remaining hidden much of the time in and beneath fallen logs, exposed root systems, and similar shelters. They are most active in the early morning or after showers.

The teeth are unlike those of most snakes in that they are flattened, producing a sharp, almost crescent-shaped cutting edge. This is an adaptation for grasping and retaining the smooth and slippery skinks (lizards), upon which they prey.

Scaphiodontophis is oviparous, but little data is available concerning the eggs or the young. Adults are thirty to thirty-six inches in length.

Some five species of this genus range throughout southern Mexico and Central America. Two additional forms of *S. annulatus* are known; the nominate race, *S. a. annulatus,* occurs in Guatemala, and *S. a. carpicinctus* is found in Guatemala and Belize.

Care. Rarely seen in captivity, conditions suitable for the Coral Snakes, *Micrurus,* should apply equally for captive requirements of this snake. A consistent supply of skinks as food is, of course, necessary.

D. Hamper

GROUND SNAKE *(Sonora semiannulata)*

Habitat. Prairies, brushy hillsides, mesquite thickets, and river beds in dry, sandy areas.

Geographic Range. Northern Mexico, north to Oklahoma, west to California and Baja California, north to Oregon and Idaho

Natural History. A small, secretive Colubrid included here primarily because of its extreme variability and extensive geographic range, and resultant taxonomic confusion. Smooth and shiny, they may be plain brown, reddish-brown or grey, black-collared, banded, speckled, or various combinations of these.

At one time this snake was classified as two distinct species with a total of seven subspecies, all now relegated to the synonomy of *semiannulata*.

Nocturnal, they spend the day beneath stones, fallen trees, trash piles or in shallow, self-dug burrows, preferring hiding places that retain some moisture.

Usually less than a foot in length, Ground Snakes seldom exceed sixteen inches. Oviparous, they deposit small clutches of five to six eggs. The five-inch young feed on arachnids (spiders, scorpions) and small insects and insect larvae. Adults add crickets and grasshoppers to the basic diet.

Care. Although many of the morphological variations are quite attractive and colorful, the difficulties in securing a steady food supply precludes proper captive maintenance, except perhaps by specialists.

R. D. Bartlett

DIADEM SNAKE *(Spalerosophis diadema cliffordi)*

Habitat. Dry, rocky plains, hillsides
Geographic Range. North Africa, east through Syria to Iraq and Iran
Natural History. Several species of Diadem Snakes range over much of northern Africa and

R. D. Bartlett

Spalerosophis arenarius, a species of Diadem Snake, occurs in northwestern India and Pakistan; they prey upon lizards and small rodents.

western Asia. They vary in color from grey, dark or light ocher, to reddish brown or reddish grey. The pattern of blotches is reddish brown. The vernacular, "Diadem Snake," alludes to the pattern and scalation of the head. The specimen illustrated is typical and was collected in Egypt.

Diadem Snakes seek shelter beneath stones, plant debris, or in burrows of small mammals. They are diurnal foragers during the cooler months, but they become nocturnal to escape the heat of summer. They prey upon a wide variety of lizards, small mammals, and birds.

Diadem Snakes breed in the spring, the females depositing a dozen or more eggs beneath stones or in burrows. Occasionally two clutches of eggs may be deposited in the same season. Hatchlings feed mostly on lizards, and reach an adult length of about four feet.

Care. Diadem Snakes may be maintained under conditions suitable for American Bullsnakes, *Pituophis.* Hiding places and a temperature of 78-85° F (26-29° C) are necessary. Specimens from western Asia hibernate for several months each year. They probably require this interval for successful captive reproduction.

Other Colubrids 205

AUSTRALIAN TREE SNAKE *(Dendrelaphis punctulatus)*

Habitat. Trees, shrubbery in open forest, wooded fields

Geographic Range. Coastal areas of eastern Australia, Queensland, and northern Australia; New Guinea (West Irian and Papua)

Natural History. One of only eight genera of Colubrids found in Australia, these unicolored snakes may be blue, grey, green, olive, or various shades of brown or black. The venter is usually yellowish; the interstitial skin is a pale blue.

Primarily an arboreal snake, they also frequently forage or shelter on the ground, in rock crevices, hollow logs, and under loose piles of debris. They are diurnal and prey upon birds, lizards, frogs, and occasionally small mammals.

They are oviparous and deposit up to twelve eggs in piles of decaying vegetation, rotted logs, and similar sites. Adults reach a length of approximately six feet.

Dendrelaphis occurs throughout Indonesia, the Malay Peninsula, and southern China. *D. pictus* occurs as far north as Hong Kong. Commonly called the "Painted Bronzeback," it shares the name with forms found in Burma and Thailand.

These snakes inflate and laterally compress the body when threatened, which exposes the brightly colored skin between the scales.

Care. As for the Tropical Chicken Snake, *Spilotes pullatus. Dendrelaphis* will accept pre-killed chicks and/or small mice as food, best offered from forceps.

This pale brown and yellow specimen of *D. punctulatus* demonstrates the color variability common to this species.

KEELED RATSNAKE *(Zaocys dhumnades)*

Habitat. Grassy hillsides, agricultural areas, open woodland, meadows

Geographic Range. Taiwan, southern People's Republic of China, Burma

Natural History. A long-tailed, large-eyed, striped snake, olive, olive-green or black; a relative of the Asian Dhamans, *Ptyas. Zaocys* are terrestrial, diurnal snakes that actively forage for the rodents and frogs that they prey upon. Good climbers, they frequently bask in low shrubs and bushes.

Oviparous, their hatchlings are dark in color and lack the adult pattern. Juveniles feed primarily on frogs and grow to an average adult length of five to six feet.

Several additional species of *Zaocys* range southward throughout the Malay Peninsula, Sumatra, Java, and adjacent islands. The yellow-spotted, black *Zaocys carinatus* is reputed to attain an adult length of twelve feet.

Care. *Zaocys* is rarely seen in collections, either public or private. Caging and conditions suitable to American Racers, *Coluber*, should satisfy its requirements.

Opisthoglyphous Colubrids—
The Rear-Fanged Snakes

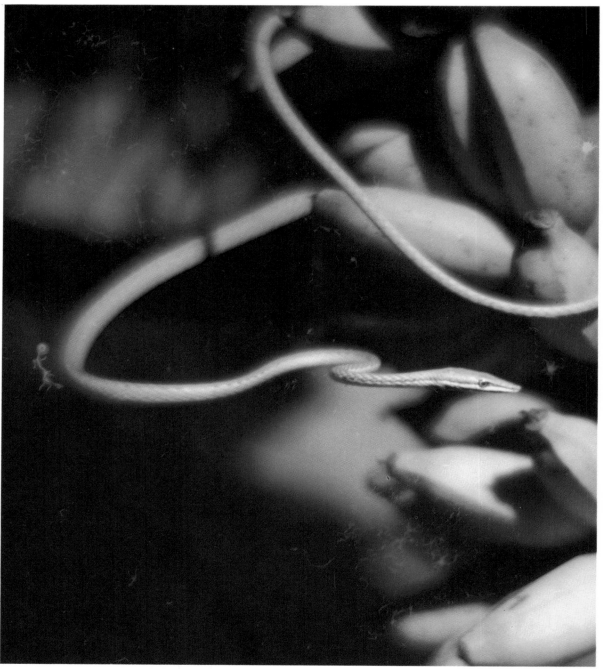

Haitian Vine Snake, *Uromacer frenatus*

Injectable venom (usually and erroneously referred to as "poison") utilized as a means of subduing prey or as a defense mechanism may be found in a wide variety of animals. The so-called "stinging cells," or *nematocysts,* of coelenterates such as the Portuguese Man O' War jellyfish, the sting of arachnids such as scorpions and insects such as the honey bee—all contain venom. The exotic Dragon or Lion fish, *Pterois,* of the Indian Ocean (and environs) injects venom through several rays of the dorsal fin. Obviously, snakes are not the only creatures to possess venom.

Snake venom, an extremely complex substance, derives from salivary secretions. Serving a two-fold function, the venom quickly incapacitates or kills prey species and thus reduces the risk of retaliation by the prey. Rodents are quite capable of killing constricting snakes that prey upon them, and adult snakes are often badly scarred as a result of such encounters. Venom is also a pre-digestant, initiating the breakdown of the food into soluble compounds allowing for proper digestion and absorption. All salivary secretions, incidentally, are pre-digestants, and should a sufficient quantity of saliva be introduced into tissue surrounding a bite, localized tissue damage will result. Such tissue damage is occasionally seen in humans bitten by harmless snakes or by dogs, cats, and horses. Moreover, if humans were inclined to bite snakes, introducing sufficient human saliva in the process, the *snake* would suffer tissue damage!

Opisthoglyphous snakes are Colubrids characterized by the presence of a venom-producing gland, *Duvernoy's gland,* and one, two, or three rear maxillary teeth that are enlarged and anteriorly grooved. *Duvernoy's gland* drains into the area of these teeth which by capillary action introduces the venom into the bitten area. Often the venom may be species specific, i.e., the venom of rear-fanged snakes that prey on frogs will be more quickly toxic to frogs than to other prey species, such as mice.

Opisthoglyphous Colubrids are as widespread and diversified in size, color, and habitat as the *Aglyphous* or solid-tooth members of the family. They range in size from the diminutive, eight-inch-long Crowned Snake, *Tantilla,* of North and South America, to the Mangrove Snake, *Boiga dendrophila,* of southeast Asia, with an adult length of seven feet.

Relatively inefficient venom apparatus as well as venom essentially specialized for effectiveness on *exothermic* (cold-blooded) vertebrates such as frogs and lizards render the majority of rear-fanged snakes harmless to man. Nevertheless, human fatalities have occurred following bites by the African Boomslang, *Dispholidus,* and the Twigsnake, *Thelotornis,* and it is, of course, prudent to consider all large, rear-fanged snakes as potentially dangerous to man.

LONG-NOSED TREE SNAKE; LONG-NOSED WHIP SNAKE
(Ahaetulla [Dryophis] prasinus)

Habitat. Trees, bushes, and shrubs in open forest
Geographic Range. Southeasten Asia and larger
Indonesian islands, e. g., Java, Sumatra
Natural History. These slender, arboreal snakes
that seldom venture to the ground, are leaf green
in color, and the interstitial skin is pale blue to indigo. The head is greatly elongated, terminating
in a pointed, flexible snout. The horizontal pupil,
which can be likened to an indented or compressed triangle, is aligned with a groovelike space
along the head, in front of the eye. This allows the
snake unobstructed, frontal vision.

Completely arboreal, they obtain water from
tree boles and/or droplets of dew or rain on leaves.
They often remain motionless for hours, with their
bodies extended and tongues protruding while
waiting for their prey of small mammals, birds,
lizards, and frogs. The prey is grasped and quickly worked to the rear of the mouth, to allow the
rear fangs to carry venom into the bitten area.

These snakes bear living young, up to two
dozen in a litter. Births apparently can take place
any time during the year. Juveniles feed on small
lizards and frogs, expanding the diet as they
mature. Adults, rarely thicker than a little finger,
reach lengths of six feet.

When molested or threatened, the body is inflated, exposing the bright blue or indigo interstitial skin, the head is greatly flattened, and the
mouth widely gaped. Envenomated bites result in
localized symptons of pain, numbness, and
swelling.

Care. Tall cages, arranged as suggested for Emerald
Tree Boas *(C. canina),* are suitable. Water should
be supplied in a manner acceptable to the snake,
and careful attention to this detail is necessary.

WEST INDIAN RACER; BIMINI RACER
(Alsophis vudii picticeps)

Habitat. Varied; open fields, sand dunes, woodland, rocky areas

Geographic Range. The subspecies illustrated occurs on East, North and South Bimini Islands in the Bahamas.

Natural History. This snake is typical of the ten (or more) species of *Alsophis,* a genus of racer-like Colubrids that are confined to and occur throughout the islands of the Caribbean. Insular isolation has produced many subspecific races, there being five subspecies of *Alsophis vudii* alone.

Unlike North American Colubrids that are called "racers," West Indian racers possess a toxic saliva (venom) that is effective on the various small mammals, birds, lizards, and frogs upon which they prey. Active predators, they are crepuscular, or diurnal in habit. They are oviparous. The average adult length is three to four feet.

When threatened or molested, *Alsophis* rears the forepart of the body, flattens the neck, and strikes at the intruder. Their venom, incidentally, has caused relatively severe reactions in humans.

Care. These snakes are rarely seen in collections. Housing suited to the Montpellier Snake, *Malpalon,* is equally suitable for *Alsophis.* They should be handled with caution.

MANGROVE SNAKE *(Boiga dendrophila melanota)*

Habitat. Mangrove swamps, edges of rain forests
Geographic Range. Malay Peninsula and adjacent Sumatra
Natural History. A large, arboreal, rear-fanged snake, immediately identifiable by its satin-smooth indigo or black color, patterned with enamel yellow bands. The supralabial scales are also yellow, each scale edged in black.

Although they are most active late in the afternoon and evening hours, they bask during the day, stretching along branches at heights of fifteen or more feet. They prey upon a wide variety of animals, including snakes, lizards, and frogs, but most frequently forage for small mammals and birds.

Clutches of up to ten eggs may be deposited in tree hollows or in suitable terrestrial sites. The hatchlings, about one foot long, are identical to the adults in color and pattern, maturing to a length of six to seven feet.

Seven forms of the Mangrove Snake are known, their identification based on the number and size of the bands that form the pattern, as well as other factors such as scale counts. In addition to the subspecies illustrated, the nominate race, *B. d. dendrophila,* occurs on Java; *B. d. annectans* is found on Kalimantan (Borneo), and *B. d. gemmicincta* is confined to the Celebes Islands. The Philippines are inhabited by three forms, which are *B. d. multicincta* of Palawan, *B. d. divergens* of Luzon, and *B. d. latifasciata* of Mindanao.

The genus *Boiga* is widespread, with over twenty species occurring in Africa, southern Asia, Indonesia, New Guinea, and Australia.

The deliberate or inadvertent introduction of a foreign species into an area in which the native fauna have not developed defenses against the introduced species usually results in a disastrous situation for the native species. The introduction of the mongoose to various West Indian islands is, of course, a well known example. The mongoose, deliberately introduced to control the snake population, embarked upon eradication of other native wildlife as well. In 1950 the Brown Tree Snake, *Boiga irregularis,* a species native to the Solomon Islands, New Guinea, and Australia, was introduced to the island of Guam, most probably through unnoticed arrival with imports of various goods. By the late 1970's many of the small native birds of Guam were rapidly disappearing,

with subsequent investigation indicating that the prolific Brown Tree Snake, with no predation checks, had increased in numbers sufficient to almost exterminate the native birds. Procedures are currently in progress to salvage the birds and control the snakes.

Care. Cages tall enough to accommodate the sturdy branches and foliage required by this arboreal snake are necessary. Shredded-bark mulch as a substrate aids in maintaining humidity. A water supply should be provided, and pre-killed laboratory rodents or chicks are acceptable as food. Temperatures of 78-80° F (25-27° C) are satisfactory. A basking spot, slightly higher in temperature, is sometimes utilized by these snakes.

Body drawn back in a striking coil, this Mangrove Snake is preparing to defend itself.

S. Reichling, Memphis Zoo

R. S. Funk   D. Hamper

(Left) The Green Cat-eyed Snake, *B. cyanea,* occurs in the forests of northeastern India, Assam and adjacent areas. It preys upon frogs, lizards and small birds. *(Right)* The Common Cat-eyed Snake, *B. trigonata,* attains a length of about four feet and occurs throughout India. It shelters in palms, thatched roofs or other vegetation; it preys on lizards, especially geckos, small birds and rodents.

D. Hamper   D. Hamper

(Left) The African species of *Boiga* are sometimes referred to the genus *Toxicodryas* by taxonomists. Blanding's Tree Snake, *B. (Toxicodryas) blandingii,* occurs in much of west and central Africa. As do other species of *Boiga,* it preys upon rodents, birds, lizards and amphibians. *(Right) B. (Toxicodryas) pulverulenta,* a slender nocturnal species which inhabits forest areas in western and central Africa. Adults attain lengths of about five feet.

214   *Colubrids—The Typical Snakes*

MUSSURANA *(Clelia clelia)*

Habitat. Open savannahs, plains, open forests
Geographic Range. Central America, south to Argentina, west to Ecuador
Natural History. A large, rear-fanged snake and a powerful constrictor that frequently preys upon venomous snakes, the Mussurana is widespread throughout the neotropics.

They shelter in and forage through mammal burrows, piles of litter, fallen logs, and other areas that shelter the rodents and snakes upon which they prey. They often kill and consume venomous as well as harmless snakes as large as themselves. Their venom has little effect on snakes, which are usually killed by constriction. Mammals, however, rapidly succumb to the venom. The Mussurana is immune to the highly toxic venoms of the neotropical pit vipers.

Adults are unicolored indigo, black, or brown. The juveniles of *C. clelia* are bright red in color, darkening with age. Juveniles of other species are usually collared with white or cream.

Females deposit up to fifty eggs. The hatchlings may be up to fifteen inches in length and can attain adult lengths of eight feet.

Six species of Mussurana are known at this time. Current studies indicate several additional species will eventually be described.
Care. As for Kingsnakes, *Lampropeltis*. Mussuranas are usually docile captives, feeding well on pre-killed rodents. They have recorded captive longevities of twelve years and more. As in the case of all large, opisthoglyphous snakes, they should be handled with caution.

HERALD SNAKE; CAT-EYED SNAKE *(Crotaphopeltis hotamboeia)*

Habitat. Dense vegetation; reeds or rocky areas adjacent to swamps, marshes, streams, and ditches
Geographic Range. The southern half of Africa in suitable habitat. It is absent from Somalia.
Natural History. A small opisthoglyphous snake of variable color, with wide distribution. The presence of a solid tooth behind its grooved rear fangs may relate it to those early Colubrids that gave rise to the cobras and other *Elapids.*

The Herald Snake may be greyish-green or olive, brown, or black, with a dark grey or black blotch usually present in the temporal area. The venter is pearly grey or white, and upper labials are often suffused with red or white.

The popular name derives from the sudden appearance of numbers of these snakes prior to or at the onset of rains, which prompt breeding aggregations of amphibians, on which these snakes prey. Nocturnal, they spend the day hidden beneath stones, vegetation, and other debris. They are good swimmers and actively forage in shallow water. They will also climb into low shrubs in pursuit of arboreal frogs.

When molested they are quick to vacate the premises, but if escape is impossible they perform a threat display, flattening the head, coiling, and striking at the threat.

Crotaphopeltis is often the prey of other snakes, birds, and large amphibians such as the Grooved-crown bullfrog, *Pyxicephalus.*

Herald Snakes are oviparous, depositing six to seventeen eggs in decaying vegetation or similar debris. The five-inch hatchlings feed on small frogs and toads. Adults may attain thirty inches in length but are usually smaller. They feed on toads, frogs, and occasionally small fish. When amphibians are scarce, lizards and small rodents may be eaten.

This genus is in need of taxonomic study. The five subspecies of *C. hotamboeia* that have been named are difficult to determine and not generally recognized. Three additional species are accepted, however, which are *C. degeni* of Sudan, Kenya and Uganda; *C. acarina* of Burkina Faso (Upper Volta); and *C. barotseensis* of Zambia.
Care. Herald Snakes often refuse all food except toads when held captive, and a supply of suitably sized toads or frogs is necessary for their successful maintenance. Shredded-bark mulch as a substrate is satisfactory, and an ample water supply should be provided. A small, twigged branch is sometimes used by these snakes. Temperatures of 78-80° F (25-27° C) are required.

R. S. Funk

BRAZILIAN SMOOTH SNAKE; "FALSE WATER COBRA"
(Cyclagras gigas)

Habitat. Well watered, open scrub and cactus woodland

Geographic Range. Eastern Bolivia, Paraguay, southern Brazil, and northern Argentina

Natural History. These large, heavy-bodied and powerful snakes are pale grey, pale brown, or yellowish in color, patterned with irregular black crossbands and spots. The venter of males is yellowish in color, striped and/or speckled with dark brown or black. Females have a brownish venter, indistinctly speckled with black.

Brazilian Smooth Snakes are diurnal, similar in habits to the tropical Cribos, *Drymarchon*. They actively forage for a wide variety of prey species, utilizing both constriction and the venom injected by the rear fangs to subdue captured prey. In well watered areas they catch frogs, toads and fish. In drier areas they catch small mammals and birds. *Cyclagras* retires to the shelter of burrows or dense clumps of vegetation during the night and between foraging excursions.

Females deposit up to three dozen eggs, the fifteen-inch hatchlings identical to the adults. They grow rapidly and soon attain the adult length of six to seven feet.

Although these snakes raise the body and flatten the neck area to intimidate potential predators, the allusion to a cobra is hardly justified. This defensive action is more pronounced in the similar *Hydrodynastes,* a snake often confused with *Cyclagras. Hydrodynastes* is known from two species, *H.bicinctus* and *H. schultzi,* found from French Guiana, west to Colombia, and in much of Amazonian Brazil. Some studies in process may show all three forms to be of one or the other genus.

Care. Quite amenable to captive conditions, *Cyclagras* should be provided with a shredded garden mulch substrate, a hiding place, and water bowl. They often shed their skin by rolling it off while crawling through a coil of their own body. Voracious feeders, they accept pre-killed rodents and chicks. To avoid obesity, care should be taken to regulate the amount of food consumed. As with any large, rear fanged snake, they should be handled with caution.

BOOMSLANG *(Dispholidus typus typus)*

Habitat. Dry woodlands, thorn scrub, savannahs, and swamps bordering or close to streams, rivers, and lakes

Geographic Range. Africa, in suitable habitat, south of the Sahara

Natural History. An arboreal, often brilliantly colored snake common in many areas of Africa. Its popular name is Afrikaans for "tree snake."

Boomslangs occur in seemingly endless color variations, varying from a solid, velvety black to dark brown, pale greyish-brown, and myriad shades of bright green. One green variation occurs with the scale edges defined in black. A black variant has a yellow spot in each scale. Some degree of sexual dimorphism occurs, since most females are usually some shade of brown, all other colors being males. The scales are keeled, with those of the neck area often having a "folded" appearance.

Boomslangs move with great speed and grace through trees and shrubbery. When foraging they often pause, with much of the body held rigidly with no support, while waiting for prey to ap-

proach within striking range. This action gives rise to the erroneous belief that they "charm" their prey.

Lizards, small mammals, frogs, birds, and their eggs comprise the diet of Boomslangs, whose venom is quickly fatal to the prey animals.

Females deposit up to two dozen eggs, which can sometimes require up to six months of incubation before hatching. The foot-long hatchlings have large heads and eyes and feed on small frogs and lizards. Adults are usually four to five feet in length, but they may attain a length of over six feet in some populations.

Two additional subspecies are recognized. *Dispholidus typus kivuensis* occurs in Zambia, Zaire, Rwanda, Kenya, and Uganda. This is an especially colorful form; males are usually a vivid green with black and/or yellow scale edges. *Dispholidus typus punctatus* is found in southern Zaire, Zambia, and Angola.

Typical of arboreal snakes, the Boomslang's threat display involves a great inflation of the throat, rearing from the ground or tree limb, and gaping the mouth. Three large, grooved teeth are located immediately below the eye, and being far forward in the mouth, allow for ease of insertion in a "normal" bite. This, in addition to a highly toxic venom (factors of which cause extensive subdermal as well as internal hemorrhages) makes the Boomslang a dangerous animal. Human fatalities are recorded. A monovalent (species specific) antisera is produced in Africa.

Care. Boomslangs are usually calm in temperament and easy to handle as captives. They readily accept pre-killed rodents and/or chicks as food. The lethal potential of their bite, however, should restrict their captive maintenance to experienced collectors and professionals. Captive reproduction has occurred.

A dark green, black-spotted variant, one of many color and pattern phases of the Boomslang.

F. Bolin, D. Hamper

TENTACLED SNAKE; FISHING SNAKE
(Erpeton tentaculum)

Habitat. Fresh and brackish water; streams, ditches, sloughs, rice paddies

Geographic Range. Coastal southeast Asia, e.g., Vietnam, Thailand, Cambodia

Natural History. A completely aquatic snake that varies in color from dark brown to tan or pale grey. Dark specimens have a pattern of tannish-yellow ventral stripes. Light specimens have a dorsal and lateral patten of brown, reddish-brown, or black bars. The color and pattern are procryptic, and the snake may resemble a twig or branch with mottled, water-soaked bark. The scales are keeled and feel like sandpaper.

Adaptations to their aquatic enviroment include nostrils that can be closed by specialized tissue and an extendable glottis that can be inserted into the internal nares. The purpose of the remarkable scaly tentacles is not known with certainty. They are possibly used as a lure to attract prey, as a device for locating prey, or as camouflage. Their probable use is sensory.

Tentacled Snakes are helpless on land and virtually never voluntarily leave the water. Underwater, they appear to rely on camouflage to escape detection by predators. If molested they extend the body and become completely rigid and remain in this position even when handled or removed from the water. Perhaps such an action further enhances their resemblance to water soaked "branches."

Tentacled Snakes bear living young. They feed exclusively upon small fish. The average adult length is eighteen inches, although some specimens may reach a length of twenty-eight inches.

The Tentacled Snakes belong to the *Colubrid*

subfamily *Homalopsinae,* a group of rear-fanged aquatic and semi-aquatic snakes that range over much of southeastern Asia, Indo-China, New Guinea, and northern Australia. Venom of the various species appears to be specialized to the preferred prey, which can be fish, frogs, and in some cases crabs.

Care. Tentacled Snakes are commonly exported by Thai animal dealers, but they are not noted for captive longevity. This is probably due to their being shipped dry in cloth sacks, the standard procedure for shipping snakes. Aquatic animals, supported by water in the wild state, may suffer un-

due pressure on, and possible damage to, internal organs when shipped dry in sacks. This supposition is supported by the fact that specimens shipped in water under oxygen, as for aquarium fish, arrive in good condition and are likely to survive. Given physically sound specimens, Tentacled Snakes do well in large aquaria arranged as for tropical fish, with aquatic plants, submerged logs, etc. They will accept most small fish, especially Barbs *(Barbus)* and small goldfish *(Carassius).* Water temperatures should be maintained at 80-85° F (26-29° C).

R. D. Bartlett

R. S. Funk

(Left) The Smooth-scaled Water Snake, *Enhydris polylepsis,* is one of many species of *Homalopsinids* which occur in fresh and brackish water throughout much of Asia. They prey primarily upon amphibians and fishes. *(Right)* Bocourt's Water Snake, *E. bocourti,* unlike most of its genus, frequently occurs in shallow water in coastal marshes.

W. Lamar

FALSE CORAL SNAKE *(Erythrolamprus bizona)*

Habitat. Forests, in leaf litter, rotted logs; exposed root systems

Geographic Range. Northern Venezuela west to Colombia, north to Costa Rica

Natural History. One of a number of tri-colored snakes collectively known as "False Coral Snakes," this species is patterned with black bands in groups of two, separated by a single white band. The black couplets are widely separated from each other, the intervening space being clear red speckled with black.

Secretive, terrestrial animals that remain hidden away in secure shelters, they emerge at dusk or after rains to forage for small snakes, lizards, and small mammals.

They are oviparous and deposit their eggs in rotted logs or decomposed litter. The hatchlings are six to eight inches in length and are patterned like the adults, which attain mature lengths of approximately thirty inches.

Six species of *Erythrolamprus* are known, the commonest being the five subspecies of *Erythrolamprus aesculapii,* ranging from central Brazil and Bolivia north through most of South America. An insular race, *E. a. ocellatus,* occurs on Trinidad and Tobago Islands.

Care. A substrate of shredded bark, covered with dry leaves, provides the contact security required.

Some may prove to be reticent feeders, but assuming caging conditions are proper, they will probably, within a short time, accept small snakes, lizards *(Anolis),* and/or nestling laboratory rodents. Temperatures of 75-80° F (23-27° C) are suitable.

W. Lamar, courtesy E. Chapman

This specimen of *Erythrolamprus aesculapii* is from extreme southern Surinam, and is probably of the nominate race.

BLUNT-HEADED TREE SNAKE *(Imantodes cenchoa)*

Habitat. Trees and shrubbery, especially those with attached epiphytic bromeliads

Geographic Range. The *species* ranges from southern Mexico, south to Bolivia and Paraguay.

Natural History. An extremely slim, arboreal snake that is pale orange or tan in color, patterned with blackish-brown saddles, often triangulate on the sides. The neck is even slimmer than the body, and the head and eyes disproportionly large.

Imantodes is a crepuscular and/or nocturnal snake that spends the day coiled beneath clumps of leaves or in the central leaf-whorl cups of bromeliads. Several snakes may share the same resting spot and habitually return to it. Their primary prey are lizards, such as anoles and geckos. Small frogs are also eaten. Reported feeding on lizard eggs may be based on secondary consumption, e.g., ingestion of gravid female lizards.

They are oviparous, although little is known about their reproductive habits. Adults may attain forty inches in length.

These snakes can bridge gaps between branches more than half their body length in width. The body is laterally compressed between the wide vertebral and ventral scales and moved rigidly forward. The snake essentially turns itself into an "I-beam girder." When proper purchase is secure on the new branch, the body assumes its normal shape.

Three subspecies of *Imantodes cenchoa* are known. The specimen illustrated, from Honduras, is probably *I. c. leucomelas.* The nominate race is confined to Panama and South America. *I. c.*

semifasciatus occurs in Guatemala and Panama. The six subspecies of *I. gemmistratus* occur from Sonora, Mexico south to Panama. The monotypic *I. inornatus* and *I. lentiferus* occur in southern Central America and much of adjacent South America. All of the varied forms are similar in habits.

Care. *Imantodes* require tall cages equipped with live or artificial foliage for climbing, and, if possible, several live broadleaf bromeliads. Temperatures of 75-80° F (23-27° C) will suit both snake and plants. These snakes will often refuse to drink from a dish, but they will drink droplets of water from their bodies or from plant leaves. Accordingly, a misting of water several times per week is required. They readily accept anolis lizards of appropriate size.

Blunt-headed Tree Snakes are readily identified by their large head and equally large eyes.

J. Mehrtens

**CAT-EYED SNAKE;
NIGHT SNAKE
(*Leptodeira
septentrionalis
septentrionalis*)**

F.R.I., Inc.

Habitat. Wooded banks of streams, ponds, and rivers in dry, semi-arid areas

Geographic Range. Sonora, Mexico and extreme southwestern Texas, south to Costa Rica

Natural History. A nocturnal, semi-arboreal snake that frequently appeared in shipments of bananas prior to the advent of containerized shipping. The ground color illustrated is typical, but may vary to a yellow tone. Juveniles are almost always some shade of orange, with a pattern identical to the adults.

Cat-eyed Snakes forage along stream banks and adjacent shrubbery for the frogs and lizards that are their usual prey. They also occasionally feed upon small snakes and rodents.

They are oviparous, with six to a dozen eggs producing hatchlings about ten inches long. Adults attain three feet in length, although average specimens rarely exceed two feet.

Three additional subspecies are known. *L. s. polysticta* occurs from southern Mexico to Costa Rica and El Salvador; *L. s. ornata* is found in Central America, Colombia and Ecuador; and *L. s. lacorum* is confined to northern Peru. Other species, such as *L. annulata,* range throughout most of Central America and northern South America.

Care. Dry cage conditions with adequate draft-free ventilation are required. An ample water supply and climbing branches should be provided, as well as a hiding place. Avoid bright light and temperatures over 80° F (27° C). Captive specimens accept frogs and small mice as food. They have attained over ten years longevity in captivity.

PARROT SNAKE *(Leptophis ahaetulla)*

Habitat. Small trees and shrubs, usually near water

Geographic Range. From southern Mexico, south through Central America to central Argentina

Natural History. A wide ranging group of snakes, essentially arboreal, Parrot Snakes are green to blue-green in color. Some subspecies have bronze or copper overtones. Seven species of *Leptophis* are known; *Leptophis ahaetulla* being represented by twelve subspecies. The specimen illustrated is from southern Surinam and is probably the nominate race.

Parrot Snakes forage in dense foliage for the lizards and amphibians that constitute their prey. They will pursue prey on the ground, if necessary. When threatened, the anterior part of the body is raised in multiple loops, the head flattened and the mouth opened widely, although they rarely strike at the source of the threat.

Oviparous, females deposit small clutches of four to six eggs. They are reputed to occasionally deposit eggs in the debris that collects about various epiphytic plants growing on tree limbs. Hatchlings are ten to twelve inches long. Adults seldom exceed four and one-half feet in length.

Care. Parrot Snakes require tall cages, equipped with branches and live or artificial foliage, and a water dish. A substrate of shredded-bark garden mulch is suitable, with temperatures of 75-80° F (23-27° C) and a warmer basking place provided. Exposure to ultraviolet and occasional mistings with tepid water are beneficial. *Leptophis* will feed only upon small frogs and lizards such as *Anolis*. As is the case for all rear-fanged snakes, they should be handled with caution.

Leptophis mexicana, a Parrot Snake found in the forests of southern Mexico. It is arboreal, as are all Parrot Snakes. Its cryptic coloration makes it difficult to see in foliage, unless moving.

R. D. Bartlett

Sometimes referred to as Asian Parrot Snakes, the popular name of Flying Snakes is more appropriate. These snakes will launch themselves from considerable heights, flattening the body into a rigid, concave shaft, which enables the snake to glide to lower levels or to the ground without injury. Once lower elevations are reached, the body is relaxed and the snake proceeds in a normal serpentine manner. The specimen illustrated is a *Chrysolopea sp.* from Thailand.

J. Mehrtens

R. S. Funk

R. S. Funk

(Left) The Ornate Flying Snake, *C. ornata,* one of the five species of *Chrysolopea* found in southern Asia. *(Right)* The Paradise Flying Snake, *C. paradisi,* a form frequently exhibited in zoological parks, is noted for its intricate and attractive pattern. All of the Flying Snakes can be maintained in much the same manner as for the Mangrove Snake, *Boiga. Chrysolopea* prey upon frogs, lizards, nestling birds and small mammals.

MALAGASY GIANT HOGNOSE SNAKE
(*Lioheterodon madagascariensis*)

Habitat. Grasslands, plains, savannahs, and forest edges

Geographic Range. Madagascar (formerly Malagasy Republic)

Natural History. Ma'ny of the animals of Madagascar are endemic, and the Colubrid snakes are no exception; only one species found on the island occurs elsewhere. One of the endemics is *Lioheterodon,* a large opisthoglyphous colubrid that is dark grey in color, blotched and spotted with dark brown and black. The snout is upturned in the manner of the American Hognose Snakes, *Heterodon.*

Lioheterodon is crepuscular, sheltering during the heat of the day in shallow, self-dug burrows, in rock crevices or beneath debris. They forage for small mammals and amphibians. Small birds *may* also be preyed upon (inasmuch as captives have accepted chicks as food).

Females deposit up to a dozen eggs, which hatch after an incubation period of slightly more than two months. The twelve-inch hatchlings prey upon amphibians such as frogs. They attain adult lengths of four to five feet.

Two additional species of *Lioheterodon, L. geayi* and *L. modestus,* occur on and are endemic to Madagascar.

These snakes flatten the neck and hiss loudly when molested, but seldom bite.

Care. Only basic arrangements are required, e.g., well-ventilated caging with hiding places and water bowl. Temperatures of 78-80° F (25-27° C) are suitable. Prior to skin shedding, increase humidity. Adults accept pre-killed mice.

J. Mehrtens

WOLF SNAKE *(Lycodon aulicus)*

Habitat. In and around rock walls, stone piles, and trash piles; in drier areas where lizards are abundant

Geographic Range. Sri Lanka and India, east to southern People's Republic of China, south through the Malay Peninsula, western Indonesia, and the Philippine Islands

Natural History. A wide ranging and variable species, represented by several subspecies that are difficult to identify without precise geographical data. The specimen illustrated is typical of the *Lycodon* exported from Bangkok.

Lycodon are nocturnal snakes, spending the day hidden in crevices or beneath stones and other shelters. They are good climbers and in rural areas may take up residence in the eaves and roofs of houses. They forage for geckos and other lizards, and also prey upon frogs and occasionally nestling rodents.

Wolf Snakes are oviparous, with up to a dozen eggs laid. Hatchlings are more brightly-colored than adults and measure about seven or eight inches in length, not often exceeding thirty inches at maturity.

These snakes are called "Wolf" Snakes because of their rather large front teeth. They also possess enlarged, non-grooved rear maxillary teeth. Although they will bite if provoked, the usual response to a threat is to loosely coil the body and hide the head. They are frequently preyed upon by various species of ophiophagous kraits, *Bungarus.*

Care. Wolf Snakes require dry, well-ventilated cages with several hiding places and climbing branches. Most refuse all food except lizards, and, unless an adequate and consistent food supply is available, Wolf Snakes should not be maintained as captives.

The Barred Wolf Snake, *Lycodon striatus,* an attractively patterned form which ranges throughout peninsular India.

D. Hamper

The sharp, recurved rather large teeth of the African Wolf Snake, *Lycophidion capense,* enable it to grasp and maintain its hold on the smooth-scaled, slippery skinks (lizards) which are its primary prey. African Wolf Snakes occur throughout Africa and are known from several species.

L. Moor

Opisthoglyphous Colubrids—The Rear-Fanged Snakes 231

MONTPELLIER SNAKE
(Malpolon monspessulanus monspessulanus)

Habitat. Dry, brushy, rocky hillsides; overgrown farmland, gullies, and semi-desert scrub

Geographic Range. Western Morocco, north through Spain and Portugal, and west to coastal France and northwestern Italy

Natural History. A large and active snake that may be greenish-grey, grey, olive or dark brown in color. An indistinct pattern of spots along the sides may or may not be present. The venter is whitish-yellow and occasionally spotted with black. A prominent ridge begins at each nostril and continues to the large supraorbital scale, creating a somewhat "hooded" effect to the eye.

This is the largest of the rear-fanged snakes found in Europe. Very similar to the American Whipsnakes *(Masticophis)* in habits, they forage actively for their prey of small mammals, birds, lizards, and other snakes. Their venom is quickly toxic to the prey species.

Montpellier Snakes hibernate through much of the range, and breed after spring emergence. Large females may deposit up to two dozen eggs that hatch in the fall, the fifteen-inch hatchlings being lighter in color than adults and patterned with rows of dark spots along the body. The hatchlings feed on lizards and insects. Occasionally an adult will exceed six feet in length, but five feet is an average size.

The eastern race, *M. m. insignitus,* occurs from the Atlas Mountains in Morocco east across Africa to Egypt and north through the Balkans and Turkey. A second species, *Malpolon miolensis,* ranges from Iran south and west through Israel, Sinai, Egypt, and Saharan Morocco.

Care. Montpellier Snakes must be maintained in large, dry, and well-ventilated cages and provided with ample hiding places. New arrivals should be checked for intestinal parasites. They require high temperatures of 85-90° F (29-32° C), which should cool to the middle 70's (low 20's) at night. Exposure to natural sunlight or ultraviolet is beneficial. Pre-killed rodents and chicks are accepted as food. Large adults should be handled with caution.

© J. Bridges

**MEXICAN
VINE SNAKE
*(Oxybelis
aeneus
auratus)***

Habitat. Brushy, overgrown hillsides; arroyos, especially near streams and creeks

Geographic Range. Suitable habitat in Mexico, north to extreme southern Arizona

Natural History. The popular name, Vine Snake, is quite appropriate, as these snakes appear vine-like in both color and form. They vary from pale grey to brownish or yellowish-grey in color, often with several shades fading into each other on the same snake. The elongated and pointed head is yellow, and sometimes white on the sides and venter.

Vine Snakes are arboreal, climbing through trees, bushes and vine tangles in search of prey. They are well camouflaged by both shape and color, and difficult to detect unless moving. A favored position is a vertical or horizontal extension of the body from a branch. The snake remains rigidly in place until suitable prey appears within striking range. Lizards are the primary prey, which quickly succumb to the venom injected by the rear fangs. Large Vine Snakes will occasionally prey on small birds and nestlings.

Data is sparse relative to the eggs and young. Available information indicates that clutches of six eggs have been deposited in early summer. Adults attain about·five feet in length.

The nominate race, *O. a. aeneus,* has a wide range from Guatemala, south through South America to Bolivia. It is similar in coloration, form, and habits. The larger and heavier-bodied *O. fulgidus* is a bright green snake, occurring at lower elevations from Mexico south throughout South America east of the Andes. They prey upon birds and lizards, which quickly succumb to the venom.

Care. Tall cages equipped with climbing branches are required for these snakes. *O. aeneus* prefers dry, well-ventilated quarters, although the snake should be misted with warm water prior to shedding. Both forms may drink from droplets rather than a dish. *O. aeneus* will accept *Anolis* lizards as food; *O. fulgidus* will accept pre-killed chicks and laboratory mice, offered from forceps.

L. Moor

AFRICAN BEAKED SNAKE *(Rhamphiophis multimaculatus)*

Habitat. Dry, sandy or rocky areas with sparse vegetation

Geographic Range. Botswana and Namibia

Natural History. One of four species of Beaked Snakes that range over much of Africa. The popular name derives from the projecting snout and hooked rostral scale that gives the appearance of a bird's beak. The specimen illustrated is typical in pattern, although the ground color may vary to light or dark brown, yellowish tan, or dark blue-grey. This species is diurnal, and spends much time burrowing in loose sand in search of lizards, its primary diet. It rarely exceeds two feet in length.

The two subspecies of *Rhamphiophis oxyrhynchus* occur from Ethiopia south throughout much of East and Central Africa to the Transvaal, inhabiting much the same type of habitat. Larger snakes, averaging three feet in length, they feed on small mammals and snakes as well as lizards.

Unlike the preceding forms, *Rhamphiophis acutus* is a striped species, the four subspecies ranging through Togo, Zaire, Uganda, Angola, and Ghana.

All of the Beaked Snakes are oviparous, depositing up to eighteen eggs, often over a period of several days.

Care. The larger, rodent-eating species fare well as captives when housed in dry, draft-free caging. A hiding place is necessary. If sand or fine gravel is used as a substrate, a buried plastic pipe provides a suitable burrow. Bright illumination and exposure to ultraviolet is beneficial, and temperatures of 78-85° F (25-29° C) should be provided.

Several species of Rhamphiophis have reproduced in captivity. Hatchlings may be fed pre-killed nestling mice and small lizards.

F. Bolin, D. Hamper

BIRD SNAKE; TWIG SNAKE
(Thelotornis kirtlandii)

Habitat. Rainforests, in trees and shrubbery

Geographic Range. Angola, north to Cameroun and west to Togo, Sierra Leone; east to Tanzania, Kenya and Somalia

Natural History. An arboreal snake, whose intricate coloration and pattern renders it almost invisible when in trees or shrubbery. Pale brown, grey, or greyish brown in color, the body is streaked and spotted with dark grey, black, or brown, creating a tree-bark effect (some white is present, especially about the head). The common name, Twig Snake, refers to its habit of maintaining a rigid body posture extended from a branch, swaying to and fro. The generic name, a Greek derivation, alludes to a mythical ability to "charm" prey.

Twig Snakes prey upon small mammals, including bats, as well as birds, lizards, snakes, and frogs. Once sighted, the prey is slowly and carefully stalked until the snake is within striking range. There is some evidence that the brightly colored tongue may be used as a "lure" to attract prey within range. Captured prey succumbs quickly to the Twig Snake's venom, and is often swallowed while the snake is hanging head downward from a branch.

Twig Snakes are timid animals, relying on their intricate coloration to remain unnoticed. If pressed, they resort to a defense display similar to that of the Boomslang. They seldom bite unless forcibly restrained, but they possess a potent venom and human fatalities have resulted from envenomated bites.

Oviparous, they deposit up to a dozen elongated eggs. The ten-inch hatchlings, as intricately colored as the adults, quickly "disappear" into low-growing bushes. Adults attain a length of five to six feet.

Another species, *Thelotornis capensis,* occurs throughout the drier regions of eastern, central, and southern Africa. More brightly colored than *T. kirtlandii,* they are similarly patterned and also are virtually invisible in the scrub bushes that they inhabit. In addition to the nominate race, a subspecies, *T. c. oatesi,* is recognized.

Care. See captive care comments for the Boomslang, *Dispholidus t. typus.*

The popular name "Twig" Snake alludes to the color and pattern which resembles tree bark.

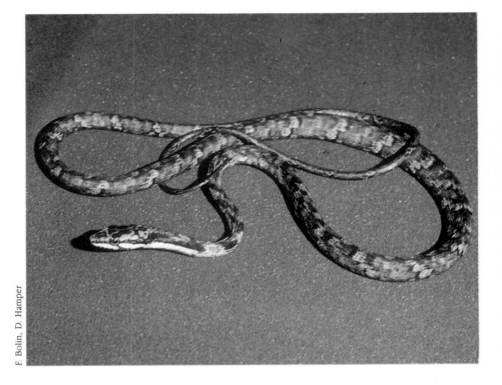

F. Bolin, D. Hamper

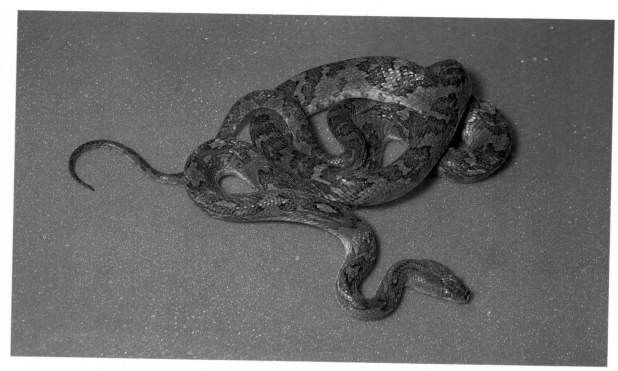

CENTRAL AMERICAN LYRE SNAKE
(Trimorphodon biscutatus quadruplex)

Habitat. Rock slides, boulder piles, and outcroppings in mountainous areas; especially in arid areas or adjacent to them

Geographic Range. Western Guatemala south to Costa Rica

Natural History. Grey, pale brown, or reddish-brown, patterned with large and small blotches. The specimen illustrated is typical of the subspecies. All Lyre Snakes have large eyes with elliptical pupils set in a relatively large head, distinct from the body. The popular name derives from the lyre-shaped marking on the head.

Nocturnal, they spend the day hidden in rock crevices, rock slides, and similar cool hideaways. The large eyes facilitate nocturnal foraging for lizards, small birds, and mammals, including bats. Prey is partially immobilized by a mild venom introduced by grooves in the enlarged upper rear teeth.

Lyre Snakes are oviparous, depositing clutches of ten to twelve eggs. The ten-inch hatchlings feed primarily on small lizards. Adults rarely attain four feet in length.

Several other subspecies of *Trimorphodon biscutatus* have been defined. Three of these occur within the southwestern United States. The Sonoran Lyre Snake, *T. b. lambda,* occurs in California, Arizona, and Sonora, Mexico; the Texas Lyre Snake, *T. b. vilkinsoni,* barely enters southwesten Texas from Chihuahua, Mexico; *T. b. vandenburghi,* is found in southern California and Baja. The nominate race ranges through southwestern Mexico.

Care. Dry caging or terraria are required. A tight hiding box or hiding space provides security and reduces any initial stress for freshly captured specimens. Small branches with multiple twigs should be provided, and substrate temperatures of 76-78° F (24-26° C) are suitable. A patient keeper can usually induce these snakes to accept small, pre-killed laboratory rodents as food.

T. b. quadruplex; the popular name of "Lyre" Snake is derived from the lyre-shaped head pattern.

R. D. Bartlett

The Sonoran Lyre Snake, *T. b. lambda,* is one of the three subspecies found in the United States. This subspecies occurs in southern Utah and Nevada, Arizona and New Mexico.

R. S. Funk

The Crowned or Black-headed Snake, *Tantilla planiceps eiseni,* is typical of the group of small, rear-fanged snakes found throughout the United States (ten species). They feed on earthworms, centipedes, insect larvae and sowbugs. In turn, they are favored prey of the American Coral Snake, *Micrurus.*

R. S. Funk

(Facing page)
Sri Lankan Cobra,
*Naja naja
(polyocellata) naja*

VENOMOUS SNAKES

R. S. Funk

Although the *Opisthoglyphous* (rear-fanged) snakes previously discussed are venomous snakes, the layman's conceptualization of a truly venomous snake is that of one of the front-fanged species such as rattlesnakes, vipers, cobras, or coral snakes. Shrouded in a welter of myths, legends, "tall tales," and often an unreasoning fear out of proportion to the potential danger that the snake may present, these species attract by far the most attention in public reptile exhibits. Although many venomous snakes are small, innocuous creatures and essentially harmless to humans, most of them can cause painful injury and/or death. Nevertheless, any given individual in the United States is statistically more likely to be killed or injured by lightning strike, vehicular, or household accident than by snakebite.

Venomous snakes are divided into two families, the *Elapidae,* which contains the cobras, mambas, coral snakes and sea snakes; and the *Viperidae,* which includes the true vipers, e.g., Gaboon Viper, *Bitis,* and the pit vipers, e.g., rattlesnakes and copperheads. The small, fossorial Mole Vipers of Africa and the Near East are the exception to the above. Although these snakes have relatively large front fangs, in some instances combined with grooved, rear maxillary teeth, they are classified as a subfamily of the Colubrids, the *Aparallactinae.*

The structure, arrangement, and number of teeth are important anatomical features used in the study of *ophidian* classification and relationships. Accordingly, the *Elapids* are often described as *proteroglyphous* snakes. The word defines the presence of venom-conducting hollow teeth (fangs) which cannot be erected, and are located at the front of the mouth. Such snakes cannot employ the fangs in a "stabbing" strike on a flat surface, but must actually bite.

The *Viperids* have greatly enlarged venom-conducting teeth, which are kept folded within the mouth when not in use. During a strike the mouth is widely gaped and the fangs erected. Thus, the vipers "stab" rather than "bite," and can deliver a venom injection on any type of surface. Snakes possessing erectile fangs are collectively referred to as *solenoglyphous.*

Venom and Antivenom

Venom is a complex substance which serves the dual function of rapidly incapacitating or killing prey as well as acting as a pre-digestant. Its role in self defense is secondary. Venoms are often prey species specific. The venom of Eastern Diamond-back Rattlesnakes, for example, is rapidly lethal to rabbits (cottontail rabbits being the habitual prey of the snake), while larger quantities of venom are required for the killing of a rat, even of smaller size than the rabbit.

Mammals, birds, and reptiles that in turn habitually prey on venomous snakes have developed varying degrees of immunity to snake venoms. Meerkats, *Suricata,* a small African mongoose, is resistant to the venom of the Yellow Cobra, *Naja nivea,* and the North American Kingsnakes, *Lampropeltis,* are either immune or highly resistant to the venoms of pit vipers such as copperheads, *Agkistrodon,* and rattlesnakes, *Crotalus.*

Extensive literature exists on the subject of venoms, and no detailed discussion is presented here. Reviewed briefly, venoms may be separated into two basic types: *haemotoxins,* which affect blood and/or tissue, and *neurotoxins,* which affect the nervous systems. All venoms contain both types; however, one or the other predominates in any given type of venom. Virtually all venoms also contain *hyaluronidase,* an enzyme that assures rapid diffusion of the venom. Haemotoxins, *generally speaking,* are the dominant factions in the venom of vipers and pit vipers. They cause extensive tissue damage, destroy the blood vessels as well as blood cells, and may act as either coagulants or anti-coagulants. Neurotoxins, *generally speaking,* are the dominant factions in the venom of *Elapids* such as cobras and kraits. Neurotoxins affect the motor nervous system and cause respiratory failure and cardiac arrest.

The physiological reactions to snakebite (envenomation) vary a great deal, and it is perhaps safe to say that no two snakebites are identical. The severity of the reaction in humans will vary depending on the age and physical size and condition, as well as the psychological attitude of the individual. The anatomical location of the bite is also a factor. Of equal significance are the age, size and physical condition of the snake, as well as the time elapsed since the fangs were last employed. All of these factors, in addition to environmental temperatures, determine both the quantity and quality of the venom injected.

The treatment of snakebite is and has been for some years as variable as the bite itself. Folk remedies such as split chickens or liver placed on the bite, snake stones, tobacco juice, and other substances gain credence when the bite is that of a harmless snake, *mistaken* for a venomous snake — or by the simple fact that many venomous bites can be survived with *no treatment at all*.

Any venomous snake bite should, of course, be considered a serious threat that can result in severe pain, permanent physical impairment, amputation, and/or death. Unfortunately, the treatment of snakebite can be as potentially dangerous as the bite itself. The immediate application of a lymph constricting band, incision of the fang punctures, and suction will remove significant percentages of venom and reduce the overall effects of the bite. However, when improperly administered, a tight tourniquet and x-shaped gashes compound rather than help solve the problem. Improper first aid is usually the result of panic, which has no place in the treatment of snakebite.

Supportive therapy and the administration, if necessary, of antisera (antivenom) require the involvement of a physician. It should be noted, however, that in the United States at least, snakebite is of such rare occurrence that physicians may not be familiar with treatment procedures or current literature. Thus, the use of cryotherapy (immersion in ice) and the drastic muscle fasciotomy are still used; the former often compounding the problem and simply delaying the inevitable diffusion of venom; the latter being of questionable value or need. The use of species specific (monovalent) antivenom, or multiple species (polyvalent) antivenom, is the only specific treatment known for snake envenomation. Individuals may be allergic to or become sensitized to horse serum and an allergic reaction may result in severe anaphylactic shock. A simple test prior to injection of antisera can determine sensitivity, and steps taken to prevent or control such reaction.

Anti-snakebite serum or antisera, antivenom, or antivenin was first developed about sixty years ago. It is produced in the United States, Europe, Africa, India, southeastern Asia, and South America. Its production is a simple yet complex process involving snake venom and horses.

In the United States all of the venomous snakes are pit vipers. The sole exception is the Coral Snake, an elapid. To produce antisera, a mixture of venoms from several species of rattlesnakes, copperheads, and cottonmouths is standardized and injected into horses in ever-increasing amounts until the horse is immunized. Blood is then extracted from the horse and processed into a whitish powder. Reconstituted with sterile water, the solution contains the factions that neutralize venom. Such an antivenom is effective against all North American pit vipers. Antisera effective against the venoms of several species of snakes are *polyvalent* sera.

Sera produced to counteract the venom of extremely dangerous snakes such as mambas, certain cobras, Gaboon Vipers, and various Australian elapids are produced in the same manner. In this case, however, the immunity developed in the horse is *monospecific* for the venom of the species involved. Such sera are referred to as *monovalent*. It might be noted here that horses involved in antivenom production are in no way harmed by the process, receive expert care, and live their normal life spans.

Snakebite occurs most frequently to those individuals involved with snakes on a daily basis, such as zoo keepers, collectors, laboratory personnel, etc. Most public reptile exhibits maintain various stocks of antivenom and are acquainted with several local physicians, often toxicologists, who stay abreast of current venom research. Most professional herpetologists consider a venomous bite a professional embarrassment, reflecting a careless or irresponsible attitude towards their charges. Certainly, individuals should not maintain captive collections of venomous snakes unless they are equipped with the knowledge and experience required and are prepared to accept the serious responsibilities and risks involved. To do otherwise is to render a gross disservice to themselves, their fellows, and to the snakes, the latter unfortunately already greatly burdened by simply being a venomous snake.

Proteroglyphous Snakes—
The Elapids

Neo-tropical Coral Snake, *Micrurus diastema*

© J. Bridges

The Elapids, a large family of venomous snakes, are circumglobal in distribution and characterized by the presence of fixed, venom-conducting hollow teeth (fangs) at the front of the mouth. Many of them are remarkably similar to the aglyphous Colubrids. Indeed, some taxonomists believe the Elapids would be more accurately classified simply as a subfamily of the *Colubridae* rather than given specific family status.

Elapids are an ancient family, and fossils are known from fifteen million year old Miocene deposits. These fossils indicate their previous presence in Europe, although none occur in Europe today. They are also absent from Madagascar as well as many other oceanic islands. Their greatest diversity occurs in Australia, called "the land of living fossils." Elapids dominate the snake fauna of Australia, ranging in size from the ten foot Taipan, *Oxyuranus* to the diminutive Bandy-bandy, *Vermicella*. One form, the Death Adder, *Acanthophis*, has evolved the morphological features of the vipers.

Elapids are represented in the Americas only by three genera of the vividly colored coral snakes. *Micrurus* encompasses almost fifty species, including the thirty inch *M. fulvius* of the southeastern United States and *M. spixi*, a five-foot species from South America.

Rudyard Kipling's delightful stories of India as well as widespread publicity of flute-playing "snake charmers" have familiarized the hood-spreading cobra to almost everyone. Cobras, *Naja*, are found throughout Asia and Africa. Several African forms have modified fangs which enable them to spray (erroneously referred to as "spit") venom at the face of an intruder. "Spitting" Cobras often occupy habitats in which antelope abound; the venom-spraying ability may have developed as a deterrent to being trampled by hooved animals, while still at a safe distance. The huge and unique King Cobra, *Ophiophagus*, is a "snake eater," as the generic name indicates, and ranges from western India throughout southeastern Asia,

as well as southern China. It reaches a length in excess of eighteen feet.

Arboreal forms occur in Africa. The various mambas, *Dendroaspis,* and tree cobras, *Pseudohaje,* are examples. Piscivorous aquatic cobras, *Boulengerina,* inhabit several of Africa's large lakes and river systems.

A number of burrowing or semi-burrowing Elapids occur throughout Asia. Some twelve species of kraits, *Bungarus,* are known. *Maticora,* a southeast Asian genus with two species, has unique venom glands that extend well into the body, causing a posterior displacement of internal organs, including the heart. Commonly called Long-glanded Coral Snakes, they are neither closely related to/nor patterned as the Coral Snakes, *Micrurus,* of the New World.

The family, *Elapidae,* has until recently been divided into three subfamilies, the *Elapinae,* which includes the many terrestrial elapids briefly discussed above. The other subfamilies classified the sea snakes into two major groups, the *Hydrophiinae* and the *Laticaudinae.* Virtually all of the available semi-technical literature follows this classification. Current studies tentatively reclassify the *Elapidae* and have erected additional subfamilies, e.g., the *Bungarinae,* which includes kraits, cobras, and mambas; the *Elapinae* for coral snakes and related forms; and sea snakes of the genus *Laticauda.* The Australian elapids are placed in the subfamily *Oxyuraninae,* and remaining sea snakes in the subfamily *Hydrophiinae,* the two subfamilies forming the family *Hydrophiidae.*

Complex taxonomic discussions are not germane to the purpose of this book; the above data is included to allow the reader to easily correlate information herein presented with both previous and future publications. For the most part, the classification used here reflects the one family/three subfamily approach to the elapids, with pertinent commentary included in the various species discussions. The marine elapids or sea snakes are discussed in a separate section.

MONOCLED COBRA *(Naja naja kaouthia)*

Habitat. Variable; occurs in virtually all habitats except dense forest; frequently occurs in cities and villages

Geographic Range. The *subspecies* illustrated is found in northeastern India, Bangladesh, south-western People's Republic of China, south through Burma, Thailand and Vietnam.

Natural History. Perhaps the most frequently seen of the ten subspecies of Asian cobras, the Monocled (more accurately termed *Monocellated,* as the hood marking is an *ocellus*) varies widely in color and pattern. They may be yellow or yellowish-tan, brown, greenish-brown, olive, or black. A black-and-white variant occurs, as well as

Proteroglyphous Snakes—The Elapids 247

albino specimens. Virtually all albino Asian cobras maintained in western collections are of this subspecies.

All Asian cobras are crepuscular, although they sometimes bask during the day. As their wide range of habitats indicate, they shelter in varied locations such as rock piles, termite mounds, fallen logs, mammal burrows, and building foundations, to name only a few. Preying primarily on rodents, they also include birds, amphibians such as frogs and toads, other snakes, lizards, and occasionally eggs, in the diet.

The Monocled Cobra, as well as all other subspecies of Asian cobras, is oviparous. Several dozen eggs are deposited in suitable sites, such as rodent burrows or deserted termite mounds, the female usually but not always staying with her eggs during the incubation period, which varies from forty-five to over eighty days, according to temperature and other variables. The ten-inch hatchlings are identical to the adults, although somewhat brighter in color. They mature to an average length of four feet, but can exceed five.

Although many elapids raise the body and spread a "hood," this defensive posture is most highly developed in the Asian subspecies of *Naja naja*. As the cobra rears the forepart of its body, the elongated ribs of the cervical area are also raised and the skin stretched over them to form the characteristic hood. Hood patterns vary from one subspecies to another and may be in the shape of spectacles, hollow discs, single or double monocles (ocelli), white bands or wavy lines.

Many interesting stories and beliefs surround the cobra. In the Far East, the spectacle mark is thought to be the fingerprints of Buddha, who blessed the snake after it had shaded him with its hood as he slept in the desert. Asian cobras are viewed as fertility symbols, phallic symbols, and as emissaries of various deities. In China they are a source of tissue reputed to be of significant medicinal value; the gall bladder, for example, is used for treatment of ophthalmic disorders.

Several species of Asian cobras "spit" or more accurately, spray venom at intruders. This habit occurs among various populations of the Chinese cobra, *N. n. atra,* as well as the Monocled Cobra, *N. n. kaouthia.* It is most highly developed in *N. n. sputatrix,* which occurs in western Indonesia and Malaya.

The Chinese Cobra, *Naja n. atra*

R. S. Funk

The Ceylonese or Sri Lankan form of the Indian Cobra is sometimes referred to a distinct subspecies *Naja n. polyocellata.*

R. S. Funk

The nominate race, *N. n. naja,* ranges from Sri Lanka north throughout much of India and Pakistan. Sri Lankan specimens are often of considerable size, exceeding five feet in length. These attractive snakes are patterned with white spots and a spectacle hood, and are often referred to as *N. n. polyocellata,* generally considered, however, to be of invalid subspecific status.

The Transcaspian Cobra, *N. n. oxiana,* is a patternless, unicolored subspecies found in Afghanistan, Iran, and throughout the trans-Caspian region of southern U.S.S.R. A glossy black in color with a yellow venter, these cobras also are large in size, reaching lengths of six feet.

Several insular races have been defined, three occurring in the Philippines. *N. n. miolepis* is confined to the Palawan group of islands and Borneo (Kalimantan); *N. n. philippinensis* occurs

throughout the islands; and *N. n. samarensis* is restricted to Leyte, Mindanao and adjacent islands. The Andaman Islands are home to *N. n. sagittifera,* and *N. n. sumatrana* occurs only in Sumatra, for which it is named.

Thousands of Asian cobras are slaughtered annually for their skins. The Indian government controls the export of cobra skins and places limited restrictions on the numbers destroyed. Such continued exploitation of this unique life form will almost certainly lead to its ultimate extinction. It would seem that the near-perfect imitation snakeskin available to a supposedly conservation-oriented society should reduce the continued use of natural snakeskins to an irresponsible frivolity.

Care. Asian cobras are adaptable animals and readily adjust to captive conditions. Newly imported specimens should be checked and treated for intestinal parasites. Avoid fine sand or gravel substrates as these are abrasive and may cause dermal or oral problems. A hiding place and ample water supply are necessary. At temperatures of 75-80° F (23-27° C), Asian cobras readily accept pre-killed laboratory rodents. They reproduce well in captivity, and all albino specimens commercially available are captive-bred and hatched. Longevity records for the Monocled Cobra exceed twelve years. Records for the nominate race exceed seventeen years, and records of other subspecies with captive longevity records in excess of twelve years are common.

Asian cobras are venomous animals, and no degree of "tame" behavior in captives precludes this fact. Bites from captive cobras are virtually non-existent, but their very lethal potential is always present. While cobras are most certainly a fascinating species, they are obviously not "pets" and should not be kept as such.

Albino cobras are popular as exhibits, and most of them are derived from captive breedings. This specimen is an albinistic Siamese Cobra, *N. n. kaouthia*.

© J. Bridges

L. Moor

BLACK-NECKED COBRA; "SPITTING" COBRA
(Naja nigricollis nigricollis)

Habitat. Savannahs and open woodland
Geographic Range. Kenya, Tanzania, west to Senegal
Natural History. A large cobra, normally dull black or brownish-black in color. Regional populations may be varying shades of brown, with black interstitial skin. The venter may or may not be banded with black on a yellowish or greyish-white ground. There is, however, almost always a wide black band across the throat from which the common name derives.

Although crepuscular or nocturnal in most cases, Black-necked Cobras frequently bask during the day in the area of a convenient shelter. Rodent burrows, unused termite mounds, tree roots, and hollows in standing trees are used. They prey upon a wide variety of food species such as mammals, birds and their eggs, other snakes, lizards, frogs, toads, and fish; juveniles also include large insects in the diet.

Up to several dozen eggs are deposited. They require two to two and one-half months of incubation before hatching. Hatchlings may be lighter in color than adults, and are ten to twelve inches in length. They are, incidentally, capable of "spitting" venom when even only partially emerged from the egg. Adults attain an average length of about five feet, although nine foot specimens are known.

"Spitting" cobras obviously are capable of biting in self defense, but prefer to "spit" venom at the intruder and quickly escape. The snake rears, spreads a slight "hood" and aims its head at the facial area of the molester. The mouth is opened slightly, venom is forced from the venom glands by muscular contraction and as it leaves the fangs, an exhalation of air carries it forward. The entire procedure takes only seconds. Although the venom leaves the fangs as twin jets, it widens into a spray over the maximum effective range of ten or twelve feet. Should the venom enter the eyes, severe pain and possible blindness results. If the venom falls on unbroken skin it is harmless. Surprisingly, these cobras will at times demonstrate no aggression towards an intruder and simply perform a death-feigning ritual, remaining "dead" until danger is past, then quietly gliding away.

Several subspecies formerly considered as races of another African "spitter," *N. mossambica,* are now assigned to the *nigricollis* group. Both are confined to southern Africa. *N. n. nigricincta* is a black-and-white banded snake found in Angola and northern Namibia. The dark, unicolored *N. n. woodi* occurs in southern Namibia and the western areas of Cape Province, South Africa. A subspecies of questionable validity, *N. n. crawshayi,* is found in Togo and adjacent areas. Dull grey-black in color, the venter is dark red, which extends up the sides, especially in the neck. These are irascible snakes and spray venom upon the slightest provocation.

Care. Black-necked Cobras adjust easily to captive conditions, in most cases soon losing any inclination to "spit." They feed readily on pre-killed laboratory rodents. Captive breeding is a frequent occurrence, and longevities exceed twenty-two years.

The Black-necked Spitting Cobra, *N. n. nigricollis*

F. Bolin, D. Hamper

W. Bazemore

W. Bazemore

(Left) The distinctively patterned Banded Spitting Cobra, *N. n. nigricincta*; this specimen was photographed in the wild in South Africa. *(Right)* The unpatterned Namibian Spitting Cobra, *N. n. woodi*; photographed in South Africa

Ringhal's Cobra, *Hemachatus haemachatus,* is a small spitting cobra, found throughout drier areas of South Africa. They prey upon small rodents and lizards; some populations prey almost exclusively upon toads (*Bufo*).

F. Bolin, D. Hamper

MOZAMBIQUE (RED)
SPITTING COBRA
(*Naja mossambica*
pallida)

A. Weber, Toledo Zoo

Habitat. Open woodland, plains, savannahs, and rocky hillsides, usually near water

Geographic Range. The *subspecies* illustrated ranges from northern Tanzania, Kenya, and Uganda north to Sudan and Egypt.

Natural History. The popular name, "Red Spitter," refers to the usually erythristic coloration of this subspecies, which may be brown-red, salmon pink, or orange-red (specimens from semi-arid regions usually being lighter in color).

These snakes shelter in rock crevices, deserted termite hills, fallen trees, or in tree hollows. They emerge to bask during the day, but forage at night, preying on a wide variety of species such as toads, small snakes, lizards, birds, and rodents. They frequently enter hen houses and feed upon both eggs and small chickens.

Up to twenty eggs are deposited, the hatchlings being twelve inches or slightly more in length. The average adult length is about five feet.

These cobras react to intruders in the manner of all "spitting" cobras, rearing the body and spraying venom at the face. Unless the venom enters an open cut or the eyes, however, it is harmless. When severely pressed they feign death, complete with preliminary writhings and spasms.

The nominate race, *N. m. mossambica*, occurs from southern Tanzania, south through Mozambique, and west to Botswana and northeastern South Africa. *N. m. katiensis* is found in northern Nigeria and Ghana as well as Mali. The subspecies *nigricincta* and *woodi* are considered to be subspecies of *Naja nigricollis*, not *mossambica*.

Care. As for Asian cobras. Red Spitting Cobras readily reproduce as captives and most specimens exhibited have been captive bred. These snakes, should, however, be maintained only by professionals. Their venom can cause blindness or permanent damage to the eyes, in addition to being potentially fatal if injected by a bite.

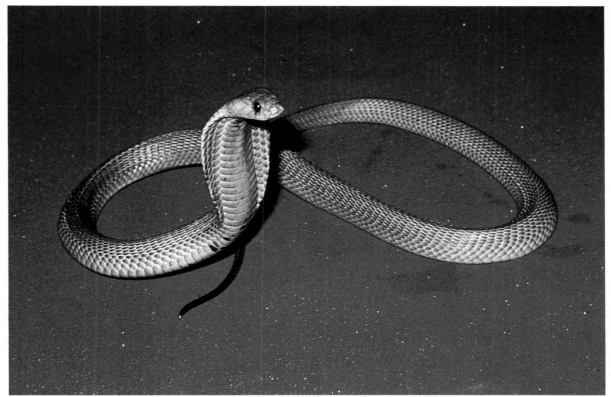

F. Bolin, D. Hamper

CAPE COBRA; YELLOW COBRA *(Naja nivea)*

Habitat. Open woodland, savannahs and range land

Geographic Range. South Africa, southern Botswana and Lesotho

Natural History. A slender, attractive snake with seemingly endless color variations and combinations. They may be straw yellow, yellow-tan, yellow-orange, or golden in color. A "buttermilk" variant that is pale yellow speckled with brown spots is fairly common. Other color variants include solid black, glossy purple-black, or greyish-black. They may also be reddish, terra cotta, or mahogany, and they may be speckled with lighter or darker spots. There are still additional variations intermediate to all of these colors.

Cape Cobras are active, diurnal snakes, foraging in burrows, rock piles, and similar places, where their primary prey of small rodents are likely to be found. They hibernate during the short South African winter. These cobras are themselves considered prey by Meerkats, *Suricata,* a small, social mongoose of South Africa.

Up to two dozen eggs are deposited in burrows, beneath stones, or in similar warm, damp places. The eight- to ten-inch hatchlings feed on toads, frogs, lizards, and nestling rodents. Several color variants may occur in any given clutch. The average adult length is about five feet; six-foot specimens occur but are rarely seen.

The neurotoxic venom of Cape Cobras is particularly toxic, and severe envenomation is rapidly fatal unless properly and quickly treated.

Care. Cape Cobras accept captive conditions readily, and conditions suitable for other cobras are satisfactory. They feed on pre-killed laboratory rodents. Captive specimens reproduce readily. Longevities exceed twenty-three years.

The red-brown color phase of the Cape Cobra, *Naja nivea*

R. D. Bartlett

The gold color phase of the Cape Cobra, *Naja nivea*

W. Bazemore

The White-lipped or Forest Cobra, *Naja melanoleuca,* occurs in forested and adjacent savannah areas in central Africa, south to Angola and the eastern parts of South Africa. Adults may attain lengths of eight feet. They prey upon a wide variety of small vertebrates.

© J. Bridges

D. Hamper

Although commonly referred to as the Egyptian Cobra, the several subspecies of *Naja haje* range widely over much of Africa. The attractively banded subspecies illustrated, *N.h. annulifera,* ranges through Zambia, Malawi, eastern Botswana and the adjacent Transvaal area of South Africa. They are heavy-bodied and robust snakes, occasionally reaching lengths in excess of eight feet, and favor savannah areas, especially with rocky outcroppings. They prey upon small mammals, birds and their eggs, lizards, other snakes and amphibians. The species was deified in ancient Egypt, and was represented on the crown of the Pharaohs.

W. Lamar, courtesy Ft. Worth Zoo

SHIELD-NOSED "COBRA"; CAPE CORAL SNAKE
(Aspidelaps lubricus lubricus)

Habitat. Areas of dry sand or sandy soil, in savannahs or open woodlands

Geographic Range. The *subspecies* illustrated
occurs in South Africa in the Cape Province and
Orange Free State.

Natural History. A small, stocky snake that is
orange or orange-red in color, patterned with
black bands. The black bands completely ring the
body in the neck area. The venter is yellow or
cream, which may extend to the sides of the body.

All members of this genus are characterized by
a greatly enlarged rostral shield (scale). This
modified rostral shield is used as a "plow," enabling the snakes to burrow in the loose soil of their
habitat. Crepuscular or nocturnal, they spend the
day in self-dug burrows, under stones or in

mammal burrows. Lizards, small snakes, toads, and
small mammals constitute their diet.

These snakes are oviparous, but little is known
concerning reproduction or hatchlings. Adults
average about two feet in length and may reach
thirty inches.

Aspidelaps rears the forepart of the body and
neck when molested, but they do not have a
"hood" as do the true cobras, *Naja.* They are
capable of producing surprisingly loud hissing
sounds for such a small snake, and they may ac-
company a defensive strike with an exhalation of
air that is quite explosive. If severely threatened,
however, they cease all aggressive actions and
feign death.

Several additional subspecific races of

Aspidelaps lubricus occur in southern Africa. *A. l. infuscatus,* a pinkish-grey form with an indistinct pattern of dark crossbands and/or spots, is found in Namibia, and the similar *A. l. cowlesi* is found in southern Angola.

A second species, *Aspidelaps scutatus,* has a more greatly enlarged rostral scale than that of *Aspidelaps lubricus,* and it is a more persistent burrower. A thick and heavy-bodied snake in relation to its short length, it is normally pinkish or pale orange in color. The head and forepart of the body is a glossy black. The nominate race, *A. s. scutatus,* is found in Namibia, Botswana, Zimbabwe, and the northeastern Transvaal. *A. s. fulafulus* ranges from southeastern Zimbabwe to southern Mozambique. *A. s. intermedius* is confined to the eastern Transvaal.

The southwest African Coral Snake (or Shield-nosed Cobra), *A. l. infuscatus.*

W. Bazemore

Care. Dry quarters and hiding places that afford an opportunity to burrow are necessary. These snakes will utilize half-buried lengths of plastic pipe as "burrows." Normally, *Aspidelaps* feeds readily on small, pre-killed laboratory mice. Captive longevities in excess of ten years have been recorded. *Aspidelap's* venom has proven fatal to humans.

EASTERN WATER COBRA *(Boulengerina annulata stormsi)*

Habitat. Brushy or wooded banks of lakes, rivers, and streams

Geographic Range. The *subspecies* illustrated occurs in the vicinity of Lake Tanganyika and adjacent streams. The shores of Lake Tanganyika border Tanzania, Burundi, Zaire and Zambia.

Natural History. A large, grey-brown, or grey unicolored snake, patterned with three to five black bands on the neck, which may or may not continue onto the whitish venter.

These are the only aquatic cobras known. They are strong swimmers and, in fact, are likely to be confused with the large aquatic non-venomous Colubrid, *Grayia,* which occurs in the same area as *Boulengerina.* Little appears to be known of these snakes in the wild other than their aquatic habits and proclivity for basking in low trees and shrubs. They are most active at night and forage for fish and frogs.

Water Cobras are oviparous, but no specific data is available. Adults average six or seven feet in

length; however, larger specimens of nine feet have been recorded.

The western subspecies, *B. a. annulata,* is a light brown or reddish-tan in color, banded with black. It occurs in Zaire, Congo, Gabon, and Cameroun. A second species, *B. christyi,* is black with yellow crossbands. This form is probably a subspecific race of *B. annulata,* although some taxonomists consider it distinct enough to warrant a genus of its own, *Limnonaja.*

Water Cobras are unaggressive, preferring to elude threats by entering nearby water. When pressed, they rear and spread a narrow "hood." Little is known about their venom or its effects.

Care. Captive conditions suitable for other aquatic snakes are adequate for these animals. Dampness is to be avoided. If the snake is given access to a sizable container of water, a means to dry off and bask should be provided. The usual precautions when feeding thawed frozen fish should be noted.

BLACK MAMBA *(Dendroaspis polylepis polylepis)*

Habitat. Dry, open woodland and scrub land, especially in areas of rocky outcroppings
Geographic Range. Kenya, south to Lesotho, west to Angola, Botswana, Zaire, and Uganda
Natural History. Although the interstitial skin of the Black Mamba may be black, the ground color can be various shades of brown, olive brown, dark olive, or greenish brown. Dark blackish-grey specimens also occur. The *interior* of the mouth is black.

Unlike the various Green Mambas that are almost exclusively arboreal, the Black Mamba is essentially a terrestrial snake that climbs in search of prey, to escape predators, to bask, or to shelter in hollow trunks. They also utilize unused termite mounds, mammal burrows, and rock piles as shelter, sometimes using the same location for months or years. Their prey is varied and includes small mammals such as rodents, shrews, bats, the rock-dwelling Hyrax, *Heterohyrax,* as well as birds.

Females deposit about a dozen large eggs in termite mounds, burrows, or other suitable, protected sites. The hatchlings vary in length from fifteen to twenty-four inches, and under optimum conditions may attain lengths of six feet during their first year. The Black Mamba is the largest of Africa's venomous snakes, and adults, averaging eight to nine feet in length, can sometimes exceed twelve feet. Specimens of fourteen feet are known.

One additional subspecies of Black Mamba, *D. p. antinori,* occurs in Ethiopia, Somalia, and northern Kenya. Other species of Mamba occur throughout Africa. The Green Mamba, *D. viridis,* is an arboreal form found throughout tropical West Africa. Several small species that rarely exceed seven feet in length are also known. These include the East African Green Mamba, *D. angusticeps,* ranging from Kenya south to Zimbabwe, and the two races of Jameson's Mamba, *D. jamesoni,* which occur throughout much of west and central Africa, east to western Kenya.

Mambas are the subject of endless tales involving unprovoked attacks, great speed, and instantaneous death from their venom. While such tales are somewhat exaggerated, the Black Mamba is a dangerous snake, quick to defend itself if attacked or prevented from gaining access to shelter. As little as two drops or so of the neurotoxic venom is fatal to a human of average size, usually through respiratory collapse. A polyvalent antivenom is manufactured in South Africa.

However, despite the Black Mamba's formidable defensive stance of spreading the neck, rearing and arching the body well above the ground, gaping the mouth and shaking the head, striking at the source of the threat does not necessarily follow. Given the opportunity, the snake will quickly retreat.

Care. Mambas are hardy and long-lived captives, with longevities of fifteen or more years recorded. Larger specimens are sometimes difficult to control, and usually light-reversal shift cages are utilized in order to secure the animals during routine procedures such as cage cleaning, feeding, etc. Captive specimens accept pre-killed rodents and/or chicks as food.

Reptile World Serpentarium

**KING COBRA;
HAMADRYAD
(*Ophiophagus
hannah*)**

Habitat. Near streams in dense or open forest, bamboo thickets, adjacent agricultural areas; dense mangrove swamps

Geographic Range. Northern India, east to southeastern People's Republic of China, including Hong Kong and Hainan; south throughout the Malay Peninsula, and east to western Indonesia and the Philippines

Natural History. Due to its broad geographic range a number of color/pattern variations, ap-parently geographically distinct, are known. Most specimens exhibited in U.S. zoological parks are exported from Bangkok, Thailand. These snakes are pale olive or yellow olive in color with a pale yellow venter. Indian specimens are similar in color, but they are crossbanded with yellow, with the posterior body and tail being black. Chinese specimens are black-brown, crossbanded with white, beige or yellow; the tail is black and the venter a pale yellow. *Ophiophagus* is a monotypic genus and no subspecies have been described. The King Cobra is diurnal, actively foraging for its near-exclusive ophidian prey. In addition to snakes, lizards are occasionally eaten. King Cobras are excellent climbers and do not hesitate to pursue prey in trees and shrubbery.

These cobras are the only snakes known to construct an actual nest for their eggs. Rotted leaves and similar vegetation are scooped into a pile by the female, using loops of the body to gather the material together. The nest may be a simple heap, in which up to fifty eggs are deposited, or a more elaborate, compartmented structure, in which the lower compartment holds the eggs and the upper is occupied by the guarding female. The female remains throughout the sixty to eighty-day incubation and hatching period. The male cobra is reputed to remain in the vicinity of the nest until hatching occurs. Hatchlings are eighteen to twenty inches in length and are banded in black and white, quite unlike the adults.

King Cobras are the largest venomous snakes in the world, with recorded lengths of over eighteen feet. The average adult length is twelve to fifteen feet, and specimens of this size are impressive. Two Philippine specimens personally observed, both in excess of seventeen feet, could only be described as "dramatic" without exaggeration. These cobras reared to a height of over four feet when they felt threatened or were merely curious about some nearby activity.

Ophiophagus is reputed to be very aggressive, capable of unprovoked attack on man and beast. However, many observations by competent field herpetologists appear to refute such tales of aggression. In captivity, for example, a sudden rush and rearing towards a cage door is more likely prompted by the expectation of food than an aggressive attack.

Care. King Cobras will accept dead snakes as food, which offers several advantages: a supply of frozen food snakes is always available; deep freezing and thawing reduces the risk of food snakes vectoring parasites; and the food snake can be packed with additional food items such as rodents or meat strips, vitamin/mineral additives, or medications. Captive specimens also respond well to odor-manipulated food; one zoological park exhibit animal accepted snake-scented strips of horsemeat. Wild-caught adults have lived more than seventeen years in captivity.

R. D. Bartlett

S. Reichling, Memphis Zoo

(Left) A typical southeast Asian color morph; the specimen illustrated is about twelve feet in length. *(Right)* A large female coiled about her clutch of eggs. The dark olive color of this specimen is typical of populations in the more northerly parts of their range.

GOLD'S TREE COBRA *(Pseudohaje goldii)*

Habitat. Rain forest

Geographic Range. The tropical forest belt of Africa, from western Kenya east to Angola and Ghana

Natural History. A large, heavy-bodied arboreal snake, black in color with a satin-smooth appearance, with the sheen sometimes imparting an indigo cast to the body. The labials and venter are ivory.

Nocturnal snakes, they spend most of their time in trees, moving gracefully and rapidly through the foliage. Their size and speed allows them to bridge sizable gaps between trees with ease. They often forage along the banks of rivers and streams for their virtually exclusive amphibian prey.

Up to eighteen large eggs are deposited early in the year. The hatchlings, perhaps fifteen inches in length, are quite different from adults, being black with yellow crossbands and an orange venter. Adults average over seven feet in length and are known to attain at least nine feet in length.

A second species, *P. nigra,* occurs in West Africa, ranging from Nigeria west to Sierra Leone.

These cobras are hoodless when adult, although juveniles rear the body and spread a narrow hood in typical cobra fashion. Adults have a reputation for aggressiveness towards the source of any threat, although such actions probably vary from one specimen to another. Their venom is known to be extremely toxic, and an untreated bite, particularly from a mature snake, would quite likely prove fatal. No antivenom is produced for this species.

Care. Tree Cobras are rarely seen as captives. Wild-caught adults often have injuries or damage to the skin that can be attributed to poor collecting technique, using nooses. The difficulty of handling a snake of this size and temperament usually restricts its captive maintenance to professional exhibits.

BLUE KRAIT *(Bungarus caeruleus sindanus)*

Habitat. Dry, sparsely wooded plains and meadows

Geographic Range. The *subspecies* illustrated occurs in Pakistan, northwestern India, and adjacent Baluchistan.

Natural History. The Blue Krait has a smooth, glossy appearance (as do all twelve species of *Bungarus*). They vary in color from a pale greyish-blue, steel-blue, or blue-black to patternless uniform black (melanistic) specimens. They are patterned with narrow white or greyish crossbands, usually arranged in pairs.

As do other nocturnal snakes, Blue Kraits remain hidden during the day in rodent burrows, piles of debris, termite mounds, and similar shelters. They prey upon rodents, lizards, and other snakes. In areas inhabited by Keelbacked Water Snakes, *Rhabdophis,* Blue Kraits may prey upon them exclusively.

Females deposit a dozen or more eggs in suitable locations and coil about them during the incubation period. The ten-inch hatchlings are identical to adults, attaining an average mature length of three to four feet.

The nominate race, *B. c. caeruleus,* is similar in appearance and has a wide range throughout Sri Lanka, India, and Bangladesh. It is sometimes referred to as the "Common Krait."

Care. Blue Kraits require dry, well-ventilated cages with hiding places, a water supply and low light levels. Humidity should be increased prior to skin shedding. At temperatures of 78-85° F (25-29° C) (cooler ranges at night), these snakes will feed readily upon pre-killed laboratory rodents. Captive specimens have attained longevities in excess of ten years.

It should be noted that Blue Kraits are extremely venomous animals. Published accounts of thirty-five envenomations inflicted by *B. c. caeruleus* indicated a 77 percent mortality rate.

BANDED KRAIT *(Bungarus fasciatus)*

Habitat. Grassy fields, meadows, cultivated areas, often adjacent to streams, rivers, and lakes

Geographic Range. Northeastern India, east through southern People's Republic of China, south throughout the Malay Peninsula; Java, Sumatra, and Borneo (Kalimantan)

Natural History. An inoffensive but potentially lethal snake, it is pale to bright canary yellow in color and banded with wide black or brown saddles that are often wider than the separating yellow color. A dorsal ridge gives them a triangular shape in cross section and a thin, emaciated appearance.

Banded Kraits are secretive and normally nocturnal. They may, however, prowl during the day during and after rains. They feed primarily on other snakes, but also on lizards, fish, and reptile eggs.

Clutches of six to ten eggs are deposited under debris or in shallow depressions, often attended by the female who remains coiled about them. There is no evidence of incubation as, for example, in the pythons. The twelve-inch hatchlings are identical to adults, but paler in color. They attain a length of five, occasionally six, feet at maturity.

Kraits hide the head beneath the body if molested, and they may twitch or writhe spasmodically but seldom attempt to bite.

Care. Ample places for concealment, both within and atop the substrate, should be provided. An ample water supply is required, and temperatures of 78° F (26° C) are suitable. Some specimens will accept pre-killed laboratory mice that have been odor-manipulated by placing the rodents in a container with a snake (a species previously accepted by the krait as food) for a short while. Banded Kraits can and have delivered fatal bites and should be handled with caution.

Proteroglyphous Snakes—The Elapids 267

D. Hamper

MANY-BANDED KRAIT
(*Bungarus multicinctus multicinctus*)

Habitat. Open woodland, grassy fields and bamboo groves adjacent to water, such as ditches, rice paddies, and streams

Geographic Range. The subspecies illustrated occurs throughout southeastern People's Republic of China (e.g., Yunnan, Guangxi, Hunan, Jiangxi, Hainan), Hong Kong and Taiwan.

Natural History. A black-and-white-banded snake, with a greyish-white venter and a glossy appearance.

Secretive and nocturnal, Many-banded Kraits are rarely seen during the day except perhaps during and after rains. Although they prey primarily upon other snakes, they also consume amphibians (frogs), fish, and occasionally small mammals.

These snakes deposit small numbers of rather large eggs. Although the Many-banded Krait is reasonably common within its range, little is known of its reproductive habits. Adults may attain a length of five feet.

Many-banded Kraits are unaggressive, preferring a quick escape from potential threats. If escape is impossible, they simply hide the head beneath the mounded coils of the body. One of the Chinese names for this species is "Umbrella Snake," based on this habit.

A subspecies, *B. m. wanghoatingi*, is found in Burma, Laos, and Yunnan province (PRC). It differs from the nominate race in scalation and pattern variations, one of which is the presence of black spots within the white bands.

Care. As for the Banded Kraits, *B. fasciatus.* Captive longevities have exceeded ten years.

MALAYAN LONG-GLANDED CORAL SNAKE
(Maticora bivirgata flaviceps)

Habitat. Loose soil and litter of the forest floor, beneath rotted logs and other debris

Geographic Range. Malaysia, Thailand, and western Indonesia

Natural History. A slim snake, indigo in color and laterally striped with pale blue or greyish-blue. The head, tail and venter are red.

Long-glanded Snakes are semi-burrowers, spending the day hidden in shallow burrows in loose leaf mould or hidden beneath forest-floor debris. They prefer the humid conditions of heavy forest, and do not occur in open or dry situations.

Maticora is nocturnal and forages for small snakes and lizards; frogs are also included in its diet. Some, but not all specimens, move about with the tail raised. If molested the head is hidden, the tail is raised still higher, and "striking" motions are made at the source of the threat with the tail.

These snakes are oviparous, but their reproductive habits are not well known. Adults reach a length of about four feet.

The extraordinary venom glands of *Maticora* are not confined to the temporal area as in most venomous snakes, but extend into the body for a full third of its length. The heart is displaced posteriorly to allow accommodation of the glands. The purpose of such greatly elongated venom glands, however, is not known.

Two additional subspecies occur in Indonesia and Borneo. A second species, *Maticora intestinalis,* with seven subspecies, ranges throughout southeastern Asia.

Care. A substrate of shredded bark garden mulch strewn with slabs of tree bark and dried leaves allows these light-shy snakes to remain comfortably hidden away. Temperatures of 78-80° F (25-27° C) and water misting several times per week maintain suitable humidity. Small snakes and occasionally lizards are acceptable food items. These snakes are dangerously venomous; the single human envenomation recorded indicated the venom is a probable neurotoxin.

R. S. Funk

ARIZONA CORAL SNAKE
(Micruroides euryxanthus euryxanthus)

Habitat. Dry, rocky, open woodland; plains, rocky hillsides, arroyos

Geographic Range. Southern Sinaloa, Mexico north to New Mexico and west throughout central Arizona

Natural History. The "other" American Coral Snake, it differs in dentitional and scalation details. The red, yellow and black rings encircle the body and are clear and well defined.

The Arizona Coral Snake is normally found in areas of loose, sandy soil in rocky areas. It shelters underground in unused mammal or other burrows, beneath stones, or in rock crevices. It emerges to forage at night or on overcast days, particularly before or after rainstorms. Its habits in the wild are poorly known, but it preys upon small snakes, especially Blind Snakes, *Leptotyphlops*.

Females deposit two or three eggs beneath stones or underground. At maturity *Micruroides* seldom exceeds eighteen inches in length.

Although possessing a potent venom, these snakes defend themselves somewhat passively by hiding the head beneath the body coils, elevating the tightly coiled tail, and waving it about. The lining of the cloaca is everted, producing a "popping" sound.

Two additional subspecies are recognized, which are the Mazatlan Coral Snake, *M. e. neglectus,* from the area north of Mazatlan (Sinaloa, Mexico) and the Sonoran Coral Snake, *M. e. australis,* of Sonora, Mexico.

Care. As for the Eastern Coral Snake, *Micrurus fulvius.* NOTE: *Micruroides* requires somewhat *drier* conditions and is not known to feed upon any prey species other than snakes.

EASTERN CORAL SNAKE; HARLEQUIN SNAKE
(Micrurus fulvius fulvius)

Habitat. Various; open woodlands, pine woods, cutover areas adjacent to streams, ditches and river banks

Geographic Range. Upper Florida Keys, north to North Carolina, west to Mississippi and eastern Louisiana

Natural History. The subject of much folklore and outlandish myth in areas in which it occurs, this Coral Snake is immediately recognizable by its brightly colored pattern of black, red, and yellow rings. This pattern, in which the red and yellow rings are adjacent, is consistent in all three of the venomous Coral Snakes found in the United States. In the case of the harmless Coral Snake "mimics," the red and yellow (or white) rings are always separated by black.

Coral Snakes are secretive and remain hidden beneath leaf litter, fallen logs, in rotted stumps or burrows. They may move about during and after rains or on humid, overcast days. They prey upon small snakes, e.g., Crowned Snakes, *Tantilla,* and small lizards, especially skinks, and sometimes nestling rodents.

Micrurus deposits up to eighteen eggs, often in rotted logs or stumps. The eight-inch hatchlings are identical in color and pattern to adults and mature to an average thirty inches in length.

The small size of the mouth and the fangs, which in elapids are fixed and non-erectile, preclude accidental bites, except under extra-ordinary circumstances. Bites inflicted upon humans are quite rare and usually the result of rough handling (of a misidentified specimen) or attempts to kill the snake. Coral Snakes are not aggressive and often hide the head and present the tail as a substitute if molested.

A western subspecies, *M. f. tenere*, is found from southern Arkansas west to central Texas and south into northern Mexico. Unlike the nominate race, its red bands are heavily speckled with black, and it occurs in some drier areas such as rocky hillsides and canyons.

Other subspecies are found farther south in Mexico. *M. f. maculatus* occurs in Tamaulipas, in swamps and adjacent areas. This subspecies inter-grades with *M. f. microgalbineus*, also found in Tamaulipas, as well as Guanajuato, and San Luis Potosi.

Care. Coral Snakes require a burrowing medium such as shredded bark garden mulch. They will utilize a clear glass or plastic plate atop the substrate as part of their burrow and thus remain visible. Temperatures of 73-75° F (22-24° C) are adequate, and they will accept small snakes or ground skinks, *Scincella*, as food. Captive Coral Snakes are best confined to professional exhibits or study collections.

Western Coral Snake,
Micrurus f. tenere

W. Lamar

R. S. Funk

BRAZILIAN CORAL SNAKE *(Micrurus frontalis subsp.)*

Habitat. Forests adjacent to swamps or streams
Geographic Range. The *species* ranges from southern Brazil, southeastward through Bolivia to northern Argentina
Natural History. Including the small coral snakes of the southeastern United States, there are (plus or minus) some fifty species of *Micrurus* known. Most of these range in South America, and it is among these tropical species that the largest coral snakes occur.

The Brazilian Coral Snake is typical of the tropical forms. Unlike the North American species, the red and yellow bands do not necessarily touch. The three colors arranged in specific sequences known as "triads" are valuable aids to identification. In the Brazilian Coral Snake, as in many other forms, the color sequence is red-black-yellow-black-yellow-black-red.

Although reasonably well-defined taxonomically, little is known of the habits of these snakes. All of the tropical species are secretive and nocturnal. They shelter within burrows and other underground retreats, beneath fallen logs, piles of drifted leaves, and other debris. Some forms are burrowers, tunnelling through the soft humus of the forest floor. Most prey upon other reptiles, especially snakes, although small mammals and fish are also included in their diet (at least in captivity). They are all oviparous, but details relative to clutch size, incubation periods, and other data are minimal.

Five subspecies of the Brazilian Coral Snake occur throughout the extensive range and include *M. f. frontalis* of Brazil, Paraguay and Argentina; *M. f. altirostris* of Uruguay, adjacent Brazil and Argentina; *M.f. brasiliensis,* which is confined to

Brazil; and *M. f. mesopotamicus,* confined to Argentina. The specimen illustrated is probably *M. f. pyrrhocryptus,* ranging through Bolivia, Paraguay, Argentina, and southwestern Brazil.

All of these forms attain adult lengths of four feet. They are sometimes popularly called "Cobra coral snakes," a reference to their habit of hiding the head and flattening and elevating the tail when threatened.

Other tropical coral snakes worthy of note are Spix's Coral Snake, *M. spixi,* known as four subspecies from Brazil, Bolivia, and northwestern South America. Attaining lengths of five feet, they are among the largest coral snakes known. They inhabit wet, swampy areas, as do the similar *M. surinamensis,* two subspecies of which occur over much of northern South America. These also attain lengths in excess of four feet.

A few tropical coral snakes lack any red color at all in their pattern. *M. p. psyches,* whose three subspecies range from Trinidad across northern South America to Colombia, is a slim indigo or black snake patterned with thin bands of dull yellow. They inhabit areas of dense forest. Another genus related to the coral snakes, *Leptomicrurus,* known from three species, is a slender, black snake, ringed with a narrow band of yellow on the neck and tail. The venter is heavily spotted with bright yellow, exposed only when the snake elevates the posterior body and tail, which is the defensive "cobra mimic" stance of many of these snakes. *Leptomicrurus* occurs throughout the northern half of South America.

Care. Comments offered for *M. fulvius* may serve as a basis for developing husbandry techniques suitable for tropical *Micrurus.* Captive *M. frontalis* have accepted snakes and lizards as food; captive *M. surinamensis* have fed upon eels and goldfish, as has *M. spixi,* which has also accepted snakes.

DEATH ADDER; DEAF ADDER
(Acanthophis antarcticus)

Habitat. Dry, sandy areas in or near open woodlands, grassy plains, rock outcroppings

Geographic Range. Australia (absent from desert areas and extreme southeast); New Guinea (West Irian and Papua); adjacent islands, west to Ceram

Natural History. A unique elapid with both the appearance and actions of a viper, the Death Adder has a triangulate head and thin tail. They are quite variable in color, and may be different shades of brown, grey, black, or reddish. The body is patterned with crossbands, always contrasting with the ground color. The pale venter is speckled with dark spots. The distinctive tail, yellow or cream in color, is tipped with a soft, spine-like scale.

The Death Adder relies upon its cryptic coloration to remain undetected during the day. As do many *true* vipers, Death Adders remain coiled and partially buried in soil, dried leaves or other debris, usually in the shelter of large stones, bushes or fallen trees. They are crepuscular and/or nocturnal, but they are not active foragers, preferring to lie in wait for potential prey, a characteristic of the vipers. *Acanthophis* feeds upon small mammals, birds and lizards, employing its brightly colored tail-tip as a lure. When prey approaches, the tip of the tail is raised and slowly waved and/or quivered in the manner of a caterpillar. The ruse is effective, and a quick strike secures the prey as it ventures towards the lure.

Death Adders are ovoviviparous; large females give birth to as many as twenty young, six inches in length. Adults are usually under two feet, but exceptional specimens may exceed thirty inches.

These snakes make little or no attempt to escape if danger threatens, remaining in their resting place, flattening the body and rapidly striking out at the intruder.

The venom of *Acanthophis* is extremely toxic and is injected deeply by fangs that are quite large for an elapid. An adult snake may inject sixty or seventy milligrams of venom in a single bite; twenty milligrams or less can be fatal to humans.

Acanthophis pyrrhus is a bright orange-brown or reddish-brown desert species, crossbanded with paler shades of the body color. The scales are heavily keeled and present a bristly appearance. It is confined to the western and central desert regions of Australia.

Additional species and/or subspecies of *Acanthophis* have been named since 1803, when the genus was first described. Of these, *A. a. laevis* of eastern Australia is considered valid by some taxonomists.

Care. Australian wildlife regulations forbid the export of living animals, and therefore, as with other reptiles from Australia, only captive-bred specimens are available commercially.

A substrate topped with leaf litter provides the necessary partial concealment for the snake. At temperatures of approximately 80° F (27° C), Death Adders feed readily on pre-killed laboratory mice. This is obviously a species suitable only for professional collections.

Los Angeles Zoo

TIGER SNAKE *(Notechis scutatus)*

Habitat. Varied; dry, grassy fields, open woodland, flood plains, and rain forest
Geographic Range. Southeastern Australia
Natural History. Extremely variable in color and pattern, Tiger Snakes are brown, reddish brown, olive, olive green, dark or light grey, and frequently crossbanded with lighter shades of the ground color. Black (melanistic), unpatterned specimens are frequent; albinos are known, but rare.

Tiger Snakes are active, diurnal elapids that become nocturnal during warm summer months. Frogs are their primary prey, but small mammals and lizards are also eaten.

Large litters of living young are produced, average sized females (four feet) bearing thirty youngsters. Exceptionally large females have produced litters of over one hundred young. The ten-inch neonates are identical to the adults in color and pattern.

The Tiger Snakes of southwestern Australia, offshore southern islands, and Tasmania are somewhat larger animals, usually black in color, and a different species, *Notechis ater.* Four subspecies are known. The insular races prey upon snakes and birds in addition to small mammals and frogs.

Notechis is an irritable snake, quick to anger if molested. They spread the neck into a small, flattened hood and strike out at the threat. Their venom is highly toxic, as little as three milligrams being fatal to humans.

Care. Frequently exhibited prior to Australia's ban on exports of native fauna, Tiger Snakes are currently shown in only a few U.S. zoological parks. Captive Tiger Snakes fare quite well under conditions as described for Asian Cobras, *Naja,* and feed readily on pre-killed laboratory rodents. Over seventeen years' captive longevities are known.

Among the many color variations of the Tiger Snake, a banded form frequently occurs, as illustrated.

B. Mealey

When nervous or threatened, Tiger Snakes flatten the neck area into a small "hood."

S. Reichling, Memphis Zoo

B. Mealey

TAIPAN *(Oxyuranus scutellatus scutellatus)*

Habitat. Varied; plains and savannahs, open woodlands, wet *and* dry coastal forests
Geographic Range. The *subspecies* illustrated occurs in northeastern and north central Australia (Queensland, Arnhemland, and Melville Island).
Natural History. A large, slender snake with both keeled and smooth scales, it is usually pale to dark brown in color, fading to beige or cream laterally; the cream color continuing onto the venter, which is spotted with orange. Juveniles are lighter in color (see illustration). Occasionally, orange or tawny specimens occur.

Diurnal in the spring, Taipans become crepuscular during the warmer summer months. When not basking or foraging they shelter in mammal burrows, rock crevices, fallen logs, and piles of forest litter. They prey upon small mammals, especially rats, which may be caught in their burrows or simply run down.

Clutches of up to twenty eggs are deposited in burrows or under stones. The hatchlings are sixteen to twenty inches in length, and more than double their length during their first year. Adults are an average six to seven feet long, but specimens eleven feet in length have been reported.

A subspecies, *O. s. canni,* occurs along the southern coast of Papuan New Guinea, in both lowland and montane habitats, although rarely occurring over 2,500 foot elevations. The Papuan Taipan is greyish-brown or black in color, patterned with an orange or red stripe posteriorly.

Taipans quickly vanish into nearby burrows or other cover when disturbed. If no retreat is available, however, they become fearsomely aggressive, and defend themselves vigorously. The long tail is raised and lashed about, the head is flattened, and several coils of the body are raised well above the ground. Should this performance fail to discourage the intruder, it is followed by a rapid series of strikes *and* bites. Due to the toxicity of their venom and their relatively large fangs, an envenomated bite delivered under such circumstances is a matter of grave concern, and many human fatalities have occurred. The Taipan is considered one of Australia's most dangerous snakes. An antivenom is manufactured in Australia.

The Taipan is sometimes confused with another Australian snake of similar size and coloration, *Parademansia microlepidotus,* the Smooth-scaled Snake, that is restricted in range to western New South Wales, and western and southwestern Queensland. Although little is known of its habits in the wild, research indicates its venom is at least four times as toxic as that of the Taipan. Based on venom yields and minimum lethal doses, the venom discharged from a single bite of the Smooth-scaled Snake is capable of killing 125,000 mice!

Care. As for the Tiger Snake, *Notechis.* Taipans are long lived as captives, albeit dangerous ones. They reproduce readily under proper conditions, one Australian institution reporting third generation captive-bred animals.

The slender form of the Taipan is typical of many fast-moving terrestrial snakes.

B. Mealey

R. D. Bartlett, R. Sayers

BANDY-BANDY *(Vermicella annulata)*

Habitat. Varied; arid plains, open woodland, and/or coastal forests

Geographic Range. Australia (absent from the southwestern and southeastern areas)

Natural History A small burrowing elapid, strikingly patterned with black and white bands which often encircle the body as rings. The numbers and width of the bands differ in males and females. The scales are smooth and glossy.

A relatively common, specialized snake about which very little is known. They are burrowers, but may emerge at night or after rains. They are oviparous. Based on records of stomach contents, *Vermicella* feeds almost exclusively on the equally fossorial Blind Snakes, *Typhlops.*

Adult specimens are eighteen to twenty inches in length. Although venomous, they seldom attempt to bite. When molested the Bandy-bandy forms the body into several rigid loops which are raised well off the ground.

Some taxonomists recognize two subspecies, which are *V. a. annulata* from southern and eastern Australia and *V. a. snelli,* occupying the balance of the range. A second species, *V. multifasciata,* found in northern and western Australia, may in fact be subspecific to *annulata.*

Care. The probable hyper-specialized diet of the Bandy-bandy prevents its successful captive maintenance outside of those areas where Blind Snakes, *Typhlops,* are found.

The Sea Snakes—
Laticaudinae and Hydrophiinae

Yellow-Lipped Sea Snake, *Laticauda colubrina*

The sea snakes are Elapids that have left the land and exploited a marine environment. Although the sea snakes have been studied for many years, their evolution and relationships to the terrestrial elapids remain unclear. Further, their tropical distribution has been until recently a hindrance to studies of their habits and their role in marine ecosystems. Researchers have relied on fish traps and trawling nets for both ecological and distributional studies. Modern research vessels allow for on-site analysis of stomach contents as well as various physiological studies, and a number of researchers are currently engaged in investigations of these unique reptiles.

Sea snakes are represented by two subfamilies of the *Elapidae*, the primitive *Laticaudinae*, represented by about five species, all of which occur in shallow water, returning to land to deposit their eggs; and the *Hydrophiinae*, represented by some forty-eight species, that are completely aquatic, laterally compressed snakes with a flattened, oar-like tail. The eyes are small relative to body size, and the nostrils, situated dorsally, can be sealed shut by specialized spongy tissue. These sea snakes never leave the water, and when accidentally washed ashore are virtually helpless.

Animals that have exploited marine environments inadvertently swallow some salt water or ingest it with their food. Although the skin is permeable to water it is not permeable to salt. Excessive amounts of salt cannot be effectively eliminated through the urine as in terrestrial animals, and specialized "salt glands" have evolved to handle this physiological aspect. (Birds such as penguins secrete excess salt through nasal glands; sea turtles by means of a lachrymal gland that allows the flow of very salty tears.) The posterior, sublingual salt glands evolved by the sea snakes are located beneath and around the tongue sheath. The glands discharge into the tongue sheath, and the excreted salt is expelled from the sheath by the action of the snake's tongue.

The scales of sea snakes vary considerably from species to species, depending upon the degree of marine specialization. Unlike the imbricate (overlapping) scales of the terrestrial snakes, the scales of most pelagic sea snakes abut one another. However, the scales of some of the species of *Aipysurus*, which live in and around coral reefs, do overlap, protecting the body from the sharp, rough-textured coral. Sea snake scales may be smooth, keeled or granular, the last often appearing as warts; or some may by spiny. The various scale types appear in the illustrations. The peg-like scales of the pelagic *Pelamis* appear as "kernels on a corn cob," while those of the sculling tail are juxtaposed plates. The ventral plates (scales) of the more pelagic species such as *Pelamis* are considerably reduced (as a result of the lateral compression of the body that reduces resistance to water), but those of the somewhat terrestrial *Laticauda* are nearly identical to the ventrals of terrestrial snakes. They assist these sea snakes in moving about on the rocky islands and shores to which they retreat during the day.

Sea snakes feed on a variety of marine organisms, especially fish such as eels. Some species that inhabit reef systems have small heads and thin necks, enabling them to extract small eels from holes in the soft bottom in which they hide. Other species may associate with patches of flotsam, beneath which small fish shelter. Two genera subsist almost exclusively on fish eggs, a most unusual "prey" for a venomous snake.

Sea snakes do not occur in the Atlantic Ocean. Most occur in the coastal waters of Australia and southern Asia. The brightly hued, yellow and black pelagic sea snake, *Pelamis,* is trans-oceanic in range, occurring in the warm waters of western Central and South America, as well as Mexico. It extends westward to the Cape of Good Hope (southern Africa). Some species inhabit mangrove swamps and other brackish water habitats. There are two "land locked" forms that live in a fresh water habitat; *Hydrophis semperi,* occurring in Lake Taal (Lake Bombon) in the Philippines, and *Laticauda crockeri,* found in Lake Tungano in the Solomon Islands.

The venom of sea snakes is considered highly toxic, that of some species several times more toxic than that of the typical cobras. Some sea snakes, such as *Pelamis,* that feed by simply gulping down small fishes, apparently utilize their venom primarily for defense, and these snakes are often quick to bite when molested. Others, such as *Laticauda,* use their venom primarily for subduing prey prior to feeding. Found ashore, some species appear to be innocuous; local fishermen who capture the Banded Sea Snakes, *Laticauda,* for food and skins apparently handle them freely and with impunity. In some localized regions large numbers of sea snakes are utilized for commericial activities. The most commonly captured are the various species of *Laticauda,* which come ashore to shelter in rocky crevices and caves. The snakes are skinned for leather and the bodies smoked for food, considered a delicacy in parts of the Far East. Specimens considered inferior for the table may be dried and used as food for domestic animals. Internal organs are used in folk medicine.

The five species of *Laticauda* regularly leave the water to shelter under rocks. Some, such as *Laticauda colubrina,* spend the day hiding in caves to escape the tropical sun. They deposit their eggs in crevices and caves above the high tidemark. All other sea snakes bear living young, and the shallow water species often enter mangrove swamps or other sheltered places to give birth.

Care. Living sea snakes are rarely exhibited by western zoological parks and aquariums, although a number of Japanese aquariums regularly exhibit them. Availability of a constant food supply is basic to the successful captive husbandry of any animal, and this obviously prevents the long-term maintenance of several species of sea snakes. Additionally, some species are extraordinarily sensitive and intolerant of handling. There is some evidence that these species may suffer cardiac arrest, apparently the result of an inability to control blood pressure when removed from the water and held in a vertical position. Several of the piscivorous (fish-eating) species have been maintained from time to time and are the most logical forms to select for exhibits.

The frequently terrestrial *Laticauda* species ship well in cloth sacks, packed in the usual manner for snakes. Others may be packed in plastic sacks containing sea water, under oxygen, in the manner used for shipping fish.

The *Laticauda* species require some provision allowing them exit from the water, as well as a basking spot exposed to ultraviolet light. Any of the several mixtures available for synthetic sea water are suitable and, of course, should be filtered. (The completely aquatic forms do not require any means of leaving the water, but do utilize a submerged shelter.) An aquarium of appropriate size, filled with filtered, synthetic sea water at a temperature of about 85° F (29° C) is suitable. The Ringed Sea Snake, *Hydrophis cyanocinctus,* widespread throughout Asian waters, has been maintained fairly successfully under such conditions. Fish, especially eels, may be offered as food.

Perhaps the species most readily available and most amenable to captive conditions is the pelagic sea snake, *Pelamis platurus.* They should be kept in sea water at all times, including time spent in transit. A number of marine organisms, sea snakes included, damage their snouts by swimming into the corners of tanks. Care should be taken to avoid this by using round or oval containers, or by modifying the right angled corners of rectangular containers with plastic inserts that present widely curved surfaces. Filtered, synthetic sea water maintained at about 85° F (29° C) is satisfactory. *Pelamis* will normally accept small fish, including goldfish, as food.

NOTE: The sea snakes have been presented here as two subfamilies of the proterogiyphous family *Elapidae.* Recent taxonomic studies have placed the sea snakes of the genus *Laticauda* in the same family as the terrestrial elapids (cobras, etc.) and separated all other sea snakes into a family including all Australian elapids. These revisions are not universally accepted and are mentioned here as a matter of interest. A more precise explanation will be found in the introductory remarks outlining the family *Elapidae.*

YELLOW-LIPPED SEA SNAKE
(Laticauda colubrina)

Habitat. Shallow water, reefs, lagoons, mangrove swamps

Geographic Range. Coastal waters of New Guinea and the Pacific islands, especially Fiji and New Caledonia, west through the Philippines and southeastern Asia to Sri Lanka, north along the coast of eastern Asia to Japan

Natural History. A smooth-scaled snake, normally a pale shade of blue or bluish-grey, and clearly patterned with black crossbands that continue on the venter, creating a ringed effect. The popular name derives from the yellow lips and snout.

These snakes are most active at night, although they may forage or bask on reefs, corals or rocks, or in mangroves at low tide. They are terrestrial except when feeding, and shelter in rock crevices and caves far removed from water.

All of the species assigned to this genus come ashore to lay their eggs in crannies and crevices above high tidemark. Large numbers may congregate in suitable areas at such times, and these aggregations are heavily exploited in the Philippines for their skins and flesh. Adults average about three feet in length; females are larger than males and may occasionally exceed four feet.

Their venom is highly toxic, but it is secreted in small quantities. They are inoffensive snakes and seldom attempt to defend themselves by biting.

Yellow-lipped Sea Snakes spend much time ashore, sheltering in rock crevices and caves. This specimen was photographed in Papua New Guinea.

Dr. W. Dunson

In addition to the Yellow-lipped Sea Snake, four other forms of Laticauda are known (all are banded and are usually referred to as Banded Sea Snakes). The specimen illustrated was photographed in the Fiji Islands.

Dr. W. Dunson

Dr. W. Dunson

DUBOIS'S SEA SNAKE *(Aipysurus duboisi)*

Habitat. Coral reefs

Geographic Range. Northern Australia, including the Great Barrier Reef; New Guinea east through Melanesia to New Caledonia

Natural History. Highly variable in color, these snakes may be creamy brown, purplish-brown, salmon or beige, with a pattern of dark bands and/or pale yellow blotches on the lower sides. A reticulated dorsal pattern sometimes occurs. The venter may be pale in color *or* dark brown.

Dubois's Sea Snake is common in the shallow water of coral reefs, but it has also been found at depths over one hundred and fifty feet. They bear small litters, although the young are quite large in size. Adults are less than three feet in length.

The genus *Aipysurus* is represented by seven species, most of which are confined to the waters of Australia, New Guinea, and Indonesia. The widest ranging form, *A. eydouxi,* occurs as far west as Malaysia, Thailand, and Vietnam. A three-foot long, salmon-colored snake, it occurs in deep, silted waters. Its habits are not well known. The heavy-bodied *A. laevis* is the largest species within the genus with adults attaining six feet in length. It occurs in the reef areas of northern Australia, New Guinea, and much of the Coral Sea. The specimen illustrated, photographed on Ashmore Reef off the coast of northwestern Australia, is an example of one of the paler color variations. *A. laevis* bears litters of up to five living young. Both juveniles and adults prey upon various species of reef fish.

(Left) An adult specimen of *Aipysurus duboisi*; note the flattened oar-like tail. *(Right)* An adult *Aipysurus laevis*; an example of the lighter-colored and patterned variation of this species

(Left) A beached specimen of *A. laevis*; note the position of the eyes and nostrils. *(Right)* A beached adult specimen of *A. laevis*; note the robust body and the laterally compressed tail.

Aipysurus eydouxi, one of the more brightly colored and patterned Sea Snake species

Dr. W. Dunson

A beached adult *A. eydouxi*; note the small head, position of eyes and nostrils, and attractive pattern.

Dr. W. Dunson

STOKES'S SEA SNAKE
(Astrotia stokesii)

Habitat. Deep, open water, especially in areas of turbid or silted water

Geographic Range. Australian waters, west through the Indo-Malayan area, to India and Sri Lanka

Natural History. These heavy-bodied snakes vary in color from black through various shades of grey, to dull white. Indistinct patterns of blotches, reticulations or crossbands may be present.

Astrotia is the largest of the sea snakes, reaching an adult length of six feet, and appearing even larger due to its thick, heavy body, which may be nine or ten inches in circumference. Despite their size, they are agile swimmers, aided by a raised ventral keel formed by the elongated and divided ventral scales.

Although it is a wide-ranging snake of considerable size and therefore presumably easily observed or studied, little is known of the habits or biology of this monotypic genus. Females bear litters of about a dozen young, twelve inches in length.

ANNULATED SEA SNAKE
(Emydocephalus annulatus)

Habitat. Shallow waters of reef areas

Geographic Range. Indonesia east to Australia and Melanesia

Natural History. A dark brown, black, or grey in color, banded and/or laterally blotched, or spotted with white. The snout (rostral shield) is somewhat conical, more obvious in males. This cone-shaped rostral shield may appear as a "spine" in fully mature males.

As is the case with so many of the marine serpents, very little factual information is available concerning the habits of this species. They are small snakes, usually maturing to an average length of thirty inches. They feed exclusively on fish eggs, a "prey" that would appear to render superfluous their possession of venom and venom-conducting fangs.

A second species, *Emydocephalus ijimae,* ranges throughout the coastal waters of the People's Republic of China, Taiwan, and Japan.

(NO "POPULAR" NAME)
(Acalyptophis peronii)

Habitat. A surface swimmer, in waters adjacent to reefs

Geographic Range. Australia

Natural History. Pale grey, beige, or pale brown in color, patterned with dark crossbands. The scales above and behind the eye (supraoculars and postoculars) are raised and form conspicuous spines. These spines are most highly developed in mature animals.

This monotypic genus is relatively rare, and its habits are all but unknown. Some herpetologists have identified sea snakes from the waters of Taiwan and the People's Republic of China as this species. However, *Acalyptophis* appears to be confined to Australian waters, and the oriental specimens remain in doubt until such time as their identification is confirmed.

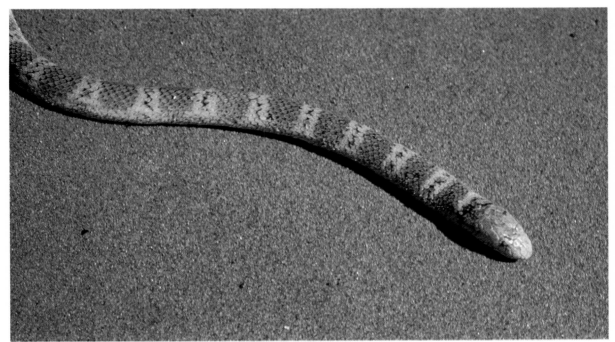

Dr. W. Dunson

(NO "POPULAR" NAME)
(Hydrophis elegans)

Habitat. Shallow coastal areas; bays and tidal rivers

Geographic Range. Waters off the north and northeastern coast of Australia and southern New Guinea

Natural History. A long "ropy" sea snake, pale brown or yellowish in color, and patterned with dorsal bars and/or blotches; laterally spotted. The posterior portion of the body is quite deeply compressed, a physical feature that undoubtedly aids or increases the sculling power of the compressed tail.

It is a common species within its range, particularly in bays with silted waters. As with many other sea snakes, its biology and habits are not well known. They feed on a variety of fishes, including eels. They bear living young, the juveniles usually pale brown in color, patterned with clearly defined crossbands. An adult length of four to five feet is average, although lengths of six feet can be attained.

The genus *Hydrophis* is represented by some twenty-five species, widespread throughout the southern Pacific area. Approximately twelve species occur in Australian and New Guinean

Dr. W. Dunson

Most Sea Snakes are helpless when washed ashore, and this adult specimen of *H. elegans* may well exhaust itself attempting to return to the water without assistance.

The Sea Snakes—Laticaudinae and Hydrophiinae 293

waters. One species, the Blue-ringed Sea Snake, *Hydrophis cyanocinctus,* found from the Philippines west to the Persian Gulf and north to Japan, is frequently indicted as the culprit in human fatalities attributed to bites inflicted by sea snakes.

Another species, *H. major,* may serve to illustrate the frequent taxomonic changes that occur in groups of animals that are little known and poorly understood. Found in the deep waters of northern Australia and southern New Guinea, *H. major* is usually placed in the composite genus *Disteira,* a genus of three species, all of whom differ from each other in form and anatomical features. The specimen illustrated is a juvenile.

Hydrophis cyanocinctus is one of the few species of Sea Snake occasionally exhibited in western zoological parks and aquariums.

F. Bolin, D. Hamper

Hydrophis major, a species found in the deep waters of northern Australia and southern New Guinea

Dr. W. Dunson

HARDWICKE'S SEA SNAKE *(Lapemis hardwicki)*

Habitat. Clear, coastal and reef waters, silted estuaries

Geographic Range. Southeastern Asia from the Bay of Bengal eastward around the coasts of the Malay Peninsula, north to Japan, and eastward throughout Indonesia and the Philippines to Australia and New Guinea

Natural History. A stocky snake, olive or olive-grey, or yellowish in color and patterned with a series of wide, darkly colored dorsal blotches. The scales of the ventral surface are much reduced in size, while those of the lower sides are much larger than the remainder of the body scales. These scales have greatly enlarged tubercles, thorn-like in appearance, and of unknown use. The thorny projections occur only in adult males.

Lapemis often enters the cloudy, brackish water of estuaries, frequently becoming tangled in fish nets. These snakes are relatively inoffensive, and fishermen, to whom they are considered pests, freely handle them to remove them from the nets. Nevertheless, several human fatalities have been recorded.

The young are born alive and attain adult lengths of about three feet.

A second species, *Lapemis curtus,* occurs in the waters of western India and the Persian Gulf.

An adult *Lapemis hardwicki.* Note the spine-like scales along the lower sides of the body.

The Sea Snakes—Laticaudinae and Hydrophiinae 295

Dr. W. Dunson

PELAGIC SEA SNAKE; YELLOW-BELLIED SEA SNAKE
(Pelamis platurus)

Habitat. Coastal and open water

Geographic Range. The west coast of Mexico, Central and South America, west throughout the Pacific and Indian Oceans, to the eastern and southern coasts of Africa

Natural History. The extensive range and the color and pattern of *Pelamis* are unique among sea snakes. The dorsum is dark brown or black, the color extending onto the sides where mid-laterally it forms a well-defined line with the light color of the lower sides and venter. The line may become indented or wavy as it approaches the tail. The lower body color is usually a vivid yellow, but may also be pale brown or beige. The oar-shaped tail is yellow, spotted with black or brown.

Pelamis is the most widely distributed of the sea snakes, and it appears to spend much time floating on the surface, drifting with currents. They also frequent mats of flotsam that attract various small fish beneath its shelter. *Pelamis* preys upon a variety of surface dwelling fishes.

These snakes bear living young that attain an average length at maturity of thirty inches.

Dr. W. Dunson

The hexagonal tail scales and peg-like body scales of *Pelamis platurus*

Solenoglyphous Snakes—The Viperids

West African Gaboon Viper, *Bitis gabonica rhinoceros*

B. Mealey

Solenoglyphous snakes have evolved a highly sophisticated dental apparatus for the injection of venom. Unlike the proteroglyphous cobras, coral snakes, and other elapids, their hollow fangs are completely enclosed, with no external remnants of a groove. The fangs are not fixed in place, but attached to a maxillary bone capable of rotation. During a strike the mouth is widely opened, the fangs erected, and a rapid stab, rather than a bite, injects the venom.

Erection of the fangs is not automatic but is controlled by the snake. Thus, both fangs may be erected simultaneously or one at a time or not at all. Each fang has a series of "embryo" or replacement fangs behind it. When a replacement reaches proper size, the functioning fang loosens at its base as the new one moves into position. At this point the snake may have three or four fangs instead of the usual two. With the new fang securely in place, the old one loosens completely and is usually left in the body of the next prey animal bitten. The process of fang replacement continues throughout the life of the snake.

The *Viperids* are the most advanced of living snakes and all are placed in the family *Viperidae*. The *Viperidae* is further divided into three sub-families, the primitive *Azemiopinae*; the old world "true" vipers, *Viperinae;* and the advanced pit vipers of Asia and North and South America, the *Crotalinae.*

The *Azemiopinae* are represented by only a single form, the very rare *Azemiops feae* of Asia. The *Viperinae* are found throughout Europe, Africa, and Asia. They range in size from the twelve-inch-long *Vipera ursinii* of Europe and southwestern Asia, which preys upon small grasshoppers, to the huge African Gaboon Viper, *Bitis gabonica,* with a recorded length of almost seven feet and a circumference of over eighteen inches, which is capable of consuming small antelope such as the Royal antelope, *Neotragus.*

The pit vipers, *Crotalinae,* characterized by the presence of a thermoreceptive pit between the nostril and eye, are represented in Asia by the various tree vipers and terrestrial Habus, *Trimeresurus,* as well as the Mamushi and its allies, *Agkistrodon.* In North and South America, the rattlesnakes, *Crotalus,* the copperheads and cottonmouths, *Agkistrodon,* and the more than sixty-five species of the neo-tropical *Bothrops* represent the family. The *Crotalinae* are discussed in the final pages of this book.

FEA'S VIPER *(Azemiops feae)*

Habitat. Mountainous areas, above altitudes of 2,000 feet

Geographic Range. Northern Burma, southeastern Tibet, Jiangxi and Sichuan provinces (People's Republic of China), northern Tonkin

Natural History. *Azemiops,* considered to be the most primitive of the vipers, is a smooth scaled snake, bluish-black or black in color, patterned with thin orange-red lateral bands that may or may not meet mid-dorsally. The venter is grey and the head, patterned with two dark stripes, can be orange-red or almost white, with only a very pale hint of the orange-red.

Virtually nothing is known about the habits of this snake, no doubt due in part to its remote habitat. First described in 1888, only two specimens had been recorded by 1935. At that time, three additional specimens were in the collections of western museums. A small number of

E. Wagner

A specimen of *Azemiops* from northern Burma.

A northern Burmese specimen of *Azemiops*. Note the *colubrid*-like non-viperine appearance.

E. Wagner

living specimens, collected in northern Burma, became available in 1985, but did not long survive. The specimens illustrated were from this group.

Although a true viper, *Azemiops* closely resembles a typical colubrid snake. The head is covered with enlarged scales and is rounded, rather than triangulate. The largest example known is just under thirty inches in length. The diet in the wild is unknown; however, a captive specimen fed upon small pre-killed laboratory mice. They are reported to be oviparous, but size of clutch and hatchlings are unknown.

Care. A great deal of knowledge could be obtained through just a few captive specimens. It is suppositioned that newly imported specimens would possibly suffer from parasitism and dehydration. Prompt identification and treatment of the former and the use of electrolyte solutions for the latter would be in order. Cooler temperatures, perhaps in the middle 70's F (low 20's C) with a warmer basking spot, ample hiding places, and a diet of small, pre-killed rodents would appear to satisfy requirements for *Azemiops*.

ROUGH-SCALED TREE VIPER *(Atheris hispidus)*

Habitat. Forests, inland swamps, reed and papyrus swamps adjacent to lakes and rivers

Geographic Range. Suitable habitat in western Kenya, Uganda, and Zaire

Natural History. Many small, arboreal vipers rely on disruptive coloration to avoid detection, which results in almost endless combinations and variations of color. *Atheris hispidus* is no exception, and its color may vary from a uniform yellow through varying combinations of green, brown or black. The venter is pale green. There is some degree of consistency in a pattern of black streaks or chevrons on the head and neck. The scales are heavily keeled and upturned, giving a very bristly appearance. They are called "hairy" vipers in some areas, a descriptive reference to these "shaggy" appearing scales.

Atheris hispidus is arboreal, with a strongly prehensile tail. They are capable of climbing reeds and stalks and often bask atop the terminal leaves or flowers. Mainly nocturnal, they may forage on the ground for their primarily mammalian prey; frogs and lizards are also eaten as well as an occasional bird.

They are ovoviviparous, with up to a dozen young being born, six inches in length. Females are larger than males and may attain an adult length of thirty inches.

Care. Tall cages are required, equipped with branches and live or artificial foliage for climbing and basking. Air temperatures of 78-80° F (25-27° C) with a warmer basking spot allows normal activity. *Atheris* may not drink from a bowl, in which case they should be misted with warm water several times weekly. They feed readily on small, pre-killed mice. Other than in very unusual circumstances their venom is unlikely to be fatal to humans, and no antisera is manufactured.

Solenoglyphous Snakes—The Viperids   301

The heavily keeled scales of *Atheris hispidus* are alluded to in the localized common name, "Hairy Viper."

BUSH VIPER; LEAF VIPER *(Atheris squamiger)*

Habitat. Rain forest, open woodland bordering forests, and swamps

Geographic Range. Angola, north to Cameroun, east through Uganda to western Kenya

Natural History. The ground color of these vipers varies from dusky pale green to olive, to olive brown, or reddish brown. The venter is pale yellow; sometimes pale green, and often thickly spotted with black. Some specimens may be cross-banded with pale yellow.

The habits of Leaf Vipers are similar to other species of *Atheris*. They are arboreal, often ascending to heights of twenty feet or more. Although they may bask during the day, they are nocturnal and frequently forage on the ground, preying on small rodents of various species.

All species of *Atheris* are ovoviviparous. *A. squamiger* bears small litters, as few as five young. Neonates are five to six inches long and have pale-colored tail tips; which *may* be used as a caudal lure for attracting the small frogs and lizards upon which they feed. Adults average about eighteen inches in length; occasional specimens, especial-

ly females, may attain lengths of thirty inches.

Bush Vipers are not well understood taxonomically, and, although numerous subspecies have been described, the various forms are currently defined only to the species level. The sole exception is the Black and Green Bush Viper, *A. nitschei*. The nominate race occurs in central tropical Africa; *A. n. rungweensis* is confined to adjacent areas of Tanzania, Malawi, and Zambia. Several species have restricted ranges such as *A. ceratophorus* of the Usumbara Mountains in Tanzania, and *A. desaixi,* with a limited distribution in Kenya; and *A. chloroechis,* occurring in West Africa.

Two small terrestrial vipers, formerly considered to be dwarf forms of the African *Bitis,* or perhaps relics of the Eurasian *Vipera,* have recently been placed in the genus *Atheris. Atheris hindii* (Hind's Viper) is confined to the Aberdare Mountains in Kenya. Peters's Viper, *Atheris superciliaris,* occurs in swamps in Mozambique, Malawi, and southern Tanzania.

Care. See *Atheris hispidus.*

B. Mealey

Atheris squamiger is an extremely variable species in both color and pattern. Its variability has led to much taxonomic confusion. The three specimens illustrated are examples; note the three different basic colors, patterns, and to a lesser extent, the head shape.

R. D. Bartlett

B. Mealey

All of the Bush Vipers have strong prehensile tails and can support their bodies while suspended from a twig or branch.

F. Bolin, D. Hamper

The rare *A. desaixi,* a species with a restricted range in Kenya

R. D. Bartlett

PUFF ADDER *(Bitis arietans arietans)*

Habitat. Occurs in all habitats *except* true deserts and rain forests; most frequent in rocky grasslands

Geographic Range. Africa, south of the Sahara; southwestern Arabia, and Yemen

Natural History. Variable in color, these heavy-bodied snakes may be yellow, yellow-brown, reddish-brown, or grey, patterned with black or brown chevrons. Some populations are heavily speckled with brown or black, often obscuring other coloration and giving the effect of a dusty brown or blackish snake. Colors and patterns often reflect environment.

Although Puff Adders are sluggish they can move with some speed when necessary. They swim and climb with ease, often basking in low-growing shrubbery. They are most active at night, but rarely forage actively. They prefer to wait quietly in a suitable spot for passing prey, which includes a wide variety of mammals, birds, amphibians, and lizards. They also frequently occur in agricultural areas, attracted by rats and chickens.

Puff Adders are the frequent prey of many raptorial birds, some mammals, and ophiophagous snakes, but are more severely threatened by agricultural development than by natural predators. Large litters of living young offset this to some degree; litters of over eighty young have been reported, and litters of fifty or sixty are not unusual. Neonates are five to seven inches in length. Adult lengths vary among populations, averaging three to four feet, although exceptional specimens, usually females, may exceed six feet. Males have been reported to engage in so-called "combat dances" when vying for the favors of a female.

Puff Adders rely on cryptic coloration to remain undetected, but if molested attempt to back away from the threat, hissing loudly and continuously.

In addition to the nominate race, the Somali Puff Adder, *B. a. somalica*, occurs in northern Kenya and the Somali Republic. This race is often vividly colored, with lemon yellow and terra cotta specimens being especially attractive.

Care. Imported specimens virtually always require treatment for endoparasites. Well-ventilated housing, hiding places, and a water supply are basic requirements. They feed well at temperatures of 80-85° F (26-29° C), which should be slightly cooler at night. Pre-killed rodents or chicks are acceptable food. Puff Adders produce a highly toxic venom that is potentially fatal to humans.

A young Puff Adder, *Bitis a. arietans.*

R. S. Funk

BERGADDER; MOUNTAIN ADDER *(Bitis atropos atropos)*

Habitat. Rocky hillsides, grassy slopes, and meadows

Geographic Range. Eastern Zimbabwe, south and west through Lesotho to coastal Cape Province, South Africa

Natural History. A montane species that is typically grey or greyish-brown in color, patterned with two buff-colored dorso-lateral stripes. These are bordered on each side by a series of dark grey, brown or black markings, often crescentric or circular. Certain South African populations are more brightly colored, the dorso-lateral crescent pattern being black edged with yellow; the lateral pattern may be bluish-grey on a black ground, bordered below with a wavy yellowish band.

Although these vipers are found in valleys at near sea level, they occur more commonly in rocky, montane grasslands. They shelter in shallow rock crevices and beneath grass clumps. At higher elevations they are diurnal and forage for small rodents, nestling birds, lizards and occasionally other snakes. Juveniles also prey upon small toads.

Bergadders are ovoviviparous, bearing six to fifteen young at a time. The length of the neonates is normally about five inches; they mature to an average length of eighteen to twenty inches.

The venom of these snakes contains a specific neurotoxin that affects the eyes and other sensory functions. In humans, the eyes cannot focus, the eyelids droop and the sense of taste and smell are lost. Recovery from these, as well as from other more typical symptoms, is a lengthy process.

A second subspecies, *B. a. unicolor,* is smaller (twelve to sixteen inches) and a uniform dark beige to reddish-brown with, at times, an indistinct pattern of spots. They have a limited distribution in southeastern Transvaal, South Africa.

Care. Thin slabs of stone (slate) or several clumps of dried grass or similar vegetation arranged to form crevices are superior to a standard hiding box. An overall temperature of 75-78° F (23-26° C), with a basking spot several degrees higher, is satisfactory. Pre-killed laboratory mice of suitable size are accepted as food.

L. Moor

HORNED ADDER *(Bitis caudalis)*

Habitat. Rocky brushland in dry, sandy areas
Geographic Range. South Africa (Transvaal) west to southwestern Zimbabwe, southern Angola and Namibia
Natural History. This is a snake so variable in color and pattern that any description of its variability would prove inaccurate even for specimens of the same litter. The specimen illustrated is reasonably typical, although they may be as vividly colored as the Gaboon and Rhinoceros Vipers, with blues, greys, reds, and yellows dominant. The foregoing applies to males; females are sandy or reddish-orange with little or no pattern. There is a soft horn above each eye, in both sexes.

Horned Adders forage at night, spending the day loosely buried in sand, the "horn" over the eye creating a small mound which leaves the eye exposed. As with other small species of *Bitis*, they employ the tip of the tail as a lure to attract their prey of small rodents and lizards.

These snakes are ovoviviparous, with litters of as few as four and as many as nineteen having been recorded. The five-inch neonates feed basically on small lizards and toads. The average adult length is about eighteen inches; females may attain twenty.

Horned Adders attempt to avoid predators by remaining quietly hidden or by flattening themselves against the ground. Such actions, especially when they are within the lights and shadows of a grass clump or stones, combine with the disruptive colors to render the animal virtually invisible. If pressed, they hiss explosively and strike out vigorously at the source of the threat.
Care. As for the Namib Dwarf Adder, *Bitis peringueyi.*

Ground and pattern colors of *B. caudalis* tend to match the color of soil or sand within its specific habitats.

D. Hamper

MANY-HORNED ADDER *(Bitis cornuta cornuta)*

Habitat. Rocky grasslands in semi-arid areas

Geographic Range. Namibia and Damaraland, south to western Cape Province, South Africa

Natural History. A snake characterized by a group of two to seven elongated scales over the eyes, giving the appearance of "horns." The horns are larger and more prominent in males. These snakes vary in color from grey to dark terra cotta, and they are patterned with several rows of brown or black angular spots that sometimes are joined on the dorsum. A large blotch patterns the head.

These snakes are diurnal, becoming nocturnal in the warmer months. They may bury themselves in loose sand, or shelter in rock crevices or grass clumps. Although they move about in the normal serpentine manner, they can side-wind over areas of loose or shifting sand. They prey upon small rodents, lizards, and toads.

As in other species of dwarf adders, the five-inch young are born alive, twelve being an average litter. Adults may attain two feet in length but average only about eighteen inches; females are larger than males.

An eastern race, *B. c. inornata,* reddish in color and patterned with black crescent shapes, is restricted to the southern Karoo area of South Africa.

Care. As for the Bergadder, *B. atropos,* note that slightly higher environmental temperatures are required for the Many-horned Adder.

L. Moor

GABOON VIPER *(Bitis gabonica gabonica)*

Habitat. Rain forests, adjacent wooded areas
Geographic Range. Tanzania, Uganda, and southern Sudan, west to Zambia, Zaire, Zimbabwe, and south through Mozambique; northern Zululand, South Africa
Natural History. Africa's largest viper, these huge snakes are colored and patterned with brown, beige, yellows, blacks and purples, in a manner that has been described as having the effect of an oriental carpet. Unlike their close relative, the Rhinoceros Viper, whose colors are bright and sharp, the Gaboon Viper's coloration is of soft, pastel shades. The silvery eye is located at the apex of a dark brown or black triangle extending to the juncture of the jaw. In common with other members of the genus, the skin above the nostrils is formed into a forward opening pocket, the use of which is unknown.

The fanciful colors are disruptive, and the snake quite literally vanishes among the debris of the forest floor, dappled with light and shadow. The broad head appears to be a fallen leaf, complete with midrib. From such hidden positions they capture their prey. Gaboon Vipers are opportunistic feeders, and a wide variety of ground birds

B. Mealey

The West African race, *B. g. rhinoceros,* is noted for its greatly enlarged rostral scales or "horns."

312   *Venomous Snakes*

and mammals, including Brush-tailed porcupines, *Atherurus,* and the small Royal antelope, *Neotragus,* are acceptable as prey. On occasion they also prey upon toads and frogs.

Up to sixty young are born, although the average litter seldom exceeds twenty-four. The neonates are normally ten to twelve inches in length, patterned and colored as the adults. Adults can attain awesome dimensions, particularly females, which are larger than the males. Average-sized adults are three to four feet in length; exceptional females may attain nearly seven feet in length with girth and weight proportionate.

One subspecies, the West African Gaboon Viper, *B. g. rhinoceros,* occurs in Guinea, Sierra Leone, Liberia, Togo, and Ghana in western Africa. This form is readily distinguishable from the nominate race (often referred to as "East African Gaboon") by the large nasal "horns," and generally softer col-or tones. The habits of both forms are identical.

Gaboon Vipers are lethargic snakes, depending upon their effective camouflage to avoid potential threats. When aroused or hungry, however, they can move with speed and agility. The fangs, which may exceed two inches in large adults, inject venom deeply into tissue. Small mammals may expire almost instantaneously when bitten. The venom, capable of causing direct damage to cardiac tissue, is almost certainly fatal to humans, perhaps even with prompt treatment. Antisera is produced in Africa and France.

Care. As for the Rhinoceros Viper, *Bitis nasicornis.* The West African race is most often seen in living collections, and reproduces readily under proper conditions. It should be noted that none of the large *Bitis* species should be kept in top-opening cages.

B. Mealey   B. Mealey

(Left) The intricate pattern and colors of the Gaboon Viper. *(Right)* A yawning Gaboon Viper. Note the divided mandible, the tongue sheath and the length of the fangs; the fang tip can be seen immediately below its protective covering sheath.

B. Mealey

RHINOCEROS VIPER; RIVER JACK *(Bitis nasicornis)*

Habitat. Rain forests, swamps and marshes, flood plains; river, stream, and lake shores

Geographic Range. Suitable habitat in western Kenya and Uganda, north to Sudan, west through Angola and Zaire, to Guinea on the western coast of Africa

Natural History. One of the world's most brilliantly colored and patterned snakes, the ground color is black speckled olive, patterned with various geometric shapes in pale blue, red, lemon yellow, white, and jet black. A black arrow-shaped mark points forward between the eyes, calling attention to a double set of enlarged scales on the nose, which have the appearance of horns, usually yellow in color.

Despite their brilliance, the colors are disruptive, and these vipers are virtually invisible among the fallen leaves and dappled light of the forest floor. Specimens that inhabit more aquatic environments acquire a coating of silt on the rough,

B. Mealey

A typical specimen from Kenya, East Africa. Eastern populations are usually darker in color than those of West Africa.

heavily keeled scales, and are anything but brilliant.

These partially aquatic snakes are good climbers although heavy-bodied, and often bask in shrubs and trees. They are nocturnal, normally waiting for suitable prey to come within striking distance rather than actively foraging. Although frogs, toads, and fish have been recorded as prey species in the wild, Rhinoceros Vipers feed most often on mammals of suitable size, especially rodents and insectivores.

Records have indicated over forty young being born, which is exceptional, the average litter being twenty-five to thirty. The eight-inch neonates are colored and patterned as the adults. Females attain greater lengths than males, having been recorded in excess of five feet. Adult lengths vary from one population to another, but an adult length of forty inches is average.

Rhinoceros Vipers are lethargic and slow to strike even in defense of themselves. Nevertheless, their venom is highly toxic and an envenomated bite sustained by a human would almost certainly be fatal unless promptly and properly treated. **Care.** Imported specimens are invariably heavily parasitized and prompt identification and treatment is necessary. Shredded-bark mulch as a substrate, with a top dressing of dried leaves, allows for normal contact security. High temperatures often inhibit feeding; 76-78° F (24-27° C) is adequate. Pre-killed rodents (presented at night) are readily accepted. Properly husbanded, Rhinoceros Vipers breed readily; the young can be reared without undue difficulty. Wild-caught adults have attained captive longevities in excess of eight years.

© J. Bridges
© J. Bridges

(Left) The well developed rostral scales (''horns'') are reflected in the common name ''Rhinoceros Viper.'' *(Right)* A large female Rhinoceros Viper. Note the heavily keeled scales.

L. Moor

DWARF SAND ADDER *(Bitis peringueyi)*

Habitat. Confined to dry, sandy coastal areas
Geographic Range. Namibia and southern Angola (the Namib desert, Africa)
Natural History. These small vipers are patterned with reddish-brown, brown and/or black spots on a grey, beige, or yellowish ground color, allowing them to blend with the sand and subtle shadows of their environment. The eyes are set high on the sides of the head; the tail tip is black.

Animals adapted to life in dry deserts are often crepuscular and/or nocturnal, and this sand viper is no exception. It spends the day beneath the sand, often in close proximity to a bush or stone that may provide some shade. The snake sinks (rather than burrowing) into its retreat, aided by a ridge of skin along its lower sides. The top of the head, the eyes, and the tail remain exposed or only lightly covered. Should a lizard, its primary prey, approach, the black tail tip is wriggled in the manner of an insect as a lure to attract the prey within striking distnce. Nestling rodents are also preyed upon.

The reproductive habits of these snakes are not well known. However, they bear living young, about four inches in length. Average-sized adults are ten inches in length, occasionally twelve.

The Dwarf Sand Adder "sidewinds," a method of moving rapidly over loose desert sand common to several other desert snakes such as the American Sidewinder Rattlesnake. The specimen illustrated was photographed in the wild.
Care. These snakes are rarely seen in collections. They require a reasonable duplication of their habitat, which includes several inches of fine, granular sand. Temperatures should be cycled from a low 70 ° F (21 ° C) to a high of 90 ° F (32 °C) daily. They accept small lizards (especially geckos) and nestling mice as food.

A Dwarf Sand Adder
about to vanish
beneath the sand; note
the position of the
eyes and nostrils.
This specimen was
photographed in the
wild, in South Africa.

L. Moor

W. Bazemore

NAMAQUA DWARF ADDER *(Bitis schneideri)*

Habitat. Coastal desert

Geographic Range. Little Namaqualand (southwestern South Africa) from Luderitzbucht south to Port Nolloth

Natural History. These small vipers are normally colored in varying shades of grey, patterned with three rows of black or brown blotches. The blotches have light centers, and those on the back may be somewhat rectangular in shape. The venter is pale yellow or pale grey and spotted with black. The eyes are quite small and set high on the head.

Confined to the dry, powdery sand deserts of its restricted range, *Bitis schneideri* is the smallest species of its genus, average sized adults being about eight inches in length.

While little is known about these snakes in the wild, they are similar in habits to the Namib Dwarf Adder, and employ the same locomotion of "sidewinding" in moving over powdery sand. The young are born alive.

Care. As for the Namib Dwarf Adder, *B. peringueyi.* Captive specimens have accepted nestling laboratory mice as food.

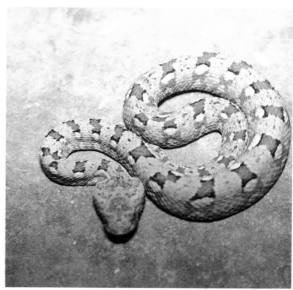

W. Bazemore

The small *Bitis xeropaga* occurs only in the Luderitz district in the vicinity of the Orange River in Southwest Africa. Little is known of this species, only discovered in 1975.

L. Moor

RHOMBIC NIGHT ADDER *(Causus rhombeatus)*

Habitat. Open woodlands, grasslands, and savannahs near streams, marshes, or other damp areas
Geographic Range. Africa, south of the Sahara (the species does not occur, however, in West Africa, southwestern South Africa or western Botswana)
Natural History. Considered a primitive viper because of the symmetrical shields of the head (resembling those of the *Colubrids*), these snakes vary from grey to pinkish brown in color, patterned with grey, black or brown rhombs, chevrons or spots. An arrow-shaped marking occurs on the neck, the point terminating between the eyes. The venter is grey, occasionally yellow or cream.

Although nocturnal, Night Adders spend much time basking during the day and/or sheltered in trash piles, rock crevices, and other hiding places. They feed primarily upon toads, but they include frogs and various small mammals in the diet.

When prey is abundant Night Adders may gorge themselves to the point of being literally unable to swallow any more food.

Causus is oviparous, the two dozen eggs (an average clutch) requiring a lengthy incubation period of about four months. Hatchlings are four to five inches long, maturing to a length of two feet; they feed upon tiny toads and frogs.

Night Adders either flatten the head and body or inflate themselves with air when threatened, either action followed by several rather frantic strikes and attempts to quickly glide away. Their venom is not as highly toxic to humans as that of other African vipers, but fatalities have been recorded. The venom glands of this genus are unique in that they extend well into the body of the animal, rather than being confined to the temporal area.

Six species of Night Adders are found throughout Africa. *C. resimus* occurs in Kenya and

Tanzania, north to the Sudan and west to Chad, Zaire, and Cameroun. The small, foot-long *C. defilippii,* found in East and Central Africa as well as Zanzibar, has an upturned snout (giving an appearance similar to that of the American Hognose snakes, *Heterodon*). *C. lichtensteini* and *C. maculatus* inhabit much of West Africa. A striped form, *C. bilineatus,* is found in Angola and portions of Zambia, Rwanda, and Zaire.

Care. *Causus* requires dry and well-ventilated caging, equipped with hiding places, drinking water and a basking spot kept slightly warmer than the substrate temperature of 78-80° F (26-27° C). They accept pre-killed laboratory rodents and are often voracious feeders. Feeding should be controlled to prevent obesity. Rhombic Night Adders have bred in captivity.

The Green Night Adder, *C. resimus*

F. Bolin, D. Hamper

This specimen of *C. defilippii* has assumed a defensive stance; note the flattened body and head.

F. Bolin, D. Hamper

HORNED DESERT VIPER *(Cerastes cerastes cerastes)*

Habitat. Dry, sandy areas adjacent to true deserts

Geographic Range. The *subspecies* illustrated occurs in the desert areas of Mali and Niger, west to Mauritania, north to Saharan Morocco, east through Egypt and Sinai, north to Jordan and Lebanon; east to Iraq and Kuwait.

Natural History. These wide ranging, side-winding vipers are varying shades of grey, pink, yellowish-brown, or yellow, the color nearly always that of the sand of the areas in which they occur. An upright spine or "horn" is over each eye.

Shelter of any nature is sparse in the arid habitat occupied by these vipers; they escape predators and excessive temperature extremes by, quite literally, sinking into the substrate. The lateral body scales have serrated, angled keels that remove sand from beneath the snake, simultaneously placing it over the snake's body whose rocking action sets the entire process in motion. The process can be accomplished whether the snake is stretched out or coiled. *Cerastes* may also bury itself in order to ambush prey. In this case, the supraorbital "horns" allow for a mound of sand over the eye, leaving the eye free of cover, yet buried. Small desert rodents and lizards constitute the diet.

Horned Desert Vipers are oviparous. Their eggs are deposited in unused mammal or reptile burrows or beneath stones. The hatchlings are six to seven inches in length and feed upon small lizards and nestling rodents. Adults may reach lengths of thirty inches, but they average about two feet.

A subspecies, *C. c. gasperettii,* occurs in Saudi Arabia. The populations of southeastern Egypt are classified as *C. c. karlharti*; those of southwestern Algeria are *C. c. mutila.*

A second species, *Cerastes vipera,* occurs in Lebanon, Israel, and Sinai, west to Saharan Morocco, Mauritania, Mali, and Niger. Popularly referred to as the Avicenna Viper, it is a small, stocky snake usually about twelve inches in length. This species has no supraorbital "horns," and it bears living young.

The native snake "charmers" of North Africa frequently use the Horned Viper in their performances, emphasizing the supraorbital "horns." Should Horned Vipers be in short supply, the *hornless* species *C. vipera,* is substituted. In this case, a porcupine or hedgehog quill is forced through the snake's head to provide suitable, if eventually fatal, cranial adornment.

Care. Several inches of fine, non-abrasive sand allows these snakes to function normally and to feel secure in burying themselves beneath it. They will sometimes use crevices that can be created by stacking flat stones. Water may be offered weekly, but it should not be left in the cage. Pre-killed mice are readily accepted. Larger specimens may also accept pre-killed small chicks as food. The Horned Viper has attained captive longevities in excess of seventeen years.

S. Reichling, Memphis Zoo

C. cerastes quite literally sinks into the loose sand of its habitat and quickly vanishes (these photographs were taken only seconds apart).

S. Reichling, Memphis Zoo

The supraorbital "horn" of *C. cerastes* serves to keep the eyes free of sand or soil, by forming an open-faced mound when the snake is buried out of sight.

D. Hamper

The Avicenna Viper, *C. vipera,* a hornless species of desert viper

D. Hamper

A. Weber, Toledo Zoo

SAW-SCALED VIPER; CARPET VIPER *(Echis carinatus leakeyi)*

Habitat. Dry plains and savannahs, open woodland, especially in areas of sandy soil and rock outcroppings

Geographic Range. The *subspecies* illustrated occurs in Kenya, Somalia, and southern Ethiopia.

Natural History. These large-eyed vipers may be various shades of brown, beige, or grey in color, patterned with brown or reddish-brown blotches. The pattern is edged with a wavy or zig-zag white stripe. The top of the head is usually marked with a dark cross. The scales are strongly keeled.

The several races of Saw-scaled Vipers are similar in habits insofar as daily activities and feeding are concerned. They are secretive and are usually securely hidden during the day. They shelter in all manner of hiding places, from deep mammal burrows and rock fissures to fallen, rotted logs. In sandy areas they may bury themselves,

leaving only the head exposed. They emerge in the evening, often most active after rains or on humid nights. They forage for small rodents and insectivores such as shrews, as well as lizards, frogs, and occasionally arthropods, including centipedes and scorpions.

Reproduction varies from one subspecies to another, and/or within populations of the same form. Thus, Carpet Vipers may be oviparous or ovoviviparous. *E. c. leakeyi* deposits about six eggs as a clutch; the five- to six-inch hatchlings initially feed on lizards and arthropods. The Indian subspecies bears living young, up to eight or ten at one time. Some populations in southern India bear smaller broods twice a year. Adults average eighteen to twenty-four inches in length, occasionally reaching thirty inches.

The popular name of "Carpet" viper refers, of

course, to the pattern of the snake. "Saw-scaled" viper refers to the serrated keel of the lateral scales. If molested or threatened, the body is thrown into a number of tight "figure eight" coils. The body then moves in a manner placing the coils in opposite directions against each other, rasping (or more properly, stridulating) the serrated scales over each other to produce a surprisingly audible sound akin to that of a saw cutting wood. This display is accompanied by loud hissing and vigorous strikes. In India, the common Hindi name for this viper is "Phoorsa," which refers to the saw-like rasping noise produced.

In addition to the subspecies illustrated, five additional races are known. The nominate race, *E. c. carinatus,* occurs in peninsular India, while *E. c. sinhaleyus* is found in nearby Sri Lanka. *E. c. sochureki,* named for an Austrian herpetologist, ranges from Bangladesh west to Pakistan. Similar in many respects to the East African *E. c. leakeyi,* the form which ranges from the Arabian peninsula north throughout the Middle East into Russian Turkestan is *E. c. pyramidium.* A spotted form, *E. c. ocellatus,* occurs in West Africa.

A pale-colored form inhabiting semi-desert areas in eastern Egypt, Arabia, and on Sokotra Island is considered distinct and represents a second species, *Echis coloratus.*

Saw-scaled Vipers are often of irascible temperament and quick to strike. Their venom is highly toxic to humans and has caused fatalities. Antivenom is produced in India.

Care. As for the Puff Adder (*Bitis arietans*). Secure hiding places are essential to proper maintenance of Carpet Vipers. Captive specimens are often disarmingly calm but are easily aroused upon slight provocation. Captives have achieved longevities of over twelve years.

LEAF-NOSED VIPER; McMAHON'S VIPER
(Eristocophis macmahoni)

Habitat. Semi-arid to arid, rocky areas
Geographic Range. Suitable habitat in Iran, Afghanistan and Pakistan (Baluchistan)
Natural History. A rare viper, these snakes are various sandy shades of reddish or yellowish-brown in color. A row of dorso-lateral brown spots partially edged with grey-white patterns each side. As the spots approach the rear of the body the greyish-white edging of the spots sometimes extends over the back as bands, creating a blotched effect. The tip of the tail is yellow. A white stripe extends backwards from the eye.

Very little is known of this snake's habits in the wild. The leaf-like scales on the nose may be used to prevent sand from entering the nostrils while the snake remains in shallow burrows, loosely covered with sand. It also has keeled ventral scales,

a feature normally seen only in arboreal snakes, which the Leaf-nosed Viper is not. It is crepuscular and/or nocturnal, and progresses over loose sand by sidewinding. Its prey includes small rodents, lizards, and occasional birds.

Reproductive data, based primarily on captive specimens, indicates that these vipers are oviparous, with up to a dozen eggs being deposited. After six to eight weeks of incubation, the six-inch hatchlings emerge. They feed readily on nestling rodents.

Care. *Eristocophis* is rarely seen in captivity. Captive conditions similar to those suggested for *Cerastes* are suitable. Drinking water should be offered weekly, but should not be allowed to remain in the cage. A longevity record for a captive male specimen exceeds nine years.

L. Trutnau

LONG-NOSED VIPER; SAND ADDER *(Vipera ammodytes ammodytes)*

Habitat. Dry, brushy and rocky hillsides at higher elevations

Geographic Range. The *subspecies* illustrated ranges from Yugoslavia north through western Hungary to southern Czechoslovakia, west through Austria to northeastern Italy; in southwestern Romania and adjacent Bulgaria.

Natural History. An attractive snake of moderate size, the ground color is normally a shade of pale grey in males, greyish-brown or reddish-brown in females. However, the ground color is variable and black, yellow-grey, and pinkish-grey specimens are common. A heavy, dark grey or black zig-zag dorsal stripe patterns males. In females the pattern is identical, but is usually some shade of brown; the underside of the tail is red in both.

Temperature determines its time of activity, although this snake is mostly diurnal except for the warmer parts of the year. They frequently bask lying in bushes or stretched on a limb of a small tree. They prefer rocky slopes where many crevices offer shelter as well as hibernation sites. Their primary prey is small mammals and both adult and nestling birds. Lizards are also eaten, especially by the juveniles.

Sand Vipers bear living young, the six- to nine-inch babies born in late summer and early fall. The average adult size is two feet to thirty inches in length, although males may reach lengths of three feet.

In addition to the nominate race, three subspecies are known. The Eastern Sand Viper, *V. a. meridionalis,* ranges from Albania east through Greece, the Cyclades Islands, Turkey, Syria, and Lebanon. This form is darker in color than the nominate race; the colors are brighter and the ventral surface of the tail is green. Bulgaria and adjacent Romania are the home of the Transdanubian Sand Viper, *V. a. montandoni,* a form with a rather small head and quite vertical rostral horn. The ventral surface of the tail is yellow-green in color. The Armenian Sand Viper, *V. a. transcaucasiana,* has a very short rostral horn and lacks the zig-zag pat-

tern common to other subspecies. It is patterned with transverse bars and spots, black or dark brown in color. It ranges throughout suitable habitat in the Transcaucasian sector of the U.S.S.R. and adjacent Turkey and Iran.

Sand Vipers are easy to care for in captivity, and numbers are maintained in European laboratories involved in the production of antivenoms.

Care. As for the Levant Vipers, *V. lebetina.* A multi-twigged branch should be provided, for climbing as well as an aid to shedding. A period of hibernation is necessary if captive reproduction is desired.

R. D. Bartlett   R. D. Bartlett

The boldly patterned *V. a. meridionalis*; the male is on the left and female on the right.

L. Trutnau

EUROPEAN ASP *(Vipera aspis aspis)*

Habitat. Well drained, rocky brush-covered or grassy hillsides

Geographic Range. The *subspecies* illustrated ranges from northwestern Yugoslavia westward through Austria, Germany, and Italy, to France.

Natural History. A relatively slim but robust appearing viper, the ground color of which may be reddish-yellow or brown, pale rust, pale brown, or grey. The body, is patterned with black crossbands, usually quite narrow, that may join to form a zig-zag dorsal stripe in some populations. Melanistic examples also occur.

The European Asp is one of only a few European snakes whose range does *not* extend into southwestern Asia or North Africa. It requires reasonably dry conditions and thus is confined to well drained, sunny areas such as occur on the southerly slopes of foothills. However, it can be a strong swimmer, and rivers, etc., do not apparently restrict its distribution. In those areas

within its range that experience lengthy winters, Asps may hibernate for as long as seven months out of the year. They are diurnal during the cooler spring and fall months, becoming crepuscular or nocturnal during the summer. They prey on small rodents, small adult and nestling birds, and lizards.

The Asp bears up to twenty living young in the fall, which average about six or seven inches in length. Juveniles feed upon grasshoppers, crickets, and small lizards. Adults average eighteen to twenty inches in length; the larger males may attain thirty inches.

Various geographic races have been accorded subspecific status. *V. a. hugyi* is found in southern Italy and Sicily. It is normally pale yellow or reddish-brown in color, with a brown dorsal pattern edged with black, which may have the appearance of saddle markings rather than bars or bands. A subspecies requiring further definition, *V. a. francisciredi* occurs in central Italy. The form found in Switzerland, *V. a. atra,* is usually darker in color and may be only a clinal color variant. The distinctively patterned subspecies from southwestern France is a small snake, patterned with a broad, black zig-zag dorsal stripe, emphasized by a pale beige or grey stripe through the center. Some specimens may have a ground color approaching clear orange. This snake is commonly called the Gascony Asp, *V. a. zinnikeri,* and is named for a Swiss herpetologist.

Several hundred miles from the mainland, the Monte Cristo Asp, *V. a. montecristi,* occurs only on the island made famous by the tale written by A. Dumas.

Care. As for other Eurasian vipers. Dampness should be avoided; it leads to respiratory and epidermal ailments that are usually fatal. A basking place, maintained at a higher temperature than the ambient, is desirable. The snakes require a period of hibernation in order to reproduce. It should also be noted that captive Asps deprived of hibernation and continually maintained at functional temperatures have considerably shortened life spans.

L. Trutnau

L. Trutnau

L. Trutnau

(Top right) The Italian Asp, *V. a. hugyi,* is found in southern Italy and Sicily. *(Top left) V. a. francisciredi,* the central Italian subspecies. *(Bottom left) V. a. atra,* a melanistic subspecies found in Switzerland.

ADDER; CROSSED VIPER; KREUZOTTER
(Vipera berus berus)

Habitat. Varied; open woodland, rocky or grassy hillsides, moors, areas adjacent to coastal sand dunes, swamps and marshes, montane meadows **Geographic Range.** The nominate race (illustrated) ranges from the British Isles throughout Europe, north to the Arctic Circle through the U.S.S.R., including southern Siberia, northern People's Republic of China to the Pacific Coast (it is absent from Ireland, southern Spain, Italy and the Balkans).

Natural History. This small viper has the greatest range (in terms of acreage) of any living snake. It is also the *only* snake found within the Arctic Circle. Obviously, there is considerable variation in color. Surprisingly, only a few subspecies have been described. The ground color may be dark

or light reddish-brown, red, yellow, olive or greenish, but it is most commonly some shade of grey. A black, dark grey, or some shade of brown, heavy zig-zag stripe patterns the back, with a "V" or "X"-shaped dark mark on the head.

Adders usually occur in colonies, based on a suitable hibernation site adjacent to an area well populated with small rodents, lizards, and birds that nest in low shrubs or on the ground. Adders are more tolerant of lower temperatures than most reptiles, and they emerge from hibernation early in the spring, shortly afterward scattering into feeding areas to forage.

These vipers bear living young, usually litters of twelve, although as few as four or as many as twenty (depending on the size of the female) may

The black, or melanistic, color phase of *V. b. berus*

L. Trutnau

The brown color phase of *V. b. berus*

L. Trutnau

be born. The neonates are normally about five to six inches in length.

In northern areas, where they may hibernate for up to nine months out of the year, young are born every other year, their development suspended during the hibernation period. The same schedule may apply to montane colonies occupying higher altitudes (up to 9,000 feet). Males indulge in "combat dances" when vying for the approval of a female. Females may reach two, and in rare instances three feet in length; adult males rarely exceed eighteen inches.

A number of subspecies have been named since Linnaeus first technically described the adder in 1758. Many of the races described have proven to be invalid. Others have proven to be sufficiently distinct to warrant species status of their own, an example being *V. seoanei* of northern Portugal and adjacent Spain, and *V. bornmuelleri* of Lebanon.

Currently accepted races of *V. berus* are the Bosnian Viper, *V. b. bosniensis* of Yugoslavia and Bulgaria, and *V. b. sachalinensis* of Sakhalin Island, off the northern Pacific coast of the U.S.S.R.

Adders possess a potent venom, rapidly fatal to the small rodents on which they feed. The small size of these snakes generally precludes a fatal bite inflicted upon a normal, adult human. However, many variables enter into any venomous snakebite, and, although rare, human fatalities have occurred.

Care. The adder is one of the most difficult of all snakes as a captive. Successful, long term captive maintenance requires involved and detailed attention to housing, lighting, and environmental conditions. Within its range, zoological parks and/or private collectors maintain these snakes in outdoor facilities, and under these natural or semi-natural conditions the snakes thrive.

L. Trutnau

L. Trutnau

The Portuguese Viper, *V. seoanei,* is considered by some taxonomists to be a subspecific race of *V. berus.* The pattern difference which occurs in both males and females is not necessarily consistent, and they cannot be called sexually dimorphic. (The male specimen is on the left; the female on the right.)

A close relative of the Adder, *V. b. berus,* Lataste's Viper, *V. l. latastei,* occurs in southern Spain, Portugal and northern Africa. They occur in several color phases, the commonest being gray and black or grayish beige and brown. One subspecies, *V. l. monticola,* occurs in the Atlas Mountains of Morocco.

Four subspecies of the diminutive *Vipera ursinii* occur in southeastern Europe, from northeastern Italy south and east through Austria and the Balkans, to the U.S.S.R., Turkey and Iran. These small vipers feed primarily on large insects and occasionally small lizards. Their venom is barely effective against such prey and their fangs are virtually never used. They are commonly caught and carried about by children as "pets." The illustration is *V. u. wettsteinii,* the most westerly subspecies and the only form not confined to southeastern Europe; it is known only from extreme southeastern France.

L. Trutnau

CYCLADES BLUNT-NOSED VIPER; LEVANT VIPER
(Vipera lebetina schweizeri)

Habitat. Brushy, overgrown rocky hillsides, ravines and valleys

Geographic Range. The Cyclades Archipelago (Greece) on the islands of Milos, Polyagos, Siphnos, Kithnos and Kinalos

Natural History. Adults of this insular race of the Levant Viper may be pale grey, beige, or pinkish-brown in color, patterned with bars and/or spots of rust, olive or dark reddish-brown. Some populations are a unicolored pale terra cotta.

These snakes are typical of the seven subspecies of Levant Vipers. Diurnal during the cooler months, they become crepuscular or nocturnal during summer, although they may bask during the morning or later afternoon. They shelter in rock crevices, burrows, or beneath stones, fallen logs, or brush piles. They prey upon small mammals, birds, and lizards, climbing into bushes and small trees in search of birds.

Levant Vipers may be oviparous *and/or* ovoviviparous, the reproduction method selected being related to environmental and climatic conditions. Oviparous populations retain their eggs for most of the incubation period required and hatching occurs within just a few weeks after deposition. *V. l. schweizeri* is such a species, the eggs hatching within four weeks after being deposited. The eight-inch hatchlings are greyish-blue in color and are patterned with rows of olive spots and bands. Adults attain thirty inches in length and are the smallest of the subspecies.

The nominate race, *V. l. lebetina,* occurs on the island of Cyprus and limited areas of the adjacent southern coast of Turkey. They bear living young, and they attain an adult length of four feet. The large *V. l. obtusa* ranges from Turkey south to northern Israel and east through Iraq, Iran, and Afghanistan to northern Pakistan. It also occurs throughout the Caucasus of the U.S.S.R. Adults of this subspecies may attain six feet in length. They lay eggs in the northern portions of the range, and bear living young in southerly areas. They are often referred to as KUFI; an Arabic name which applies to the North African forms as well.

One of the most attractively colored forms, the Turan Viper, *V. l. turanica,* is a pale-colored race, some populations being a dusty greyish-white, patterned with pink and gold spots and bars. It is found in the Uzbek and Turkmenistan regions of the U.S.S.R., northeastern Iran, Afghanistan, and portions of Kashmir. In northern Iraq, the Euphrates Viper, *V. l. euphratica,* occurs throughout the valley of the Euphrates River. This is a darkly colored snake, patterned with indistinct crossbands. Adults are heavy-bodied and attain a length of five feet.

In northwestern Africa, two large vipers often

V. lebetina schweizeri, the Cyclades Viper from the Aegean island of Milos

R. D. Bartlett

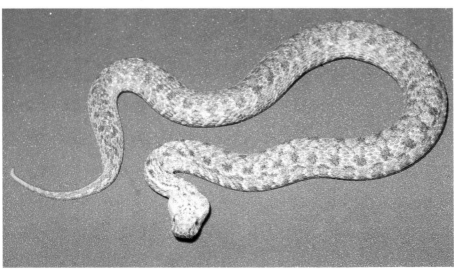

The Turan Viper, *V. l. turanica,* occurs in parts of southern Russia, Iran, Afghanistan and adjacent Pakistan.

D. Hamper

referred to as *V. mauritanica* are in fact subspecific races of the Levant Viper. The Libyan Desert Viper, *V. l. deserti,* occurs in the dry, southern foothills of the Atlas Mountains in Algeria, Libya, and Tunisia. The Atlas Viper, *V. l. mauritanica,* is found within the coastal areas of Tunisia and Algeria as well as Morocco. This viper is reddish-brown or grey in color, patterned with darker blotches often coalescing to form a zig-zag dorsal pattern. Average adult lengths are three to four feet, although some specimens far exceed the average and may attain over five feet in length.

The Libyan Desert Viper, *V. l. deserti,* is found in the dry, desert foothills of the Atlas Mountains.

R. D. Bartlett

Throughout their extensive range the Levant Vipers are the subject of myth and speculation. They have been suggested as the serpent or viper included in a number of Biblical stories, such as that of the apostle Paul; another tale purports their venom to be the perspiration of the devil. Needless to say, various incantations and prayers are invoked to keep them at bay, several of which involve mystical circles and symbols drawn on the ground, especially about the camps of the many nomadic peoples who live within the range of these snakes.

Levant Vipers have a dangerously toxic venom and a bite, particularly from a larger specimen, is potentially lethal. Fatalities have been recorded for domestic animals such as dromedary camels and horses, as well as humans.

Care. The Levant Vipers adjust readily to proper captive conditions, and longevities of over ten years are not unusual. Dry, well-ventilated cages simply furnished with a hiding place, water bowl and stones or heavy branches to assist shedding are adequate. Temperatures of 72-80° F (22-27° C) allow normal activity. Pre-killed laboratory rodents and/or chicks of appropriate size are acceptable as food. Well-adjusted specimens tend to become obese, a physical condition to be avoided.

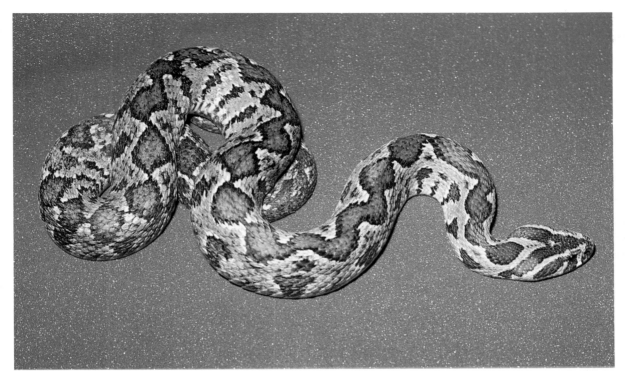

PALESTINIAN VIPER *(Vipera palaestinae)*

Habitat. Rocky hillsides, open woodland, agricultural areas, adjacent or close to rivers, streams or other water sources

Geographic Range. Israel, north through Lebanon and Syria, east through Jordan

Natural History. A robust snake, which may be reddish-brown, beige, olive, or greyish-yellow; a wide, wavy dorsal stripe may be broken into several segments or rhombs. The pattern may be dark grey, black, or reddish, edged with dark black. The sides are spotted and/or barred. A dark V-shaped marking adorns the head. The venter is pale grey in most males; that of females usually pale yellow, speckled and streaked with black or brown.

These vipers do not occur in semi-arid areas, preferring rocky areas overgrown with brush and small trees. They often frequent the banks of streams, or irrigation ditches within settled areas. They are nocturnal during the warm summer months, spending the day in the shelter of

The dark color phase of the Palestinian Viper

L. Trutnau

R. D. Bartlett

V. x. xanthina occurs in several color morphs. The pale-colored specimen on the left is from the southerly part of the range; the dark form on the right is from the northerly range.

L. Trutnau

L. Trutnau

(Left) A specimen of *V. x. xanthina* photographed in the wild in western Turkey. Rocky terrain illustrated is typical habitat for this species. *(Right) V. x. raddei,* the Armenian Viper, photographed in the wild in eastern Turkey.

crevices, burrows, or clumps of vegetation. They usually remain quietly coiled in suitable locations to ambush their prey of small mammals. They also forage in low shrubs and trees for adult and nestling birds.

Palestinian Vipers deposit up to twenty eggs in typical sites. The eight-inch long hatchlings emerge in five to six weeks, and feed upon nestling rodents and probably also lizards. Thirty-six to forty inches is the average length at maturity; even the largest specimens seldom exceed four feet.

The relationships of many vipers is not clearly understood, and the correct classification of the Palestinian Viper is not to be considered a closed book by any means. It is presented here as a separate species, but it has been previously considered a subspecies of the closely related Ottoman Viper, *Vipera xanthina xanthina,* which occurs in western Turkey and several islands of the adjacent southern Sporades. This is a grey or greyish toned snake, with a black pattern similar in design to that of the Palestinian Viper. A subspecies, the small, thirty-inch Armenian Viper, *V. x. raddei,* found in Turkish and Russian Armenia, is a dark grey snake patterned with irregular yellowish-orange dorsal blotches.

Two additional species of *Vipera* occur within the general range of both the Palestinian and Ottoman vipers. *V. bornmuelleri* is found in Jordan, Israel, and Lebanon, and *V. latifii* is known only from the Albors Mountains in Iran. These species may well prove to be further subspecific races of the species initially discussed. The United States, incidentally, considers the Iranian species to be endangered.

Care. As for the Levant Viper, *V. lebetina.* The five forms discussed all accept pre-killed laboratory rodents and/or chicks as food. The Armenian Viper is a secretive animal and requires tight-fitting hiding places.

Kaznakov's Viper,
Vipera kaznakovi, an
attractively patterned
and colored viper
occurring in the
western Caucasus area
of the U.S.S.R. and the
northeastern Anatolian
region of Turkey. They
rarely exceed two feet
in length and prey
upon small rodents,
lizards and large
insects.

R. S. Funk

RUSSELL'S VIPER; DABOIA; TIC-POLONGA
(Vipera russellii russellii)

Habitat. Occurs in many varied habitats *except* dense forests

Geographic Range. The *subspecies* illustrated ranges throughout Pakistan, India and Bangladesh.

Natural History. The ground color of these large vipers varies from a dark brown to a brownish-yellow or brownish-grey. A commonly seen adult ground color is brownish-orange, a color that has darkened from clear-orange-colored juveniles. Although variations occur among the five subspecies, the typical pattern consists of brown or black oval or circular spots edged with white and black. The tail is striped.

Russell's Viper is a nocturnal snake, especially during hot weather. When not foraging, they shelter in rodent burrows (having, in all probability, first consumed the residents), old termite mounds, rock crevices, piles of leaves, or other debris. They often occur in and around rural settlements, attracted by rodents and domestic fowl. Although found most often in plains, savannahs, and foothills, they occur in open montane areas as high as 7,000 feet above sea level. They prey primarily on rodents and birds.

These snakes are ovoviviparous, bearing large litters of thirty to forty young; litters of over sixty have been recorded. The nine- to ten-inch neonates are identical to the adults, although more brightly colored. In addition to nestling rodents they also prey on lizards, small snakes, and various arthropods. Adult lengths vary among the subspecies, most attaining three to four feet. Very large specimens may, however, exceed five feet in length.

Russell's Viper is generally considered to be one of the more dangerous Asian snakes. They possess an exceedingly toxic venom, and several antivenoms are produced. Although collecting is more or less controlled currently, a number of Indian populations of this snake have been totally exterminated as a result of excessive exploitation by skin hunters supplying the exotic leather trade.

In addition to the nominate race, other subspecies are *V. r. pulchella* of Sri Lanka, *V. r. siamensis* occuring in Burma, Thailand, and southern and southeastern People's Republic of China (Yunnan, Fujian, Guangxi and Guangdong provinces). *V. r. formosensis,* a generally darker-colored snake, is found on Taiwan. The insular *V. r. limitis,* found on the Indonesian islands of Java, Lomblen, Flores, and Komodo, is a dark to light grey color, with a variable body pattern. The typical ovals and spots may be elongated into wavy bands that can coalesce to form a zig-zag pattern. Inhabitants of the islands on which this subspecies occurs are fearful of this snake, as its bite more often than not proves fatal.

Care. As for the Levant Vipers, *V. lebetina.*

D. Hamper

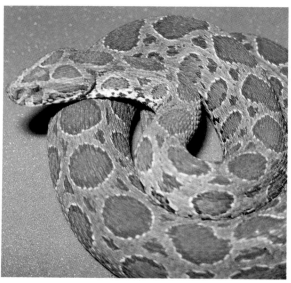

D. Hamper

(Left) An albinistic specimen of the Siamese Russell's Viper, *V. r. siamensis. (Right)* The Formosan Russell's Viper, *V. r. formosensis.* The dull coloration of this specimen is due to the fact that the snake is about to shed its skin.

R. D. Bartlett

A classically colored and patterned Russell's Viper, *V. r. russelli,* which was collected in Pakistan

PIT VIPERS—THE CROTALIDS

Honduran Palm Viper, *Bothriechis (Bothrops) marchi*

B. Mealey

The Pit Vipers are solenoglyphous snakes of the family *Viperidae*. They are characterized by the presence of a thermoreceptive cavity or "pit" located on either side of the head between the nostril and the eye. The Pit Vipers are placed in a subfamily of their own, the *Crotalinae*.

The thermoreceptive "pit" is complex in structure, akin to but far more sophisticated than the labial thermoreceptive pits found in the boas and pythons. In the Crotalids the pit is quite deep and secured in a maxillary cavity. A diaphragm (similar to an eardrum) divides the pit into two sections of unequal size, the larger being the forward section, that is exposed to the environment. The two sections are connected by a narrow tube (duct), which can be opened or closed by a group of muscles that surrounds it. Through control of the duct, the snake is able to balance air pressure on either side of the pits.

All warm-blooded animals radiate heat in the form of infra-red rays. When potential prey (or predator) is discerned by odor (scented particles are gatherered on the tongue and differentiated by the Jacobsen organs located in the roof of the mouth), the snake moves its head towards the odor. Infra-red rays, falling on the heat sensitive diaphragm, allow the snake to determine the direction of the prey (or other object). Further movement of the head will place the heat source directly in front of the snake and radiation, entering both the pits simultaneously, allows the snake to triangulate the heat source and thus determine distance as well as direction. Objects that emit fewer heat rays and are thus cooler than the air temperature can be located with equal ease, as the pits are sensitive to temperature variations as minute as two-tenths of a degree centigrade.

Several genera of Crotalids occur in Asia, reaching their greatest diversity in the eastern and southeastern areas. Only one form, the Russian Meadow Viper, barely enters Europe. Meadow Vipers belong to the same genus as the American copperheads, cottonmouths, and cantils, *Agkistrodon*. *Agkistrodon* is the only genus of Crotalid that occurs in *both the old and new world*.

The greatest diversity of the Crotalids occurs in North and South America. The neo-tropical genus, *Bothrops* (recently revised into several genera), contained over sixty-five species, and includes several primitive or at least unspecialized forms, such as the Fer-de-Lance, *Bothrops atrox*.

Rattlesnakes, unique to the new world and unique among reptiles by the presence of their caudal appendage, are represented by two genera and probably over thirty species. During the process of shedding the skin, a new rattle segment forms at the base of the tail and snaps into the base of the one preceding it. Since the skin is shed several times per year, several new segments are added to the rattle. Normal movement and activity usually disposes of several terminal segments per year; the central clip of the remaining terminal segment is often erroneously called the "button." Obviously, the age of the rattlesnake cannot be determined by counting the segments, a belief still adhered to in many areas of their range.

R. D. Bartlett

CANTIL; MEXICAN MOCCASIN *(Agkistrodon bilineatus bilineatus)*

Habitat. Swamps, marshes, lowland forest and cane fields adjacent to slow moving streams, lakes, and ponds

Geographic Range. The *subspecies* illustrated ranges from southern Mexico south through Guatemala, El Salvador, Nicaragua, Honduras and Belize.

Natural History. An indigo to cocoa-brown in ground color, this snake is patterned with thin enamel-white or cream-colored crossbars formed by the light-colored tips of lateral scales. Two stripes of the same color outline the sides of the head. The venter is brown with a scattering of white or cream spots.

Similar in habits to their northern relatives, the Cottonmouths, Cantils forage for a wide variety of prey species, including rodents, birds, reptiles, amphibians, and fish. On occasion they leave their usual habitats, prowling about canefields, farmland, and humid coastal forests. Environmental conditions determine whether they are diurnal or nocturnal; in either case they frequently bask, quickly vanishing into the water or undergrowth if disturbed.

Cantils are live-bearing snakes, about a dozen ten-inch young to a litter. The neonates are brown in color, more brightly patterned than the adults. The neonate's sulphur-yellow tail is used as a caudal lure to attract prey within striking distance.

The brightly colored and more vividly patterned Taylor's Cantil, *A. b. taylori,* is limited in range to the states of Tamaulipas and Nuevo Leon, Mexico. The similar *A. b. russeolus* occurs in the Yucatan peninsula.

Care. A dry, well-ventilated cage, arranged to suit other terrestrial pit vipers, is adequate for Cantils. They accept pre-killed rodents as food. Cantils are easily irritated and capable of rapid and repeated strikes, and they are sometimes difficult to handle. They reproduce in captivity, and longevities in excess of twenty years are recorded.

A juvenile Cantil, *A. b. bilineatus.* Note the yellow tail, which is sometimes used as a caudal lure.

D. Hamper

Taylor's Cantil, *A. b. taylori,* a brightly patterned subspecies

S. Reichling, Memphis Zoo

Dr. R. Goris

MAMUSHI *(Agkistrodon blomhoffi blomhoffi)*

Habitat. Varied; marshes, swamps, rocky hillsides, open woodland, montane rock outcroppings, and meadows

Geographic Range. Japan (including most of the smaller islands)

Natural History. A pale grey, reddish-brown, or yellow-brown in color, patterned with irregularly shaped lateral blotches, often with lighter centers and bordered with black. The head is dark brown or black with pale grey or beige sides.

The Mamushi is primarily a diurnal snake, but it becomes crepuscular when summer temperatures are too high for comfort. They forage for small rodents and birds and often occur in and around rural agricultural areas due to the rodent populations usually associated with such areas.

These snakes are ovoviviparous, with as few as three or as many as ten to twelve young born at

a time. As do other species inhabiting the colder areas of the temperate zone, females may retain the developing embryos during the lengthy hibernation period, giving birth only every second or third year. Adults average eighteen to twenty-four inches in length. Lengths of three feet have been recorded, but are uncommon.

In addition to the nominate race, four other subspecies of the Mamushi are known. Korea (north and south) and Manchuria are inhabited by *A. b. brevicaudus.* The range of *A. b. ussuriensis* extends from Vladivostok (U.S.S.R.) north to the Amur Valley, and west to northeastern Manchuria (Heilong Jiang province of the People's Republic of China). *A. b. dubitatus* is restricted to the northern portion of the prairie-like habitat in Hebei province, People's Republic of China. The Chinese Mamushi, *A. b. siniticus,* has an extensive range in the People's Republic of China, extending south from Shandong, Jiang Su and Anhui provinces to the Ch'ang Chiang Basin and eastern Sichuan, Jiangxi and Hunan.

Large numbers of Mamushi are used in the preparation of "Viper Wine," a popular tonic and restorative. A single snake is placed in each bottle of wine and remains sealed in the bottle until used. The tonic and medicinal qualities of the snake are supposedly dissolved into the wine. The Mamushi is also considered by some to be a table delicacy. It is doubtful that these unaggressive snakes are eager participants in such activities, and apparently the greatest number of reported bites are inflicted upon individuals involved in collection and preparation of these gustatory "delights." The mortality rate is low, perhaps due to the antivenom manufactured in Japan.

Care. The Mamushi is a hardy captive, with longevities in excess of twelve years recorded. A substrate of shredded-bark garden mulch, hiding place, and a brushy branch for climbing and as an aid to shedding should be provided. Temperatures of 68-75° F (19-24°C) are preferred. They feed readily on small, pre-killed laboratory mice. Captive reproduction requires a hibernation period.

W. Lamar

Dr. R. Goris

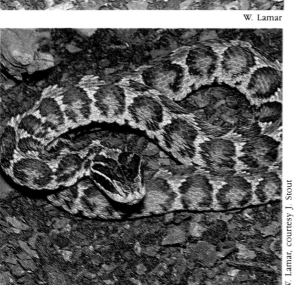

W. Lamar, courtesy J. Stout

(Top left) The gray color morph of *A. b. blomhoffi. (Top right)* A brown color morph of *A. b. blomhoffi.* The specimen was photographed on a mountain path in Japan. *(Bottom left) A. b. ussuriensis,* one of the several mainland subspecies of the Mamushi.

R. D. Bartlett

NORTHERN COPPERHEAD *(Agkistrodon contortrix mokasen)*

Habitat. Open woodland, especially hillsides with rock outcroppings near streams, lakes, and ponds

Geographic Range. The *subspecies* illustrated occurs over much of the eastern United States, from Massachusetts south (at higher elevations) to Georgia and Alabama, and west to Illinois.

Natural History. A cryptically colored snake of coppery or orange-brown color, often suffused with pink, and patterned with dark reddish-brown or chestnut crossbands that may or may not meet mid-dorsally to form saddles. The snake's head is unpatterned.

After spring emergence from communal hibernation sites, Copperheads disperse into feeding areas, sheltering in or under fallen logs, piles of drifted leaves, old rock walls, and similar retreats. As do their Asian relatives, they bask during the day, becoming nocturnal during the warmer months. Their coloration allows them to coil unnoticed among dead leaves, a vantage point from which to catch or strike passing prey such as mice, birds, or frogs. They also prey upon insects such as cicadas and may climb through bushes in search of them.

Copperheads bear living young, females normally returning to the hibernation site or "den" for delivery. The eight-inch young are identical to the adults, except for brighter colors and a yellow or yellow-green tail, which is used as a lure to attract prey. Adults vary from two to three feet in length.

A. c. mokasen, with a litter of typical size; note the yellow tail tips of the neonates.

R. S. Funk

Including the Northern Copperhead, there are five subspecies, all of which occur in the United States. The Southern Copperhed, *A. c. contortrix,* the nominate race, occurs in the coastal areas of North Carolina, south to northern Florida, west to eastern Texas and Oklahoma, and north to southern Illinois. It is lighter in color but similar to the Northern Copperhead, with which it frequently intergrades. *A. c. phaeogaster,* the Osage Copperhead, ranges from Nebraska east through parts of Iowa, Kansas, and Oklahoma.

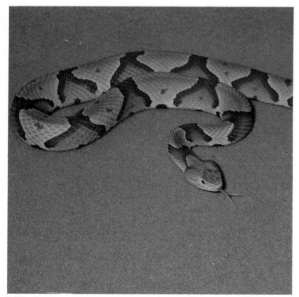

D. Hamper

R. S. Funk

A. c. contortrix, the Southern Copperhead; like many brilliantly colored and patterned snakes (cryptic coloration) they become almost invisible in their native habitat.

Unlike the preceding subspecies, the Broad-banded Copperhead, *A. c. laticinctus,* is patterned with wide bands of vivid, coppery brown. It occurs from Oklahoma south to central Texas. Almost identical, except for its colorful, patterned venter, the Trans-Pecos Copperhead, *A. c. pictigaster,* occurs in the Big Bend and Davis Mountains of western Texas. It inhabits canyons and canebrakes near permanent water sources.

Copperheads often utilize communal hibernation sites, often in company with other snakes. The habit renders them vulnerable in large numbers to destruction by target shooters. Suburban development also takes it toll of these snakes. Despite widespread belief to the contrary, bites from Copperheads are virtually never fatal. As all snakes do, they play important ecological roles within their habitats and deserve better than being shot and left to rot on a sunny hillside.

Care. Copperheads are long-lived snakes (up to thirty years recorded) and require simple, well-ventilated cages floored with shredded garden mulch. They feed readily on pre-killed laboratory rodents, at a temperature of about 78° F (26°C).

The Osage Copperhead, *A. c. phaeogaster*

R. S. Funk

The Trans-Pecos Copperhead, *A. c. pictigaster,* is perhaps the most attractive of the Copperheads; its darker color resembles that of the Broad-banded Copperhead, *A. c. laticinctus.*

© J. Bridges

AMUR VIPER *(Agkistrodon intermedius saxatilis)*

Habitat. Open woodland, rocky, grassy hillsides, and adjacent flatland

Geographic Range. People's Republic of China (Heilong Jiang province), North and South Korea to the lower Amur River

Natural History. A pale to ruddy-brown in color, patterned by irregular crossbands of greyish-white, thus forming an ovoid pattern with pale centers on the sides.

These pit vipers occur throughout the same area as the Korean Mamushi, *A. b. brevicaudus,* and the habits of the two snakes are similar. Amur Vipers are ovoviviparous, and may retain the eggs over hibernation, thus giving birth every second or third year.

The Amur Viper is included here primarily as an example of a highly adaptable species of pit viper, which has exploited a vast geographic range. The nominate race, *A. i. intermedius,* occurs from southern Siberia (U.S.S.R.) east into central Asia (Kazakhstan); *A. i. stejnegeri* ranges from eastern central People's Republic of China north to southeastern Nei Mongol province. *A. i.* *caucasicus* extends the range westward across Afghanistan and northern Iran.

Care. As for the Mamushi, *A. b. blomhoffi.*

A dark color morph of *A. i. saxatilis.* The specimen illustrated was collected near Vladivostok, U.S.S.R.

COTTONMOUTH; WATER MOCCASIN
(Agkistrodon piscivorous piscivorous)

Habitat. Swamps, marshes, fields adjacent to slow moving bodies of water, e.g., ditches, streams, ponds, and lakes

Geographic Range. The nominate race ranges from east central Alabama, east through central Georgia, and north to southeastern Virginia.

Natural History. A heavy-bodied snake with an olive or light to dark brown ground color, patterned with darker brown or black irregularly edged crossbands, often with lighter markings within them. Darkly colored and patternless specimens, as well as light and faintly patterned individuals, occur.

A primarily nocturnal snake, it is nevertheless a confirmed basker. A large cottonmouth, artfully draped along a half submerged log in the middle of a southern swamp, is an impressive sight.

When disturbed in such situations, Cottonmouths slide quickly into the water, either diving out of sight or swimming off with the head elevated above the surface. They often wander far from water and forage in fields, farmlands, and open woodlands. They may share hibernation sites with other venomous, as well as harmless, snakes. The rock outcroppings that afford protection during the winter may be at considerable elevations.

Cottonmouths prey upon a wide assortment of species, which includes mammals, fish, amphibians, and occasionally birds. They also consume other snakes, small turtles, and juvenile alligators.

Relatively small litters of up to sixteen living young are born, reddish-brown in color and vividly patterned. The bright yellow tail is used as a lure in attracting prey.

Similar in habits, but darker in color and with noticeable brown and white or grey stripes on the head, the Florida Cottonmouth, *A. p. conanti,* is found in southern Georgia and Florida. The Florida and Eastern Cottonmouth are the larger of the three subspecies, averaging three to four feet, but often attaining lengths of five and six feet. The Western Cottonmouth, *A. p. leucostoma,* occurs in western Kentucky and Tennessee, south through Oklahoma and central Texas. A smaller snake than the two preceding subspecies, it seldom reaches four feet in length.

F. Alvey

D. Hamper

(Left) The Eastern Cottonmouth, *A. p. piscivorous* in the classic defensive posture of Cottonmouths; its popular name is derived from this action. Specimen photographed in the wild, in Georgia. *(Right)* An adult Florida Cottonmouth, *A. p. conanti*; this subspecies often lacks any pattern when mature.

A juvenile Florida Cottonmouth, *A. p. conanti.* This specimen is typical in color and pattern of all juvenile Cottonmouths. As they mature, the vivid pattern fades. This subspecies is often completely black.

R. D. Bartlett

When molested, Cottonmouths vibrate the tail and with head thrown back, gape widely, displaying the startling white interior of mouth and throat. The popular names of "Cottonmouth," "Gaper," "Snap Jaw," and other localized names refer to this characteristic.

Cottonmouths, *unlike* their relatives, the Copperheads, have a potent venom which can result in extensive tissue damage and may possibly prove fatal. Despite a popular belief to the contrary, Cottonmouths are capable of biting underwater.

Harmless watersnakes are often mistaken for Cottonmouths, although both are relatively simple to identify.

Drainage of wetlands prior to development and weekend target shooting take a heavy toll of Cottonmouth populations.

Care. Housing suitable for watersnakes, *Nerodia*, or Copperheads, *Agkistrodon*, are adequate for Cottonmouths. Well fed, captive-raised specimens often attain impressive lengths. They readily accept pre-killed rodents and chicks as food.

B. Mealey   B. Mealey

(Left) A severely stressed Florida Cottonmouth, *A. p. conanti,* in a rigid defensive posture; note the fangs still enclosed in their protective sheath. *(Right)* An albinistic specimen of the Florida Cottonmouth.

R. D. Bartlett

MALAYAN PIT VIPER *(Calloselasma rhodostoma)*

Habitat. Coastal forest, bamboo thickets, overgrown, unused farmland; forest adjacent to plantations

Geographic Range. Southeastern Asia (Thailand, Laos, Vietnam, Malaya, Sumatra and Java)

Natural History. These snakes may appear triangular in cross section, which enhances the pattern of angular or triangulate dark brown lateral markings that meet or alternate mid-dorsally. The ground color is grey, pale brown, or pale reddish-brown, except for the lips, which are pinkish or pinkish yellow and usually spotted with black.

Malayan Pit Vipers usually occur in open areas within or adjacent to forests having thick layers of leaves and other debris on the ground. They shelter in piles of litter, beneath and within fallen logs, or in clumps of grass or bamboo. They forage in the evening or at night, preying upon various rodents, lizards, and frogs.

An oviparous species, up to thirty eggs are deposited in a clutch, usually with the embryos already developing. The female deposits the eggs within hollow, rotted logs or piles of decaying vegetation, remaining with them for the five to six weeks of incubation. The six-inch hatchlings are identical to the adults. They prey upon small frogs and nestling rodents. Females attain greater lengths than males, thirty inches being average; occasionally, they reach three feet in length.

Envenomated bites inflicted by this snake are apparently rarely fatal. Antivenom is produced in several European and Asian laboratories.

Care. As for the Okinawan Habu, *T. flavoviridis.* Malayan Pit Vipers prefer the shelter of a thick layer of dead leaves to a box or plastic pipe. Fresh imports normally require treatment for intestinal parasites.

SHARP-NOSED VIPER; HUNDRED PACER
(Deinagkistrodon acutus)

Habitat. Wooded mountain slopes, rocky hillsides, and/or brushy valleys

Geographic Range. People's Republic of China (central and eastern provinces of Hubei, Hunan, Zhejiang, Fujian and Guangdong), northern Vietnam and Taiwan (NOTE: May range slightly farther west and north in the People's Republic of China than provinces listed)

Natural History. This attractively colored and patterned viper is also referred to as the "Snorkel" Viper due to the pronounced soft "horn" on the snout. The body color is greyish or reddish-brown, patterned with brown or reddish-brown lateral triangles with grey or beige centers. These join mid-dorsally, creating an effect of alternating triangles of different color. The head is dark brown except for the sides, which are beige or

pinkish. The colors darken considerably with age.

Active at night or in the evening hours, this viper normally spends the day coiled among dried, dead leaves or bracken, in sheltered rock ledges, fallen logs, and in other locations where its color and disruptive pattern blend into the surroundings. They prey upon small mammals, birds, and frogs.

Sharp-Nosed Vipers deposit up to two dozen or more eggs in typical sites. It is possible that the eggs are retained during initial incubation, a procedure that shortens post-deposition incubation time. Hatchlings are lighter in color and more vividly patterned than adults, maturing to an average length of three to four feet, with the largest specimens known attaining five feet.

Dangerous animals of any species almost always become the subject of folklore and/or myth, which often exaggerate the characteristic most impressive to those who develop the stories. The popular name "Hundred Pacer" refers to the belief that if a human is bitten by this viper, the victim can walk one hundred paces before expiring. Apparently, certain areas within its range are inhabited by people even more impressionable, who refer to the viper as the "Fifty Pacer." Many snakes held in fear and dread by some are deified by others. The aboriginal inhabitants of Taiwan claim the Sharp-Nosed Viper as their maternal ancestor, their first leaders having hatched from the eggs of the snake. The dramatic and acclaimed art produced by the aborigines (the Paiwan) consistently features this viper, usually in a highly stylized manner.

Varying degrees of rostral elongation are not unusual among vipers and pit vipers. This is quite pronounced in *Deinagkistrodon;* they are often called "snorkel vipers" because of it.

Dr. R. Goris

This viper is in fact dangerous, and fatalities from bites, especially among rural populations, are not unusual. An antivenom is produced in Taiwan. **Care.** Sharp-Nosed Vipers are not often seen in western collections, a reason for which has been the suggestion that demand and price paid for the alleged medicinal and tonic properties of this viper preclude its sale as a zoological specimen. Newly imported specimens are usually dehydrated and/or parasitized; these conditions should be promptly corrected. Captive maintenance requirements of the Malayan Pit Viper, *Calloselasma,* are equally suitable for these vipers.

Asian Pit Vipers—Trimeresurus

White-Lipped Pit Viper, *Trimeresurus albolabris*

INDIAN TREE VIPER *(Trimeresurus gramineus)*

Habitat. Bamboo thickets, vine tangles, dense foliage adjacent to streams and other water sources
Geographic Range. Southern and central India
Natural History. This is a variable form sometimes difficult to identify (one consistent characteristic is a combination of smooth and keeled scales.). These snakes may be unicolor green, with an irregular pattern created by a scattering of black-tipped scales, or a bronze green such as the specimen illustrated. The eye is golden; the tail is russet.

Indian Tree Vipers (more accurately pit viper) are slow-moving, nocturnal snakes similar in habits to other Asian arboreal pit vipers. The prehensile tail aids in their arboreal activities, also functioning as an anchor during periods of rest. Adults forage for various small rodents and other mammals of similar size.

Females bear litters of up to six living young about five to six inches long. The tail of the juvenile is more brightly colored than that of the adult, and it is used as a caudal lure to attract its prey of small frogs and lizards. This small viper matures to a length of thirty inches.

Several other pit vipers are confined to India. *T. huttoni,* a montane form, is found in the Madras area of southern India, and another montane species, the Large-scaled Pit Viper, *T. macrolepis,* occurs in the mountainous areas of the south. An essentially terrestrial species, the Rock Viper (Hara Gonus in Hindi), *T. malabaricus,* ranges in the western Ghats.

Care. As for the Bamboo Pit Viper, *T. stejnegeri.*

OKINAWAN HABU
(Trimeresurus flavoviridis flavoviridis)

Habitat. Sparsely wooded plains and fields adjacent to forests; brushy, rocky hillsides

Geographic Range. Ryu Kyu Islands (south of Japan), on Okinawa and Amami

Natural History. The largest of the Asian terrestrial pit vipers, this Habu normally is pale or dark brown, greenish-brown, or olive in color. It is patterned with irregular blotches, varying in shades of green or brown and bordered with yellow or greyish-yellow. The arrangement of the pattern may present a marbled effect. The head is large and markedly triangular, quite distinct from the slim neck.

These snakes are restricted to islands of volcanic origin and do not occur on adjacent islands of coral origin. They are nocturnal, but they may bask during the day. They shelter in lava caves, rodent burrows, stone walls, and similar cover. As do some other habus, they frequently enter rural houses and barns in search of rodents.

Okinawan Habus mate in early spring, with up to eighteen eggs being deposited in mid-summer. The eggs hatch after an incubation period of five to six weeks. The ten-inch hatchlings are identical to the adults. The average adult length is four to five feet; exceptional specimens may, however, exceed seven feet.

Sizable populations of these snakes, as well as large human populations, occupy Okinawa and Amami, and accidental bites are not infrequent. Only a small percentage of these terminate fatally, although permanent physical damage or impairment often results. An antivenom is produced by two Japanese laboratories.

A subspecies, the Kume Shima Habu, *T. f. tinkhami,* was described in 1955, and is confined to Kume Shima Island in the Ryu Kyus.

Care. All of the terrestrial races of *Trimeresurus* may be housed in caging floored with shredded-bark garden mulch. Partially buried plastic pipe is normally more suitable for these snakes than the usual hiding box. Temperatures of 72-78° F. (22-26° C) are adequate, and pre-killed laboratory rodents, offered in dim light or at night, are accepted. Imported specimens should be cleared of intestinal parasites.

R. D. Bartlett

KANBURIAN PIT VIPER; TIGER PIT VIPER
(Trimeresurus kanburiensis)

Habitat. Forests and open woodland, in areas of limestone hills

Geographic Range. Hilly, limestone areas of southwestern Thailand (Siam); first collected in the vicinity of Kan Buri (Kanchanaburi Prov.)

Natural History. Initially described in 1943, this snake varies from the faintly patterned, brown specimen illustrated to tawny-colored animals, patterned with dull brown blotches and spots and a white ventro-lateral stripe; hence the fanciful popular name of "Tiger" Pit Viper. These snakes are often confused with the Mangrove Pit Viper, although easily distinguishable by the first three supralabial scales, which are obviously and disproportionally large.

Not a great deal of information is available concerning this snake's habits in the wild. They are nocturnal, but also diurnal baskers, retiring to

R. D. Bartlett

sheltering foliage during the heat of the day. They prey upon mammals and birds. Juveniles probably add frogs and lizards to the diet. The young are born alive. Kanburian Pit Vipers are rather heavy-bodied for an arboreal species, and while their maximum length is unknown, specimens supplied by Thai animal dealers have exceeded thirty inches in length.

The Mangrove Pit Viper, *T. purpureomaculatus purpureomaculatus,* is a brownish-purple, olive, or greyish snake with green or brown spots which may be distinct, very faint, or sometimes entirely absent. These pit vipers are somewhat terrestrial, frequenting rocky coastal areas in the vicinity of mangrove or coastal swamp forests. They occur most often on offshore islands and freely enter and swim in salt water. Their prey consists of rodents and birds, the juveniles feeding more frequently on frogs and lizards. The young are born alive and mature to a length of about three feet.

The Mangrove Pit Viper, *T. p. purpureomaculatus*

R. D. Bartlett

The nominate race occurs in eastern India and southern Burma, ranging south and east in suitable habitat through Malaya and Indonesia to Sumatra. An insular subspecies, *T. p andersonii,* is found on the Nicobar and Andaman Islands, south of the Bay of Bengal.

Envenomated bites by these pit vipers result in the typical, painful symptoms, but are rarely fatal. **Care.** As for the Bamboo Viper, *T. stejnegeri.* Care should be taken to eliminate probable intestinal parasites in newly imported specimens.

R. D. Bartlett

HIMEHABU; KUFAH *(Trimeresurus okinavensis)*

Habitat. Open woodland, fields, agricultural areas close to streams, ponds, or other water sources

Geographic Range. RyuKyu Islands (Japan), on Okinawa and Amami Islands

Natural History. A somewhat dull-colored, heavy-bodied snake, grey in color and crossbanded with darker grey or greyish-black. A pattern of black ventrolateral spots on a grey-white ground is present. Superficially this snake resembles a rather "overweight" cottonmouth.

Although it occupies the same range as the Okinawan Habu, *T. flavoviridis,* it inhabits slightly different environments, and the two species do not necessarily compete. Kufahs forage for rodents as well as other vertebrates during their nocturnal forays.

The Kufah may deposit eggs in the usual manner, or retain them internally during incuba-tion, in which case living young are born. Apparently environmental conditions determine which method is used. Adults average three or four feet in length.

Kufahs are sluggish, and despite the large human rural populations within its range, bites do not occur nearly as frequently from this snake as from the more active and wider ranging Okinawan Habu.

Two additional species of Habu occur in the Ryu Kyu Islands. The Sakishima Habu, *T. elegans,* is found on Irimote, Ishigaki, and Miyako Islands. It resembles the Okinawan Habu in color and pattern, but it is a smaller snake, usually about three feet in length. The Takarashima Habu, *T. tokaren-sis,* is found on Takara Island, part of the Tokara group northeast of Taiwan.

Care. As for the Okinawan Habu, *T. flavoviridis.*

CHINESE TREE VIPER; BAMBOO VIPER
(Trimeresurus stejnegeri formosensis)

Habitat. In bamboo thickets, bushes, and trees along water courses; prefers hillsides to level terrain

Geographic Range. The *subspecies* illustrated occurs on Taiwan.

Natural History. A medium-sized, arboreal pit viper that is green in color, with no pattern other than a thin ventrolateral stripe. The body color can vary from a leaf green to chartreuse and often has a dull cast. The thin side stripe is white in females; males may have an additional stripe of red below the white. The stripe is narrow, involving only one or two scale widths. The venter is pale green; the tail is terracotta or rust.

Bamboo Vipers spend the day in bushes, trees, and other arboreal shelters, securely anchored to a perch by the prehensile tail. They are nocturnal foragers, often descending to the ground to hunt for small mammals and amphibians, particularly frogs. Streams well populated with frogs may attract a great many of these snakes, and considerable numbers may often be found in such locations.

These snakes are ovoviviparous, with up to six young forming a litter. The neonates average about five inches in length and feed on small frogs. Adults are usually about twenty inches in length, sometimes attaining thirty.

The nominate race of the Bamboo Viper *T. s. stejnegeri,* occurs throughout many of the southeastern provinces of the People's Republic of China, as well as on Hainan. It was named in honor of Leonhard Stejneger, a prominent American herpetologist active in the latter half of the last century. *T. s. kodairi,* a subspecies apparently confined to two mountains in Taiwan (Mount Arisan and Mount Daiton) requires further study to determine its validity as a subspecies. *T. s. yunnanensis,* ranges from Yunnan province in southern People's Republic of China west to Nepal and northeastern India and south to northern Burma.

Bamboo Vipers have a rather calm disposition, but they strike quickly if surprised or brushed against while in their arboreal shelters. If threatened on the ground they may coil and rapidly vibrate the tail. Accidental bites are reported with reasonable frequency in agricultural areas, but the mortality rate is quite small.

Care. Bamboo Vipers should be provided with tall cages, equipped with climbing and resting branches and live or artificial plants. They will not usually drink from a bowl, but one should be provided. The cage should be misted with warm water several times weekly, in a manner that allows droplets to remain on the leaves. Temperatures of 75-80° F (23-27° C) are suitable. They accept small pre-killed rodents.

R. D. Bartlett

SRI LANKEN PIT VIPER *(Trimeresurus trigonocephalus)*

Habitat. Montane forests, woodlands, and plantations

Geographic Range. Sri Lanka

Natural History. The illustration is of a typical specimen of this attractively colored and patterned snake, although variables occur. Specimens of a dark, leaf-green color, patterned and speckled with indigo, are common.

These arboreal snakes are diurnal, becoming nocturnal during the warmer months. Sheltering in dense foliage, their cryptic coloration effectively "vanishes" them among the leaves and dappled light. Adults prey primarily upon small rodents and birds.

The eight-inch young are born alive and initially prey upon frogs and lizards. Adults may attain lengths in excess of three feet but usually mature at twenty inches.

Tea plantations are frequented by these pit vipers, where they reportedly present a hazard to field workers. However, fatalities from envenomated bites are rare.

The technical species name of this viper equates the shape of the head to an ancient Greco-Roman musical instrument, the trigon, a heavy, triangular lyre.

Care. As for the Bamboo Viper, *T. stejnegeri.*

The dark color morph of the Sri Lankan Pit Viper, *T. trigonocephalus*

WAGLER'S PIT VIPER; TEMPLE PIT VIPER
(Tropidolaemus [Trimeresurus] wagleri)

Habitat. Lowland forest, in low shrubs and bushes, and small trees

Geographic Range. Malaysia, Indonesia (large and small islands), and the Philippines

Natural History. A vividly colored snake, with a disproportionately large head. The specimen illustrated is typical in color and pattern, although there is much variation from one population to another. They may be a uniform green, green with black-tipped scales, or black with green-tipped scales. The development of the typical pattern is unusual in that juveniles are a bright green with a reddish tail, patterned with rows of half white, half red spots (see illustration). As the animal matures, the spots become stripes and/or bars,

which in turn are speckled with blackish-blue spots; eventually the adult pattern emerges.

Their activity period varies with temperature, and they may be diurnal or nocturnal, foraging for the typical arboreal pit viper prey of small mammals, birds, lizards, and frogs.

Twelve to fifteen young comprise the average litter, the neonates being five or six inches long. Adults are thirty inches in length on average, but occasionally forty inches may be attained.

These snakes are sluggish in their actions and rarely strike, even when severely threatened. As would be surmised by their popular name of "Temple" Pit Viper, these snakes are incorporated into religious activities, and numbers of them are

Asian Pit Vipers—Trimeresurus 371

kept at the well-known snake temple on Penang Island where they are freely handled by the priests, who consider the snake to be a reincarnated rajah. In parts of their range they are also kept in bushes around houses, to bring good luck and to keep evil spirits at bay. Temple Pit Vipers can and do bite, of course, but envenomation apparently causes only localized symptoms.

Care. As for the Bamboo Viper, *T. stejnegeri*. It should be noted that Wagler's Pit Vipers are prone to respiratory infections, and prompt veterinary care is indicated should symptoms such as nasal discharge or wheezing appear.

A juvenile *T. wagleri* of the dwarf form of this species, which occurs in the Philippines

W. Lamar, courtesy Dallas Zoo

Abilene Zoological Gardens

SIAMESE PALM VIPER; WIROT'S PIT VIPER *(Trimeresurus wiroti)*

Habitat. Palm jungle

Geographic Range. Southwestern Thailand

Natural History. A rare and unusual Asian pit viper, the species was first discovered in 1979, incidental to field studies conducted on other reptiles. The snakes were found in montane jungle with heavy palm growth above 1,500 feet.

A characteristic unique to these snakes is the indented, projecting snout. The species is sexually dimorphic, the coloration of both sexes evident at hatching. As the animals mature, females become more robust, their heavy bodies more akin to a terrestrial *Agkistrodon* than the usual slim, arboreal *Trimeresurus*. Male *T. wiroti* remain slender, also appearing more rugose than females, due to slight curling of the perimeter of the scales. Females apparently are terrestrial in habits, rarely climbing into bushes; males tend to be arboreal.

T. wiroti is oviparous, data from captive females noting one clutch of eight eggs and one of fourteen. Females coil about the clutch, guarding them, and becoming aggressive if molested. The eggs may be retained during the early stages of development, for they hatch after a minimal external inclubation period of only a few weeks. Hatchlings measure six inches in length. Adults probably do not exceed thirty inches; females are larger than males.

The species has been reported as preying upon small mammals, birds, lizards, especially geckos, and frogs.

Care. The few captive specimens have apparently thrived to date in caging similar to that suggested for other Asian arboreal pit vipers. They have an apparent need for moist, but well-ventilated conditions. Females with eggs have been noted to leave the eggs, enter a water bowl, and return to the eggs while still wet. These captives feed on pre-killed laboratory mice.

Abilene Zoological Gardens

A male *T. wiroti*; note the difference between this specimen and the female illustrated.

The Sumatran Tree Viper, *T. sumatranus,* a pale green, red-tailed arboreal viper widely distributed through Malaysia and Indonesia. It is similar in habits to other species of Tree Viper which inhabit much the same areas. It preys primarily upon small mammals and birds. A subspecies, *T. s. malcolmi,* is confined to a small mountainous area in Kalimantan (Borneo).

R. D. Bartlett

Pope's Tree Viper, *T. popeorum,* is found in northeastern India, Burma, much of the Malay Peninsula and Indonesia. It reaches an adult length of about three feet, and has unusually large litters (as many as twelve). The species is named in honor of Clifford Pope, a well-known American herpetologist.

R. S. Funk

Neo-Tropical Pit Vipers

Eye Lash Viper, *Bothriechis (Bothrops) schlegeli*

R. D. Bartlett

YELLOW-LINED PALM VIPER *(Bothriechis [Bothrops] lateralis)*

Habitat. Shrubbery, trees, and palms in cloud forests

Geographic Range. Costa Rica and Panama

Natural History. A typical, neo-tropical arboreal pit viper, this snake is unicolored pale to dark leaf green. A pale yellow, narrow ventrolateral stripe and irregularly scattered yellow dorsal markings form the pattern. The latter may have a few blue and/or black-tipped scales adjacent to the yellow. The cryptic colors and patterns serve as camouflage.

Yellow-lined Palm Vipers are arboreal and shelter in the thick foliage of forest trees and shrubbery. A favored place is at the juncture of palm frond and trunk. The prehensile tail is employed as an anchor when resting or sleeping,

as well as when the snake strikes out to grasp its prey, which consists of small birds, rodents, lizards, and frogs.

The six- or seven-inch young are born alive, and prey upon small frogs and lizards. Adults average twenty-four to thirty inches in length.

These snakes do not aggressively defend themselves, remaining quietly coiled and relying on their coloration to remain unseen. However, they will quickly strike if brushed against or touched. Their venom is rarely fatal to humans, and no monovalent antivenoms are produced.

Care. Tall cages equipped with branches and foliage are required, as described for Asian arboreal pit vipers. Most specimens will accept small, pre-killed mice.

B. Mealey

HONDURAN PALM VIPER *(Bothriechis [Bothrops] marchi)*

Habitat. Shrubbery, palms and vine tangles adjacent to streams and rivers

Geographic Range. Honduras

Natural History. One of several typically green, arboreal, neo-tropical pit vipers, the Honduran Palm Viper is a unicolor bright green or turquoise. The lower sides and venter may be pale yellow or cream, tinged with green. In some specimens the dorsal scales may be edged with black.

Crepuscular or nocturnal snakes, Palm Vipers shelter in the crotches of branches hidden by foliage, or at the base of palm fronds. They forage for, or ambush their prey of small mammals, birds and nestlings, lizards, and amphibians, particularly frogs.

The six- to seven-inch young are born alive, the litter size varying with the size of the female. Juveniles occupy lower levels than adults, their prey of small frogs and lizards more abundant closer to the ground. Adults are an average two feet in length.

As noted with other species of neo-tropical pit vipers, their relationships are not well understood, and taxonomic revisions are not universally accepted. The Honduran Palm Viper has been regarded as a subspecies of the Speckled Palm Viper, *Bothrops n. nigroviridis* (currently viewed as *Bothriechis nigroviridis,* a full species). By either name this arboreal pit viper is green in color, heavily spotted with black, and occurs in Costa

Rica and Panama. A similar taxonomic situation exists with the very attractive Guatemalan Palm Viper, *Bothriechis aurifer* (previously *Bothrops n. aurifer*). This green snake is patterned with yellow dorsal blotches edged in black, and occurs in Guatemala and nearby Chiapas, Mexico.

B. aurifer, the Guatemalan Palm Viper

The probably closely related Guatemalan Tree Viper, *Bothriechis (Bothrops) bicolor*, which ranges from the mountainous areas of southern Chiapas, Mexico through the foothills of the Pacific coast of Guatemala, is a large-headed form, leaf green in color with a yellow venter; and the characteristic prehensile tail.

Care. As for *Bothriechis (Bothrops) lateralis*.

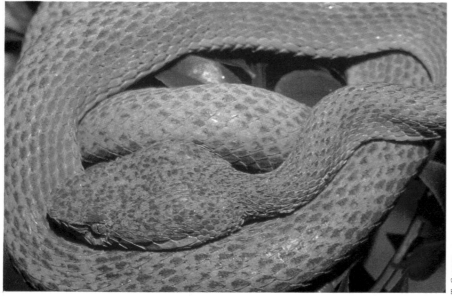

B. bicolor, the Guatemalan Tree Viper

EYELASH VIPER; SCHLEGEL'S VIPER *(Bothriechis [Bothrops] schlegeli)*

Habitat. Shrubbery, vine tangles, trees and palms; usually adjacent to streams and rivers

Geographic Range. Southern Mexico, south through Central America to Colombia, Ecuador, and western Venezuela

Natural History. Easily identified by the presence of several spiny scales above the eyes, giving the appearance of "eyelashes," this snake is quite variable in color, ranging from solid reddish-yellow, golden or lemon yellow, through various shades of grey-brown to green. The darker colors are often spotted with black and/or red; yellow specimens may be spotted with white and/or black and/or red.

Eyelash Vipers are similar in habits to other arboreal, neotropical pit vipers. They are nocturnal and prey upon small mammals, birds and nestlings, lizards, and frogs. As do Palm Vipers, the Eyelash Viper grips the food animal firmly until the venom has dispatched the prey, after which it is swallowed. The snake is often suspended in midair by the prehensile tail during the entire process.

Twelve or more young are born alive and resemble the adults in all respects. They prey primarily on small frogs, especially tree frogs *(Hylids)*. Although thirty-inch adults are not uncommon, a mature length of eighteen to twenty-four inches is average.

Variously treated taxonomically as a subspecies *or* species, *B. supraciliaris* is a montane form known only from the province of San Jose in Costa Rica.

Care. As for *B. lateralis.* Eyelash Vipers are common in collections and are long-lived, longevity records exceeding sixteen years. They reproduce readily in captivity, and many commercially available specimens are so bred.

The spotted, brown color morph of *B. schlegeli*

R. S. Funk

B. Mealey

AMAZONIAN PALM VIPER
(Bothriopsis [Bothrops] bilineatus bilineatus)

Habitat. Shrubbery, trees and palms, most often adjacent to streams, rivers, and ponds

Geographic Range. French Guiana, Guyana, Surinam, Venezuela, and northern Brazil

Natural History. Neo-tropical arboreal pit vipers resemble in color and habits the related arboreal pit vipers of Asia, *Trimeresurus*. The Amazonian Palm Viper is unicolor green, which may or may not be relieved by a narrow yellow stripe or scattered yellow spots. The tail is usually, but not always, russet in color.

Palm Vipers are nocturnal, spending the day in sheltered locations such as thick foliage, tree hollows, or at the base of palm fronds. They select resting sites that allow them to anchor themselves securely with the prehensile tail. They are somewhat sedentary and catch their prey from "ambush" rather than actively foraging. Small mammals such as mouse opossums (*Marmosa*), mice, both adult and nestling birds, lizards, and frogs comprise their diet.

The young are born alive and remain closer to the ground than the adults, where small frogs and lizards are readily available. The average adult length is thirty inches.

Other than the nominate race, one subspecies, *B. b. smaragdinus*, is known, which occurs in the Amazonian regions of Colombia, Ecuador, Peru, Bolivia, as well as adjacent Brazil. Green in color, this snake is heavily spotted with black on the head and dorsum.

Care. As for *B. lateralis*.

All of the neo-tropical Palm Vipers rest or shelter in a tight coil, secured to branches or twigs by their strong, prehensile tails. The specimen illustrated is *B. b. bilineatus.*

T. Granes

FER-de-LANCE; BARBA AMARILLA *(Bothrops andianus asper)*

Habitat. Forested areas, adjacent fields, cultivated areas; brushy areas along streams and ditches
Geographic Range. The *subspecies* illustrated ranges from southern Mexico, south through Central America to western Colombia and Ecuador.
Natural History. Often referred to as "Lance-heads," a name based on the distinct, sharply triangular head and its frequent pattern of a dark arrow or lance-head marking. A number of species and subspecies are found through much of South America, Trinidad, and St. Lucia Island in the Caribbean. Quite variable, they are usually some shade of brown, patterned with dark-colored triangles or "near-triangles." The young specimen illustrated (collected in Costa Rica) will darken with age. As with many common, wide-ranging and variable snakes, their relationships are poorly understood and undergo frequent taxonomic

changes or adjustments. Formerly considered a subspecies of *Bothrops atrox,* it is now considered to be more accurately defined as a subspecific race of the Andean Fer-de-Lance, *Bothrops a. andianus,* a montane form from Peru.

These snakes may move about at any time, but they are most active at night, foraging or waiting in ambush for their prey. Adults feed primarily on mammals and birds; juveniles on frogs and lizards as well. They shelter in a wide variety of hiding places, although they often simply coil in forest litter or drifted piles of leaves, their colors and pattern creating an effective camouflage.

The Fer-de-Lance is a prolific snake, and larger females may produce litters in excess of seventy young, twelve inches in length. The juveniles are somewhat brighter in color and pattern than adults, and mature to an average length of four feet. Larger specimens are not uncommon, however; the largest length for *B. a. asper* recorded is in excess of eight feet.

These snakes possess a virulent venom and have caused many human fatalities. Although they are quick to take flight when disturbed, a threatened animal will defend itself vigorously. In addition to being potentially fatal, the venom is destructive of tissue, destroying blood cells and mucous membranes as well.

Care. As for the Urutu, *B. alternatus*. Wild-caught Fer-de-Lance should be checked for intestinal parasites and treated if necessary. They reproduce readily under captive conditions and captive-born specimens usually present fewer problems to the keeper. Longevity of over twenty years is known.

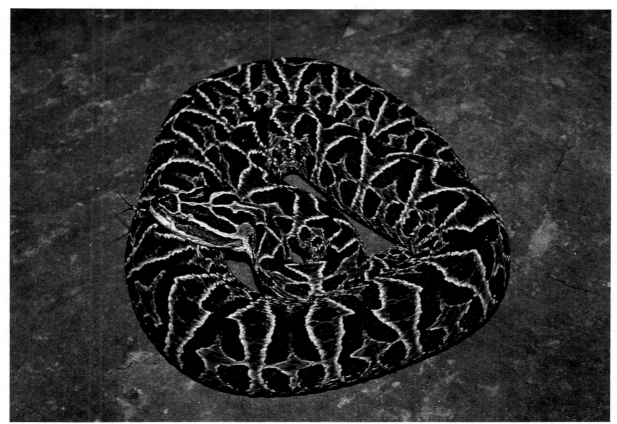

T. Granes

URUTU; WUTU *(Bothrops alternatus)*

Habitat. Open forest or forest edges in the vicinity of streams, ponds and lakes

Geographic Range. Southeastern Brazil, northern Argentina, Uruguay and Paraguay

Natural History. A dark grey, brown or reddish-brown, stout-bodied pit viper, vividly patterned with dark brown or black crescents edged with white or cream. The vernacular "Urutu" or "Wutu" refers to the crescent markings. The complex pattern is better illustrated than described.

Nocturnal, they shelter during the day in mammal burrows, hollow logs, and root tangles. They locate pathways used by their prey (small mammals) by scent, and remain coiled adjacent to them, quickly striking a careless rat or mouse. The prey is released and found later, as the snake follows the scent trail.

The litters of living young vary in number according to the size of the female. The eight- to ten-inch youngsters are identical to adults, but they are more brightly colored. Adults average about four feet in length; usually larger, females may attain five feet.

The venom of these snakes generally causes extensive tissue damage, but it is not often fatal. A polyvalent antibothropic antivenom is produced by several laboratories in South America.

Care. Draft-free caging, floored with shredded-bark garden mulch, a secure hiding place and a water dish provide the basics. Urutus require a temperature of 75-80° F (23-27° C), and feed upon pre-killed rodents of appropriate size. Properly maintained pairs reproduce regularly.

BUSHMASTER *(Lachesis muta muta)*

Habitat. Primary and secondary forests; adjacent fields and cleared areas

Geographic Range. The nominate race ranges from western Ecuador and Peru, east across northern South America to French Guiana, south throughout suitable habitat in Brazil, north of the Amazon Basin.

Natural History. A yellowish, reddish, or grey-brown ground color, patterned with dark brown or black dorsal blotches that form lateral, inverted triangles of the same color. The lateral pattern may be precisely or indistinctly defined, normally pale at the center. The scales are heavily keeled, appearing bead-like. Those on the tail tip are divided and resemble the burrs of a round wood rasp.

Bushmasters are secretive and shelter in fallen logs, burrows, or the exposed root systems of trees. They bask during the day, but are nocturnal snakes, foraging for the small mammals that form their basic diet, along with occasional birds and amphibians.

The only neo-tropical pit viper that lays eggs (about twelve constituting an average clutch), females are reputed to remain with the eggs during incubation. If they do in fact guard the nest site, the many tales of aggressive behavior by this species may be associated with females so involved. The hatchlings are more vividly colored than adults and about twelve inches in length. Average adults are seven to eight feet in length, although ten-foot specimens are not too unusual. The largest recorded length is slightly under twelve feet. Thus, this species is the largest of all pit vipers and the longest venomous snake of the western hemisphere.

Several subspecies are known in addition to the nominate race. *L. m. stenophrys,* a darker-colored form than the nominate race, occurs in the forested regions of Costa Rica and Panama. The forests of eastern Brazil are occupied by *L. m. rhombeata*. *L. m. melanocephala* has been recently described, and is apparently confined to the Peninsula de Osos in southwestern Costa Rica. The generic name, *Lachesis,* is a fanciful allusion to one of the Three Fates of mythology, who determine the length of an individual's life.

L. m. stenophrys, the Central American Bushmaster, is more somberly colored than the South American subspecies.

J. Mehrtens

The reputation of the Bushmaster as an aggressive, savage denizen of the jungle is undeserved, and is probably based upon the overactive imaginations of "explorers," who perhaps felt that the usually impressive size of most adult specimens called for a formidable reputation as well. While it is certainly a dangerous snake, fully capable of inflicting a lethal bite, the Bushmaster is no more so than other venomous snakes less burdened with romantic reputations.

Care. Bushmasters do have a reputation for being difficult to maintain in captivity, although this is due in large part to rough collecting methods, e.g., nooses, and misinterpretation of their physical requirements. On occasion, properly collected and transported specimens have done well in plain cages, simply equipped with a hiding box and water bowl. Ideally, Bushmasters require tight hiding places, low light levels and temperatures not exceeding 80° F (27° C). Small, freshly killed laboratory rats are the most readily accepted food. Careful observation of skin shedding cycles should be made and cage humidity increased just prior to ecdysis. Captive-hatched animals have been reared a number of times by several institutions.

T. Granes

UNDULATED PIT VIPER
(Ophryacus [Bothrops] undulatus)

Habitat. Brushy, rocky slopes and arroyos adjacent to streams

Geographic Range. Southwestern Mexico. The range is not well defined, but the species occurs in the Sierra Madre del Sur and portions of Oaxaca and Puebla.

Natural History. An attractive, silvery-grey snake, patterned with black dorsal blotches that fuse to form a wide, wavy dorsal stripe. The sides are speckled with black. The dorsum of the head is black, and the supraorbital scales are elongated to form a spine or "horn" over the eyes.

The little that is known about its habits indicates it is semi-arboreal and nocturnal, spending the day coiled in shrubs or vine tangles. Captive specimens have accepted small, pre-killed mice as food, and it may be assumed that in the wild state they forage for small mammals, birds and nestlings, lizards, and amphibians. They bear living young.

The removal of this species from the genus *Bothrops* to a monospecific genus of its own attests to the poorly understood relationships of the neo-tropical pit vipers. These generic revisions are not accepted by all taxonomists, and considerable research will be necessary before universally acceptable interpretations can be made.

Care. As for the various arboreal pit vipers.

BARBOUR'S PIT VIPER
(Porthidium [Bothrops] barbouri)

Habitat. Rocky, montane pine forests; bunch grass clearings

Geographic Range. Confined to Guerrero and Sierra Madre del Sur, in southwestern Mexico

Natural History. A small pit viper, blackish in color, patterned with an ill-defined dorsal zig-zag stripe extending laterally, which gives the appearance of trangular markings. Small triangular blotches pattern the lower sides. The interstitial skin is rust colored, as are the sides of the head.

This is a montane snake, inhabiting areas some 9,000 feet in altitude. Its remote and inhospitable home is difficult to access and little is known of its habits. It is diurnal and almost certainly basks frequently in order to maintain activity temperatures in the cool mountains. Captives have fed upon pre-killed mice and small rodents, and amphibians are probably also preyed upon in the wild. They bear living young, although litter size and size of the young have not been accurately defined. Adults probably do not exceed thirty inches in length.

Care. Living specimens of this species are rarely available, except perhaps to professional institutions. A captive environment suited to the European Asp, *Vipera aspis,* should prove a reasonable basis on which to develop a proper husbandary program for this pit viper.

GODMAN'S PIT VIPER
(Porthidium [Bothrops] godmani)

Habitat. Rocky, grassy hillsides; forest edges
Geographic Range. Oaxaca and Chiapas, Mexico, south to Panama
Natural History. A small, "chunky" pit viper, varying in color from shades of grey to dark brown, patterned with dark brown or grey blotches. Specimens from some populations in Costa Rica are reddish in color.

Montane populations tend to be diurnal; those at lower elevations tend to be nocturnal. They shelter beneath fallen logs and other debris. They frequently bask, often climbing into bushes for this purpose. They prey upon mice, lizards, and occasionally frogs.

Up to ten young, five to six inches in length, are born, the number depending on the size of the female. Adults can attain a length of two feet, but they are usually smaller.

Godman's Pit Viper is an irritable snake, and if molested, it rapidly vibrates its tail and vigorously strikes at the intruder.

Care. As for the Jumping Viper, *P. nummifer.*

BLACK-TAILED HORNED PIT VIPER
(*Porthidium [Bothrops] melanurus*)

Habitat. Dry, rocky, sandy hillsides and adjacent flats

Geographic Range. Northern Oaxaca and southern Puebla states, Mexico

Natural History. A terrestrial, neo-tropical pit viper similar in appearance and habits to several of the true vipers of Eurasia. They vary in color from shades of grey, often suffused with terracotta, to dusky orange-red. The pattern is a series of dark grey to black, angular dorsal blotches that unite to form a zig-zag dorsal stripe. The sides are spotted; the tail is black. The raised supraorbital shields form a "horn" over each eye.

These little-known pit vipers are crepuscular and/or nocturnal in habits. They shelter in rock crevices and similar retreats, or bury themselves in shallow troughs in loose sand, the supraorbital "horns" keeping the eyes free of sand. Small rodents and lizards are their primary prey.

The young are born alive and are identical to the adults in color and pattern, maturing to an average length of two feet.

Care. As for the Western Hog-nosed Viper, *P. ophryomegas*. *P. melanurus* is uncommon in collections. One published record indicates a captive longevity of four years, with the specimen still living at that time.

A dark color morph of the Black-tailed Horned Pit Viper, *P. melanurus*; note the supraorbital "horn."

T. Granes

R. D. Bartlett

HOGNOSE VIPER *(Porthidium [Bothrops] nasutus)*

Habitat. Humid, open forests

Geographic Range. Southern Mexico (Vera Cruz), south on the Caribbean coast of Central America to Colombia and Ecuador

Natural History. Among the smallest of the over sixty-five described species of *Bothrops,* a genus of neo-tropical pit vipers recently split taxonomically into six genera. Dark to light reddish-brown in color, it is patterned with a narrow cream mid-dorsal stripe, flanked on either side by small, square, brown or black markings. There is a dark band on the side of the head that accentuates a sharp, upturned snout.

Climatic conditions and temperature determine periods of activity for the Hognose Viper; thus, they may be observed either day or night. They prefer to shelter in locations that retain some moisture, even in the drier areas of their habitat,

such as piles of litter, stumps, or fallen logs. They often occur among the overgrown, fallen stones of pre-Columbian Indian temple ruins. They forage for small rodents and lizards.

Other than the fact that they bear living young, little information is available concerning size of litters or young. Adult specimens average about eighteen inches in length, perhaps occasionally attaining two feet.

In those portions of its range in which both occur, *P. nasutus* is often confused with Lansberg's Pit Viper, *Porthidium (Bothrops) lansbergii,* a small snake of similar coloration and pattern. Inhabiting a drier habitat than *P. nasutus,* the three subspecies of Lansberg's Pit Viper have a discontinuous range in Central and South America. *P. l. lansbergii* is found in the semi-arid areas of the eastern coast of Colombia. *P. l. rozei* occurs in similar habitat in northern Venezuela; and *P. l. annectans* is found in Honduras.

Care. Both species are uncommon in collections. *P. nasutus* requires slightly lower temperatures, 74-78° F (23-26° C) and higher humidity than does *P. lansbergii*. Both are secretive snakes, and *P. nasutus* will utilize the tight shelter of cork bark, partially buried in shredded bark, in preference to the standard hiding box. Both will accept small, pre-killed mice.

A typically colored and patterned specimen of the Hognose Viper, *P. nasutus*.

R. D. Bartlett

JUMPING VIPER
(Porthidium [Bothrops] nummifer occiduus)

Habitat. Rain forests, forested hills; adjacent clearings such as plantations

Geographic Range. Western Guatemala and El Salvador

Natural History. A stocky, terrestrial pit viper that varies from grey to brown or beige, patterned with angulated blotches that meet mid-dorsally. The blotches vary from brown to black in color. The head is unpatterned except for a dark, oblique band on the side, extending back from the eye.

During the day these snakes bask or remain sheltered beneath or inside fallen logs, piles of leaves, or other debris. Becoming active at dusk, they may forage or wait in ambush for their primary prey of small rodents. Lizards and frogs are also consumed.

The five- or six-inch young are born alive and feed upon small frogs and lizards. Adults may attain lengths of thirty inches, but they average eighteen to twenty-four.

Jumping Vipers live up to their name by sometimes striking at intruders with such force as to actually leave the ground. If thoroughly frightened they flail about, striking wildly and quickly turning to keep the threat in view.

Two additional subspecies are known. The nominate race, *P. n. nummifer,* occurs in Mexico (Oaxaca north to San Luis Potosi). *P. n. mexicanus* is found on the eastern (Caribbean) side of the mountains from southern Mexico south to Honduras to Panama. It inhabits lower elevations and is not a montane species.

Care. Caging floored with shredded garden mulch, topped with a thick layer of dead leaves to shelter in, is more suited to this pit viper than plain cages. A piece of cork bark may also be used as shelter by some specimens. Temperature in the high 70's F (mid 20's C) are adequate. They accept small pre-killed mice as food.

© J. Bridges

WESTERN HOG-NOSED VIPER
(Porthidium [Bothrops] ophryomegas)

Habitat. Rocky, semi-arid, or arid slopes and hillsides

Geographic Range. Western Guatemala, south on the Pacific coast to Panama and Honduras

Natural History. Although popularly referred to as a "Hog-nosed" Viper, the snout does not terminate in any raised scales as in *P. nasutus*. The ground color varies, quite often matching the soil or sand colors of the habitat. Some shade of grey, overtones of yellow or reddish-brown may be prevalent in some populations. They are patterned with numerous black dorsal blotches and spots.

While they may bask during the day in the cooler months, these pit vipers are nocturnal, foraging among stones and debris for small rodents and lizards.

The six-inch-long young are born alive and primarily prey upon lizards. If available, small frogs are also eaten. Some specimens may attain thirty inches, although two feet is the average length at maturity.

These pit vipers vigorously defend themselves when threatened, often striking with such vigor that the body is thrown forward or off the ground.

Care. Dry, well-ventilated caging is required, with suitable hiding places. Temperatures of 78-80° F (25-26°C) are suitable, while cooling several degrees at night will allow for normal activity. Prekilled, small mice are accepted as food. They are not often seen in collections, although longevity records of more than five years are known.

Rattlesnakes

Mexican Green Rattlesnake, *Crotalus b. basiliscus*

© J. Bridges

EASTERN DIAMONDBACK RATTLESNAKE
(Crotalus adamanteus)

Habitat. Flatwoods (pine, oak), palmetto hammocks, abandoned agricultural and logging areas
Geographic Range. Florida (Keys and peninsula), north in coastal areas to North Carolina, west to Mississippi and Louisiana
Natural History. An impressive, heavy-bodied snake, the ground color may be blackish-brown, olive or dusty grey, patterned with black or blackish-brown diamond-shaped blotches dorsally, each edged with a narrow band of cream, beige, or yellow-gold. The side of the head is patterned with two white, oblique stripes. The tail may be ringed with white and black bands.

These rattlesnakes shelter in mammal and gopher tortoise burrows, exposed root systems of uprooted trees and stumps, and similar sites,

emerging in early morning or afternoon to bask. They become nocturnal during the warm summer months. They actively forage or lie in ambush for their prey of small mammals, especially rabbits, and rice rats, *Oryzomys;* birds are also included in their diet. Prey animals are usually struck and released, the snake later following the scent trail to the deceased prey. Eastern Diamondbacks are secretive, and surprisingly little is known of their habits and activities in the wild. Field studies, utilizing electronic implants for tracking of individual specimens, will certainly provide much additional data.

Up to twenty young, twelve to fourteen inches in length, are born during late summer and early fall. Although known to attain an adult length in excess of eight feet, the average size at maturity is about four feet. Larger specimens exist, for the most part, only in those areas that still remain remote from frequent human activity.

When threatened, Eastern Diamondbacks retreat from the threat, maintaining a striking coil and facing the intruder, maneuvering their body backward to shelter, at which point they quickly disappear.

The majority of rattlesnakes are afforded no protection, and the Eastern Diamondback is rapidly disappearing from many areas in which it formerly occurred. Suburban housing and agri-cultural development annually destroys vast areas of habitat, but perhaps the most needless destruction of this uniquely American species is the result of the so-called "rattlesnake roundups" held annually in several states of the U.S.

Care. Adult specimens, especially when improperly collected, are often difficult to maintain as captives. Captive-born young, on the other hand, are quite stable as captives, feeding readily on pre-killed laboratory rodents.

They require dry, well-ventilated caging and a secure hiding place. A temperature of 75-80° F (23-27° C) is satisfactory for normal activity.

An albinistic specimen of the Eastern Diamondback, *C. adamanteus,* considered something of a rarity in this species of rattlesnake

B. Mealey

WESTERN DIAMONDBACK RATTLESNAKE
(Crotalus atrox)

Habitat. Varied; dry or semi-arid areas; brushy plains, canyons, hillsides and montane areas; also river bluffs, cedar brakes

Geographic Range. Northern Mexico, north through Texas to central Arkansas, west to southeastern California

Natural History. A large snake of variable color, often matching or blending with the soil color of the area in which a given population occurs. They may be brown, grey, reddish, reddish-pink, or a brownish-yellow, patterned with pale-bordered diamond-shaped blotches, usually a darker tone of the body color. The tail is ringed with black and white bands.

This wide ranging snake frequently occurs in close proximity to both large and small cities and often runs afoul of its human neighbors. In those areas that provide suitable sites, large numbers gather in the late fall prior to hibernation, often in company with non-venomous snakes such as Whipsnakes and Bullsnakes. Western Diamondbacks are secretive animals, a fact demonstrated by a den site located just a short walk from a large house, the owners of which being completely unaware of the many dozens of snakes gathered there twice a year. Although they bask during the early spring and late fall, Western Diamondbacks are nocturnal snakes. They feed on a wide variety of small mammals and birds. These rattlesnakes bear up to two dozen young, twelve inches in length, in late summer or early fall. Adults may attain lengths slightly in excess of seven feet, but these are rare and even then occur only in remote, undisturbed areas. The average adult length is about four feet.

Western Diamondbacks are quick to escape should they feel threatened, although they are equally quick in defending themselves if escape is impossible, remaining in place and raising the head and striking coil well above the ground. Envenomated bites are potentially fatal, even when treated.

While its vast geographic distribution perhaps assures its continued existence as a representative of North America's fauna, target shooters frequently decimate populations emerging from hibernation. Many localized populations have been extirpated by "rattlesnake roundups," rattlesnakes being caught elsewhere and released, in order for the activity to continue.

Care. Dry, well-ventilated cages simply furnished with a hiding place, water bowl, and a rock or branch to aid in shedding are sufficient. Pre-killed laboratory rodents are acceptable as food, at temperatures of 75-80° F (23-27° C). Captive specimens reproduce readily under proper conditions and have attained longevities in excess of twenty-five years.

A denning site used by rattlesnakes, whipsnakes and copperheads in central Texas; the limestone outcropping has many deep crevices, through which the snakes find access to the hibernation areas deep underground.

J. Mehrtens

MEXICAN WEST COAST RATTLESNAKE
MEXICAN GREEN RATTLESNAKE;
(Crotalus basiliscus basiliscus)

Habitat. Dry, coastal cactus (thorn) forest; rocky areas and canyons

Geographic Range. Western Mexico, from southern Sonora south through Michoacan and Guerrero

Natural History. This is a large rattlesnake that may be pale brown, pale greyish-green, or pale green in color, patterned with dark diamond-shaped dorsal blotches, appearing as lateral triangles. The triangles are edged in white; sometimes terracotta may border the white or appear as scattered specks of color. The keeled scales have a beaded appearance.

Crepuscular, Mexican West Coast Rattlesnakes become nocturnal during the warm, summer months. They bask in close proximity to shelters of unused burrows, rock crevices, and similar sites, quickly disappearing if disturbed. They are active after rains and engage in the dangerous habit of coiling upon, or crossing, roads. They prey primarily upon mammals, although birds are also included in their diet.

The young are born alive, measuring about fourteen inches in length. Captive neonates readily accept small mice; in the wild, lizards are probably also suitable prey. Large, adult specimens of nearly seven feet in length have been recorded, although the average length at maturity is four to five feet.

A subspecies, the Oaxacan Rattlesnake, *C. b. oaxacus,* is confined to the mountains of Oaxaca. Habitat destruction has eliminated this subspecies from much of its former range.

Care. As for *C. atrox.*

The Oaxacan
Rattlesnake, *C. b.*
oaxacus, a rare
subspecies confined to
montane areas of
Oaxaca, Mexico.

T. Granes

© J. Bridges

SONORAN SIDEWINDER
(Crotalus cerastes cercobombus)

Habitat. Arid, sandy areas, desert sand dunes, rocky, sandy hillsides, especially in areas of mesquite or creosote shrubs

Geographic Range. Western, central Sonora, Mexico; north to south central Arizona

Natural History. A pale-colored, desert rattlesnake, the ground color often resembling or matching the color of the soil and/or sand of the areas in which they occur, e.g., beige, pinkish-grey, grey, or tan. They are patterned with small dorsal blotches of pale brown or brownish-grey; the sides may be spotted with the same color. The supraocular scales are elongated and form a "horn" over each eye.

The popular name refers to the method of locomotion used by these snakes to rapidly traverse the soft, shifting sands of their habitat. The body moves forward in rolling loops, forward of the head, which is then moved forward and the body loop repeated. A series of "J" shaped tracks are left in the sand.

Nocturnal snakes, they shelter in rodent burrows or shallow troughs in the shade of a rock or bush, the supraocular "horns" keeping the eyes free of sand. They prey upon small desert rodents such as Kangaroo rats, *Dipodomys,* and lizards.

Females give birth in early fall, up to eighteen young in a litter. The seven- or eight-inch neonates initially prey upon small lizards. Adults seldom exceed thirty inches in length; large specimens are usually females.

The Sidewinder of the Mojave Desert area

(California, Nevada, and Utah), *Crotalus c. cerastes,* is similar to the Sonoran, except for the color of the basal rattle segment, which is brown rather than black. The Colorado Desert Sidewinder, *C. c. laterorepens,* ranges through southeastern California and adjacent Arizona, south into northwestern Mexico (including Baja).

Care. Caging as suggested for the African dwarf desert vipers, *Bitis,* is equally suited to these rattlesnakes. Specimens collected in areas in which lizards are primary prey will often refuse to accept rodents and may refuse to feed entirely. Successful husbandry of Sidewinders can be difficult and requires both a skilled and experienced keeper.

R. D. Bartlett

F. Bolin, D. Hamper

(Left) A dark-colored specimen of the Sonoran Sidewinder; as with many desert snakes, its colors match those of the habitat. *(Right)* A dorsal view of a Sonoran Sidewinder; note the supraorbital "horns" and the ventrolateral scales, which aid the snake in burrowing in loose sand.

TROPICAL RATTLESNAKE; CASCAVEL; CASCABEL
(Crotalus durissus durissus)

Habitat. Dry grasslands, thorn scrub; rocky, sandy hillsides; forest clearings, and farmland

Geographic Range. The nominate race, illustrated, ranges from southeastern Mexico south through Central America to Costa Rica. It is absent from the eastern portions of Honduras and Nicaragua.

Natural History. The only rattlesnake species found south of Mexico, its thirteen subspecies range widely throughout South America. Usually some shade of brown, brownish-grey, or olive in color, they are patterned with large, dorsal diamond-shaped blotches that extend onto the sides, creating an effect of lateral triangles. The head and neck are patterned with parallel stripes; the tail is usually dark brown or black. The heavily keeled scales give the body and pattern a beaded effect.

Crepuscular, especially during the cooler months, these snakes shelter in abandoned burrows, drifted piles of leaves and similar debris, rock crevices, and, in or under fallen trees and cacti. They forage for various mammals, birds, and large lizards.

Up to two dozen living young are born; the twelve- to fourteen-inch neonates are more vividly colored than the adults. Juveniles prey upon lizards, nestling rodents, large grasshoppers, and crickets. Average adults measure four feet in length.

Several subspecies occur in Mexico, which include the Totonactan Rattlesnake, *C. d. totonacus,* found in southern Tamaulipas, San Luis Potosi, and northern Vera Cruz. The southwestern areas of the states of Michoacan, Morelos, Guerrero, and Oaxaca are inhabited by *C. d. culminatus.* The Mayas, as well as other groups of Meso-American Indians, venerated the rattlesnake as an earthly representative of various deities, the most well known probably being Quetzalcoatl, the Feathered Serpent. The periodic shedding of the skin, the snake emerging from its dusty, dingy scarf skin, and appearing in fresh, vibrant colors, demonstrated the Mayan belief in an endless cycle of birth and rebirth. The rattlesnake, or *Tzabcan,* carved in stone, appears in many of the ruins of the great cities and ceremonial centers in Mexico and Central America. The subspecific name of the form occurring in Yucatan and northern Belize, *C. d. tzabcan,* commemorates the role of this snake in the Indian cultures. They are patterned as the other subspecies, but of a soft grey ground color,

The Mexican Cascabel, *C. d. culminatus*

T. Granes

The Tzabcan or Yucatec Cascabel, *C. d. tzabcan*

F. Bolin, D. Hamper

the dorsal rhombs outlined with terra cotta. Three subspecies often seen in collections are *C. d. terrificus* of Bolivia, Paraguay, Uruguay, and southern Brazil; and *C. d. dryinus,* found in Guyana, Surinam, and French Guiana; and *C. d. cumanensis,* which ranges throughout Venezuela and northeastern Colombia.

The venom toxicity of these snakes varies from subspecies to subspecies, as well as from one locality to another. The venom has profound neurotoxic effects, one of which is paralysis of the neck muscles. A number of localized names for this rattlesnake loosely translate as "neck breaker," an appropriate vernacular for this snake.

Care. As for *Crotalus atrox.*

The Cascavel, *C. d. terrificus*

D. Hamper

The Venezuelan/ Colombian Cascabel, *C. d. cumanensis*

T. Granes

J. Mehrtens

TIMBER RATTLESNAKE *(Crotalus horridus horridus)*

Habitat. Rocky, sparsely wooded hillsides, rock outcroppings, adjacent fields, meadows, and pastures

Geographic Range. The *subspecies* illustrated ranges from southern New Hampshire, south in higher elevations to northern Georgia, west to Illinois, southeastern Minnesota, Wisconsin, and south to northeastern Texas

Natural History. A variably colored, medium-sized rattlesnake, the ground color ranges from sulphur yellow through various shades of grey-green, brown or black, patterned with dark brown or black chevrons and crossbands. The tail is black. Yellow specimens are often, but not always, females; black specimens are often, but not always, males. Both melanistic (black) specimens and albinos occur in wild populations. The specimen illustrated is a female from western Massachusetts.

Timber Rattlesnake populations are usually associated with a specific hibernation site or "den." In the northeast such sites are usually montane rock outcroppings, with a southerly or eastern exposure and with numerous, deep crevices. The snakes emerge in the spring, basking in the sun and mating. They then leave, foraging through lower elevations for rats and mice, which are their primary prey, or for squirrels, chipmunks, small rabbits, and birds, which are also included in their diet.

Depending upon temperatures, they may be active day or night, and when not prowling or lying in ambush for prey they are secretive and remain hidden. Local residents are often completely unaware of their presence.

Females, especially in northern areas, give birth every other year, usually in the vicinity of the "den." Hatchlings are ten- to twelve inches long, and unlike most young, rather dull in color but otherwise similar to the adults. Specimens in excess of six feet have been recorded, although adults average three to four feet in length.

Once abundant throughout the northeast, Timber Rattlesnakes have been exterminated in many parts of their range. They are now protected by several northeastern states, although, unfortunately, the regulations are difficult to enforce.

Suburban and rural development, "rattlesnake roundups," target shooting, and dynamiting of den sites have taken a significant toll. During both early and late colonial times the "Belled Viper," as it was called, figured prominently in the activities, communications, and folklore of the colonists. During the Revolutionary War the Timber Rattlesnake was often used as a heraldic device on both the state and battle flags, as well as that of the infant naval forces. The snake was always depicted with thirteen segments to the rattle (representing the thirteen colonies) and bore the motto "Don't Tread On Me." This symbolic use of the snake was quite popular and widespread, and the Timber Rattlesnake came quite close to becoming the symbol of the United States, rather than the Bald Eagle.

Southern Virginia, south to the panhandle of Florida and west to central Texas, is home to the Canebrake Rattlesnake, *C. h. atricaudatus,* which unlike its northern cousin, occurs in lowland areas such as swamps, cane brakes, and riverine thickets. Recognized subspecifically for many years, some taxonomists consider it to be merely a clinal variant of the Timber Rattlesnake. It intergrades with the northern form in many areas. A larger snake, it is often pinkish or reddish in color, and with the exception of a rust-colored dorsal stripe, is identical to the Timber Rattlesnake in pattern. **Care.** As for *C. adamanteus* and *C. atrox.* Captive longevities in excess of thirty years are known.

The Canebrake Rattlesnake, *C. h. atricaudatus.* Unlike its northern cousin, it inhabits lower elevations such as riverine forests.

B. Mealey

OAXACAN SMALL-HEADED RATTLESNAKE
(Crotalus intermedius gloydi)

Habitat. Montane forests of pine and/or oak

Geographic Range. Suitable habitat in the mountains of Oaxaca, Mexico

Natural History. One of three subspecies of a rare and little understood rattlesnake, the Oaxacan form is soft grey or bluish-grey in color, patterned with irregularly shaped, black edged blotches that are pale terracotta. The blotches are leaf-like in appearance. The female specimen illustrated is typical.

Climatic conditions apparently play a significant role in their periods of activity, as they may be diurnal or nocturnal and are especially active after rainstorms and other barometric disturbances. They prey upon lizards and small rodents.

Little data is available concerning reproduction, but litters are probably similar to those of the other subspecies, whose litters consist of five or six young, seven to eight inches in length. Adults rarely exceed two feet in length.

A montane form found most often in rocky areas, *C. i. omiltemanus*, occurs in central Guerrero state, Mexico. The nominate race, *C. i. intermedius*, is found in east central Mexico, e.g., Vera Cruz, Puebla.

Care. As for *C. willardi*. Unlikely to be seen in collections, the small number of captives known have fed on small, pre-killed rodents and/or swifts, lizards of the genus *Sceloporus*.

DURANGO ROCK RATTLESNAKE *(Crotalus lepidus maculosus)*

Habitat. Open rocky, grassy areas in montane pine and/or oak forests

Geographic Range. Poorly defined. Occurs in southeastern Sinaloa, northeastern Nayarit and western Durango, Mexico

Natural History. The least known of the four subspecies of *Crotalus lepidus,* this subspecies was first described in 1972. The illustration of a sexual pair is typical in pattern and coloration.

Unlike the wide ranging Mottled and Banded, this rattlesnake apparently inhabits humid, montane forests, especially in open, grassy areas strewn with rocks. They prey primarily upon lizards, although small rodents are also consumed, at least by captive specimens.

Little is known of the size of litters or young, other than a record indicating one litter of eleven. Adults probably do not often exceed two feet in length.

Another little known subspecies, *C. l. morulus,* occurs in southeastern Tamaulipas in the same type of habitat as that of the Durango form, in montane forests above three thousand feet.

The nominate race, *C. l. lepidus,* has an extensive range from San Luis Potosi, north to southern and western Texas and southern New Mexico. It inhabits dry, rocky montane areas often in the vicinity of streams. Its varied diet includes small rodents, lizards, small snakes, some amphibians, and large insects. The Banded Rock Rattlesnake, *C. l. klauberi,* occurs in western and central Mexico, from Jalisco north to southwestern New Mexico and southeastern Arizona. The young of this subspecies have bright yellow tail tips, which may serve as a lure to attract the lizards that are the primary diet of juveniles.

Care. As for the Ridge-nosed Rattlesnake, *C. willardi.*

T. Granes

T. Granes

The Tamaulipan Rock Rattlesnake, *C. l. morulus,* occurs in several color and pattern variants, two of which are illustrated here. The specimen on the right is male; specimen on the left is female (they were collected from two different populations).

© J. Bridges

© J. Bridges

The Mottled Rock Rattlesnake, *C. l. lepidus,* is an extremely variable subspecies, but readily recognized by the presence of a dark streak on the side of the head. Their mottled pattern makes them difficult to see among the rocky areas in which they are found.

The Banded Rock
Rattlesnake, *C. l.
klauberi,* has an
extensive range in the
southwestern United
States, extending well
into Mexico. It
intergrades with the
nominate race in areas
of range overlap. This
snake is named in
honor of Laurence
Klauber, an American
authority on
rattlesnakes.

SOUTHWESTERN SPECKLED RATTLESNAKE
(Crotalus mitchelli pyrrhus)

Habitat. Talus slopes, rocky hillsides and canyons; rock ledges

Geographic Range. The subspecies illustrated is found in western Arizona, north to southern Utah and west to southern California.

Natural History. A rattlesnake of variable color, which normally closely resembles the sand, soil, and rock of the habitat. They may be shades of pink, brown, grey, yellow, or nearly white and speckled with black and white. The pattern, when present, may consist of bands, rhombs, or blotches. The overall effect is that of a sandy, pebbled surface and hue. The tail is ringed.

Diurnal during the cooler months, they retreat to the shelter of rock crevices and mammal burrows during the heat of summer days, emerging only at night. They forage for small rodents such as ground squirrels and birds and lizards.

During midsummer females bear litters of up to twelve young. The twelve-inch-long neonates prey primarily on lizards. Adults may occasionally exceed four feet in length, but usually average about three feet.

Four additional subspecies are known. The Panamint Rattlesnake, *C. m. stephensi,* is found in southern Nevada and adjacent California. The nominate race, *C. m. mitchelli,* occurs in southern Baja California and several offshore islands. Two insular forms, *C. m. angelensis* and *C. m. muertensis,* are confined to Angel de la Guarda and El Muerto Islands, respectively (both are in the Gulf of California).

Care. As for the Red Rattlesnake, *C. ruber.* Water should be provided several times each week, but water bowls should not be left in the cage.

NORTHERN BLACK-TAILED RATTLESNAKE
(Crotalus molossus molossus)

Habitat. Cliffs and rock slides along streams, rocky outcroppings; talus slopes

Geographic Range. The *subspecies* illustrated ranges from central Texas (Edwards Plateau) west through much of Arizona and south to northern Mexico.

Natural History. Attractively colored and patterned, Black-Tailed Rattlesnakes may be grey, olive, or greenish-yellow. They are banded and blotched with dark brown or black; the blotches may be diamond-shaped and have pale centers. The pattern is edged with white or pale grey, and the tail is black.

Almost invariably found in rocky areas, they occupy a variety of habitats and may be associated with deciduous or pine woodlands, open grassy hillsides, or cactus and agave groves. They often climb into low-growing bushes, possibly foraging for nestling birds, or to bask. They are active both day and night but seek shelter during hot summer days. They prey primarily on small rodents.

Females bear small litters of five or six young, each about twelve inches long. Adults may attain lengths in excess of four feet, but average thirty-six to forty inches.

The Mexican Black-tailed Rattlesnake, *C. m. nigrescens,* ranges from southern Sonora to Puebla, Mexico. San Esteban Island, in the Gulf of California, harbors *C. m. estabanensis.* There is some evidence that the Black-tailed Rattlesnakes are closely related to the Mexican West Coast Rattlesnake, *C. basiliscus*.

Black-tailed Rattlesnakes do not aggressively defend themselves when molested and seldom rattle. Some specimens may form a body loop and gape the mouth, in the manner óf Cottonmouths.

Care. As for Speckled Rattlesnakes, *C. mitchelli*. Black-tails will occasionally utilize a basking spot. A brushy branch is useful for this purpose as well as an aid to skin shedding.

Populations of Northern Black-tailed Rattlesnakes from New Mexico often have yellowish or yellowish brown ground colors, as opposed to the gray usually seen in Texas populations.

R. Pawley

T. Granes

LANCE-HEADED RATTLESNAKE *(Crotalus polystictus)*

Habitat. Rocky areas in grassland and mesquite scrub

Geographic Range. The Mexican plateau, from central Vera Cruz, west and north to southern Zacatecas, eastern Jalisco and Michoacan

Natural History. A number of small rattlesnakes inhabit Mexico, one of the most attractive being the Lance-headed Rattlesnake. The specimen illustrated is typical in color and pattern.

During the dry season these snakes are nocturnal, becoming diurnal as rains encourage the growth of high grass and brush that provides cover for the snakes. Although they prey on small rodents, lizards are an important part of the diet, especially for juveniles. Females give birth to about a dozen young, usually in late spring (June), the seven- to nine-inch neonates maturing to an average length of about two feet.

Another small montane species, the Long-tailed Rattlesnake, *Crotalus stejnegeri,* occurs in southwestern Durango and adjacent Sinaloa. A rather primitive rattlesnake, it occurs on rocky hillsides and valleys in areas of pine forest as well as deciduous forests. When molested, the long tail as well as a portion of the body is held stiffly in a vertical position while a typical striking coil is assumed. Their primary prey are lizards and small rodents. Adults are about two feet in length.

Also considered a primitive form, the Tancitaran Dusky Rattlesnake, *Crotalus pusillus,* has a limited range in central Michoacan and southern Jalisco, Mexico. It occurs in humid, montane forests of oak and/or pine. These snakes give birth to small litters of six- to seven-inch young early in the year (January). Several adult males may vie for the favors of a female by engaging in ritualized "combat dances." Lizards and small rodents form their diet.

Care. These rattlesnakes are not often seen in collections. They require secure hiding places, cool temperatures of 70-75° F (21-24° C), with a warmer basking place such as raised stones or cork bark. They prefer lizards such as swifts, *Sceloporus,* as food but can usually be induced to accept small rodents. Both *Crotalus polystictus* and *C. pusillus* have attained captive longevities of more than five years.

The Long-tailed Rattlesnake, *C. stejnegeri,* a rare, primitive rattlesnake with a limited range in Mexico

T. Granes

The Tancitaran Dusky Rattlesnake, *C. pusillus,* another primitive form with a limited Mexican range

T. Granes

D. Hamper

TWIN-SPOTTED RATTLESNAKE *(Crotalus pricei pricei)*

Habitat. Montane pine and/or oak forests
Geographic Range. Southeastern Arizona, south to northwestern Mexico
Natural History. The popular name of this small rattlesnake refers to its pattern of two rows of dorsal spots or blotches. The ground color is grey or greyish-brown, overlaid with brown stippling.

This snake occurs at high elevations, inhabiting rock slides, outcroppings or rocky slopes within the forest. Diurnal, it basks and forages as air temperatures warm, preying upon lizards and small mammals.

In mid-summer up to eight young are born, six to eight inches in length. Very large adults may be two feet in length, but eighteen inches is an average size.

Another subspecies, *C. p. miquihuanus,* occurs in northeastern Mexico (Tamaulipas), Coahuila, and Nuevo Leon.

Among the many small rattlesnakes found in various montane habitats in Mexico, only *C. pricei,* in addition to the Rock Rattlesnake, *Crotalus lepidus,* and the Ridge-nosed Rattlesnake, *Crotalus willardi,* ranges northward into the United States.

All others are confined to Mexico, including the rare *Crotalus transversus,* known from only a very small number of specimens, and the common Dusky Rattlesnake, *Crotalus triseriatus,* known from four subspecies that range widely through central and southwestern Mexico.
Care. As for *C. willardi.* Montane rattlesnakes should not be subjected to temperatures over 80° F (27° C).

T. Granes

The Western Dusky Rattlesnake, *C. triseriatus armstrongi,* one of the four subspecific races of the Dusky Rattlesnake occurring in Mexico

D. Hamper

RED DIAMOND RATTLESNAKE
(Crotalus ruber ruber)

Habitat. Brush or cactus-covered foothills, and adjacent brushy grasslands

Geographic Range. Baja north to southwestern California

Natural History. A robust rattlesnake, reddish-tan, pink or terracotta in color, patterned with pale-edged, diamond-shaped dorsal blotches, which may be indistinct or nearly absent. The tail is ringed with black and white bands.

Secretive and nocturnal, these snakes occur in cool, coastal areas as well as desert. They prey upon a variety of small mammals, large adults often taking rabbits and large, terrestrial squirrels, and also birds.

Up to twenty young, twelve to fourteen inches in length, are born in late summer. Large adults may exceed five feet in length.

Several insular races are recognized and occur on islands in the Gulf of California; *C. r. elegans* on Angel de la Guarda, and *C. r. lorenzoensis* on San Lorenzo Island. The San Lucan Rattlesnake, *C. r. lucasensis,* occurs in southern Baja California.

Red Diamond Rattlesnakes are surprisingly inoffensive for large rattlesnakes. Even when severely pressed they appear reluctant to strike or use the rattle. Nevertheless, they can and do bite, and an envenomated bite from a large specimen is a serious matter.

Care. As for *C. atrox.*

MOJAVE RATTLESNAKE *(Crotalus scutulatus scutulatus)*

Habitat. Semi-arid grassland, brushy flats, open scrub areas

Geographic Range. The nominate race ranges from southern Nevada, adjacent California, south and east through Arizona, New Mexico, and west Texas, through central Mexico to Queretaro

Natural History. A wide ranging, attractive rattlesnake often confused with the Western Diamondback, *C. atrox,* although it has a slimmer body. Greenish brown, olive, or greenish-yellow in color, it is patterned with brownish-green diamond-shaped blotches, bordered with white. The tail is banded in black and white.

Mojave Rattlesnakes may bask during the early hours of the day, but they retreat to shelter as the temperature rises, emerging at night to forage for small mammals. They often coil upon roads and many are killed by vehicles, a not uncommon fate for snakes inhabiting open, flat areas.

About a dozen ten- to twelve-inch young are born in mid-summer. The juveniles prey upon lizards in addition to small rodents. Adults may slightly exceed four feet in length but average about three.

Salvin's Rattlesnake, *C. s. salvini,* occurs at the southern edge of the range of that of the nominate race, in Puebla and western Vera Cruz, Mexico. It inhabits the dry plains that occur at higher elevations in this area. The diamond pattern is somewhat irregular, and dark in color, appearing as blotches and spots.

The Mojave Rattlesnake has a highly toxic venom, which particularly affects the respiratory system. They aggressively defend themselves if molested, and a fully envenomated bite, even from a juvenile, is a most serious cause for concern.

Care. As for *Crotalus atrox.*

TIGER RATTLESNAKE *(Crotalus tigris)*

Habitat. Dry, rocky valleys, hillsides in areas of mesquite and cactus brush

Geographic Range. Southern Sonora, Mexico, north to central Arizona

Natural History. A small rattlesnake that is pinkish-grey, pale grey or reddish in color, cross-banded with grey or brown. The crossbands are comprised of dots of color and may appear to have a pebbled effect. Occasional specimens may be bluish or lavender in color.

Although considered a desert species, its occurrence is restricted to limited areas within its habitat. They are not as widespread as are many desert forms. They may be either diurnal or nocturnal, depending upon temperature and time of the year. Usually active after rain showers, they forage through rock piles and other suitable areas for the small mammals and lizards upon which they prey.

The nine-inch young, lighter and brighter in color than the adults, are born alive, and prey primarily on lizards. Adults average between twenty-four to thirty inches in length, not often exceeding three feet.

Care. As for *C. atrox.* Dampness should be avoided, and water bowls should not be left in the cage but offered two or three times weekly. Small, pre-killed laboratory rats are sometimes preferred by these rattlesnakes in lieu of mice.

ARUBA RATTLESNAKE *(Crotalus unicolor)*

Habitat. Rocky hillsides, rock slides, and adjacent rocky, sandy fields

Geographic Range. Aruba Island, Netherlands West Indies

Natural History. A small, pale grey or grey-brown rattlesnake, patterned with pale brown dorsal rhombs often giving the appearance of inverted triangles laterally. The head and neck are patterned with a pair of stripes that may extend well onto the body. The pattern is often vague or virtually absent.

Obviously related to the rattlesnakes of South America, and formerly viewed as a subspecific race of them, this insular snake is now recognized as a full and distinct species. Nocturnal during the warmer months, they are active in early morning and late afternoon the rest of the year. They prey upon small rodents and birds, and undoubtedly also take the numerous *Teiid* lizards found on the island.

Small litters of young, about eight inches in length, are born. Adults attain three feet in length, but are normally shorter, twenty-four to thirty inches being average.

Resort development and other habitat pressures now restrict the dwindling populations of this rattlesnake to just a few rocky, inhospitable parts of the island. The U.S. Endangered Species Act (USFWS) lists the species as "threatened."

Care. As for *Crotalus atrox*. The Aruba Rattlesnake is regularly bred in several North American collections.

J. Mehrtens

SOUTHERN PACIFIC RATTLESNAKE
(Crotalus viridis belleri)

Habitat. Brush-covered rocky canyons, talus slopes and abandoned quarries; sandy fields in coastal areas

Geographic Range. Southern Baja, north to San Luis Obispo and Kern Counties, California

Natural History. A medium-sized snake with a pattern of black blotches edged with creamy yellow or gold, and a white tail ringed with black. Southern Pacific Rattlesnakes are adaptable animals, surviving in such inhospitable environments as suburban and agricultural areas.

Normally crepuscular, they become diurnal during cool weather or at higher altitudes. At lower altitudes they become nocturnal during the warm summer months. They utilize rock crevices, vegetation clumps, exposed tree roots, and mammal burrows as shelters. In suitable sites, usually at higher altitudes, large numbers gather for hibernation. Breeding takes place after spring emergence, large females producing litters of up to twenty live young, averaging eight to ten inches in length. The tails of neonates are bright yellow and may serve as a lure to attract the lizards upon which they prey. The three-. to four-foot adults feed on rodents and occasionally birds.

The Southern Pacific Rattlesnake is one of nine subspecies of the Prairie Rattlesnake, *C. v. viridis.* These are the Northern Pacific, *C. v. oreganus,* the Hopi Rattlesnake, *C. v. nuntius,* Grand Canyon Rattlesnake, *C. v. abyssus,* the Midget-Faded Rattlesnake, *C. v. concolor,* Great Basin Rattlesnake, *C. v. lutosus,* the Arizona Black Rattlesnake, *C. v. cerberus,* and the Coronado Island Rattlesnake, *C. v. caliginus.* Collectively, these rattlesnakes range from northwestern Mexico and Baja north through most of the western United States and into southern Canada.

Care. Uninjured, properly captured specimens or captive-born juveniles adjust readily to dry quarters provided with hiding places. Most of the subspecies readily accept pre-killed laboratory rodents or chicks as food. Any of the Prairie Rattlesnakes can infict a bite potentially lethal to humans, and they should not be kept as "pets" or by inexperienced people.

The Prairie Rattlesnake, *C. v. viridis*

D. Hamper

The Northern Pacific Rattlesnake, *C. v. oreganus*

F. Bolin, D. Hamper

The Arizona Black Rattlesnake, *C. v. cerberus.*

C. v. lutosus, the Great Basin Rattlesnake

CHIHUAHUAN RIDGE-NOSED RATTLESNAKE
(Crotalus willardi silus)

Habitat. Montane and canyon forests of pine, oak, and manzanita

Geographic Range. Suitable habitat in the montane areas of Sonora and Chihuahua, Mexico

Natural History. These are small, montane rattlesnakes that are usually some shade of brown or reddish-brown, patterned with narrow crossbands, white or greyish-white in color and bordered with brown or black. The ground color often closely resembles the color of leaf litter within the area of a specific population. Specimens which are light grey in color may occur in rocky areas and canyons. The snout is conspicuously ridged.

Although these snakes are usually found at rather high elevations, they also occur in well watered, rocky canyons that support broad-leaf, deciduous woodland. The five subspecies are essentially similar in habits. They are most active before and after rainstorms. As are most montane species, they are diurnal, often basking in direct sunlight. Their coloration is somewhat cryptic, and when coiled in leaf litter they are difficult to detect. They actively forage for lizards, especially *Sceloporus,* or lie in ambush for small rodents and birds.

Females give birth to up to nine young, six to eight inches long, in late summer. Adults average about eighteen inches in length, some specimens occasionally attaining two feet.

The subspecific name *silus* at one time applied to a population of these rattlesnakes with an ex-

T. Granes

T. Granes

(Left) The Del Nido Ridge-nosed Rattlesnake, *C. w. amabilis*. *(Right)* The Southern Ridge-nosed Rattlesnake, *C. w. meridionalis*.

tremely limited range in southern New Mexico. This form, now considered distinct, is known as the Animas Ridge-nosed Rattlesnake, *C. w. obscurus*. This small population could easily be eliminated by habitat destruction or overly zealous and irresponsible collectors. It is protected by the federal government.

The nominate race, *C. w. willardi*, occurs in southern Arizona, south to northern Sonora, Mexico. *C. w. amabilis* ranges in the mountains of north central Chihuahua, Mexico, while the frequently greyish-colored form, *C. w. meridionalis*, has the most southerly range, occurring in very restricted habitats in Durango and Zacatecas, Mexico. They are found in high, grassy meadows bordering montane forests.

Care. Conditions suitable for other rattlesnakes are basically acceptable for these snakes. Captive breeding has often occurred, and the species has attained longevities in excess of twenty years. These snakes may sometimes prove difficult as captives, and require experienced care.

The Lower California Rattlesnake, *C. enyo enyo,* is known from three subspecies. The nominate race occurs in Baja California. It inhabits arid desert and adjacent montane areas throughout its range. It preys upon small rodents and lizards.

D. Hamper

The Uracoan Rattlesnake, *C. vegrandis,* is unique in being the only rattlesnake found on mainland South America which is not a subspecies of the Cascavel. The Uracoan Rattlesnake occurs in the grassy, savannah areas of western Venezuela. It shelters in armadillo burrows, apparently emerging for short periods of time to bask and forage.

© J. Bridges

DUSKY PYGMY RATTLESNAKE
(Sistrurus miliarius barbouri)

Habitat. Flat, open woodland and fields near swamps, marshes, and ponds

Geographic Range. The *subspecies* illustrated ranges from Florida, north to southern South Carolina and west to southeastern Mississippi.

Natural History. Pygmy Rattlesnakes and Massasaugas are small rattlesnakes that differ from their larger cousins by the presence of nine large scales on the top of the head. All other rattlesnakes, *Crotalus,* have a mixture of both large and small scales. The specimen illustrated is typical in color and pattern.

These rattlesnakes almost always occur in dry, sandy areas close to water. They may be active at any time of day or night, ambient temperatures largely determining the activity period. They shelter beneath piles of leaves, pine needles, or the shallow space along fallen logs. Their diet is varied, and they prey upon mice and other small mammals, small snakes, lizards, and frogs. Some specimens also consume large insects such as grasshoppers and crickets.

Females bear six or eight young in late summer, the six- or seven-inch young identical to the adults in both pattern and color. Average-sized adults are usually less than twenty inches in length, but specimens in excess of thirty inches have been recorded.

Another subspecies, the Carolina Pygmy Rattlesnake, *S. m. miliarius,* occurs in the Carolinas and extends westward to Alabama. Normally pale grey in color, some populations of this subspecies are brick-red or orange. The Western Pygmy, *S. m. streckeri,* named in honor of an early Texas herpetologist, ranges from southwestern Kentucky to Louisiana, Oklahoma, and eastern Texas.

The Carolina Pygmy Rattlesnake, *S. m. miliarius*

D. Hamper

A second species of *Sistrurus* is popularly referred to as the Massasauga, the name originally applied to it by the Chippewa Indians. The three subspecific races of *S. catenatus* range from southern Canada (Ontario) south to southeastern Arizona and northeastern Mexico.

The Mexican Massasauga, *S. ravus,* occurs as four subspecies in south central Mexico. It is most abundant in grassy valleys and logged forest areas. They are heavier-bodied than their northern relatives and average about thirty inches in length. They feed primarily on rodents.

The Western Pygmy Rattlesnake, *S. m. streckeri*

W. Lamar

Care. Caging basic to the needs of other rattlesnakes is suitable for *Sistrurus*. Some specimens seem to prefer a pile of dried leaves or pine needles, instead of a box or log as shelter.

NOTE: The small size of these rattlesnakes does not reduce the gravity of their bite. The venom is highly toxic and produces serious physiological problems such as respiratory collapse, and it is potentially fatal.

S. ravus exiguus, one of the four races of the Mexican Massasauga. They are more robust than North American Massasaugas and Pygmy Rattlesnakes.

T. Granes

GLOSSARY

aestivate (estivate) to become dormant during the summer or dry season

aglyphous the absence of any teeth modified in any manner for venom injection

albino any animal congenitally deficient in epidermal pigment

ambient encompassing on all sides; surrounding

anaphylactic (shock) a physiological condition resulting from protein sensitization

anterior front or front portion

antibothrophic antivenom effective against venoms characteristic of the neo-tropical pit vipers, other than rattlesnakes; e.g. Bothrops, et al.

antisera a serum containing antibodies; an antitoxin

antivenom (antivenin) an antitoxin to a venom

arachnids a class of invertebrates which includes spiders, scorpions, mites, and ticks

arboreal inhabiting or frequenting trees and/or high bushes

basal (rattle) relating to or forming the base

bifurcated forked

binomial a name consisting of two parts, e.g., a genus name and a species name

cervical pertaining to the neck

cline (clinal variant) a gradual change of a variable characteristic over a given geographic range

cloaca (cloacal) a chamber present in most vertebrates (other than mammals) into which the intestinal, urinary, and reproductive tracts empty

coelentrates a group of invertebrate animals which includes jellyfish, sea anemones, and similar creatures

constrictor a snake which kills its prey by enveloping it within the muscular constricting coils of its body

crepuscular active during the hours of twilight

cretaceous (lower) a geological period characterized by chalk and coal deposits

crustaceans a group of invertebrates which includes shrimp, lobsters, crabs, and water fleas

cryotherapy therapeutic use of cold temperatures

cryptic (coloration) patterns and colors which obscure, rendering an animal difficult to detect in its natural habitat

cyanomorph a color phase (morph) in which the dominant color is blue

deciduous a shedding (as of antlers), falling off (as leaves) or falling out (as of teeth) at a given season or age

dichromatism (sexual) an obvious color difference between sexes of the same species

dimorphic morphological differences between members of the same species, e.g., color or pattern phases

disruptive (coloration) colors which disrupt or confuse bodily outline or shape; camouflage

diurnal active during the daytime

dorsal pertaining to the back or upper surface

dorso-lateral the upper sides

ecdysis shedding of skin, specifically shedding the outer epidermal layer or cuticle

Glossary (continued)

ectoparasite   external parasites such as mites and fleas

ectothermic   animals that cannot maintain an internal (body) temperature independent of external temperatures

endemic   confined (indigenous) to a given area or region

endoparasites   internal parasites, such as protozoans or worms

erythritic (erythristic)   a color phase in which the dominant color is red

evolution (parallel or convergent)   the phenomenon of two unrelated species confined to two distinct geographical locations developing similar or identical morphological characteristics and habits as a result of exploiting similar or identical habitats

family   a group of related animals ranked above a genus and below an order

fasciotomy (muscle)   removal of muscle fascia (connective tissue)

fauna   all animal life of a region, period, habitat, or environment, e.g., desert fauna, woodland fauna, etc.

fossorial   adapted for digging or burrowing

friable   easily crumbled or pulverized

genus (genera)   a group of phylogenetically related animals which may be divided into a number of subordinate species

gestation   the period of time that young develop within the body of the female prior to birth

gular (skin)   pertaining to the throat

haemotoxin   a toxin specifically affecting the blood

husbandry   the care and management of captive animals or plants both wild and/or domestic

hyaluronidase   an enzyme present in virtually all reptile venoms that acts by dissolving the gel present about normal cells, resulting in a more rapid absorption of the venom toxins

hypapophyses   spine-like projections of the vertebra

imbricate (scales)   to overlap, as overlapping roof tiles

interstitial (skin)   between the scales

keeled   ridged

labial   pertaining to the lips or area of the lips

lateral   side

leucistic   absence of all color (white)

mandible   lower jaw

maxilla   upper jaw

maxillary   pertaining to the upper jaw

nares   nostrils

neonates   the newborn

neo-tropical   tropical areas of the New World; e.g. the Americas

neurotoxin   a toxin specifically affecting the nervous system

new world   North, Central and South America

nocturnal   active at night

nomenclature   A system of names used in a specific branch of knowledge, e.g. zoology, botany, etc.

nominate (race)   the first defined of a species upon which subspecies, if any, are based

ocellus (ocelli)   circular or eye-like markings

old world   the eastern hemisphere, e.g., Europe, Asia, and Africa

ontogenetic   pertaining to the life history and/or development of an organism

Glossary (continued)

ophidian   a snake, or relating to a snake

ophiophagous   snake-eating

opistoglyphous   the presence of grooved venom-conducting (usually enlarged) teeth at the rear of the maxilla

oviparous   egg laying

ovoviviparous   specifically the retention of unshelled eggs within the body of the female until "hatching," e.g., live-bearing; the term is often replaced by viviparous, which implies the presence of a rudimentary placenta in reptiles

parthenogenetic   reproduction without males

pelagic   pertaining to the ocean or open seas

permian (upper)   the last period of the Paleozoic, characterized by glaciation over much of the southern hemisphere

photo-period   hours or change of hours of light and dark (day and night) to which an animal is exposed (lengthening of the diurnal photo period often plays a role in the reproduction of many animals)

piscivorous   fish-eating

posterior   at or toward the rear or the end

postocular   behind the eye

prehensile   adapted for grasping

prey species specific   exclusive utilization of a specific prey species, e.g. stenophagy

procryptic   camouflaging colors and/or patterns

proteroglyphous   the presence of fixed, non-erectile venom conducting teeth (fangs) in the front of the mouth

pupae (insects)   the quiescent stage between larva and adult forms

rear-fanged   enlarged grooved venom conducting teeth located at the rear of the upper jaw (maxilla)

relict   isolated, left behind, a survivor

rhomb   diamond shaped

rostral (shield)   tip of the snout; the scale found on the tip of the snout

rugose   wrinkled

scutes   an external bony or horny plate

solenoglyphous   the presence of movable (erectile) venom conducting, hollow teeth (fangs) at the front of the mouth

subdermal   below or beneath the skin

sublingual   below or beneath the tongue

subocular   below the eye

subspecies   a variety or sub-division of a species

substrate   the surface on which an organism lives and functions

supralabial   one of several scales on the upper lip

supraocular   scale(s) above the eye

supraorbital   above the eyes, e.g., a "supraorbital ridge"

stridulating   a shrill noise or chirp, such as sounds produced by crickets, cicadas, and similar insects

sympatric   two or more populations occupying an identical geographical range or territory

synonomy (synonomous)   the correct and incorrect technical names which have collectively been used by various systematists to designate a given species

taxonomy   the science of the classification of animals and plants according to their natural relationships

thermoreceptor   a device or organ sensitive to heat or fluctuations in temperature

triads   the grouping of color bands on certain species of snakes, e.g., Coral snakes

trinomial   referring to a three-part technical name, e.g., genus, species, and subspecies

triassic   the earliest period of the Mesozoic era, characterized by reddish sandstone rock

tubercles   a small, knob-like prominence or nodule

vectors (of parasites)   organisms capable of transmitting parasites or disease-causing organisms

vent   the anal opening

venter   refers to the lower (under) surface of the body

ventral   the lower (under) surface of the body

vestigial   an imperfectly developed or degenerate part or organ more highly developed in previous generations

xanthic   a color morph in which the dominant color is yellow

Metric Conversion Chart		
Unit	Equivalent in Other Units of Same System	Metric Equivalent
Foot	12 inches, 0.333 yards	30.480 centimetres
Inch	0.083 feet, 0.027 yards	2.540 centimetres

ABOUT THE AUTHOR

An eminent zoologist and herpetologist, John M. Mehrtens was the curator of reptiles at the zoological park in Fort Worth, Texas, as well as those in Cleveland and Columbus, Ohio. He brings to this study over twenty-five years of progressive experience in zoologically oriented environments.

As a result of positions that range from departmental curator to executive director, including curator of exhibits, general curator, associate director and professional consultant in the areas of design, husbandry, funding programs, management and administration, his knowledge and know-how span virtually every aspect of the field.

Responsible for the re-design of the highly acclaimed reptile department at the Fort Worth Zoo, he established all its husbandry techniques, training programs and interpretive graphics systems. As Executive Director, he conceived and brought to successful operation a major new zoological park in Columbia, South Carolina.

He has done extensive field work in the United States, Mexico and Central America and was the leader of a collecting expedition to Central America for the Forth Worth Zoo. He has instituted several regional herpetological societies and written numerous technical papers, as well as popular articles and books.

Currently a zoological park animal broker and consultant, he lives in Miami, Florida.

TECHNICAL NAME INDEX
(Arranged by Genera)
Page number in italics refers to photograph.

A

ACALYPTOPHIS
  peroni, 292
ACANTHOPHIS
  antarcticus antarcticus, 246, 275, *275*, 276
  antarcticus laevis, 276
  pyrrhus, 276
ACANTOPHIS
  dumerili, 22, *23*
  madagascariensis, 22, *23*, 23
ACROCHORDUS
  granulatus, 79, *79*
  javanicus, 78, *78*, 79
AFRONATRIX
  anoscopus, 154
AGKISTRODON
  bilineatus bilineatus, 347, *347*, 348, *348*
  bilineatus russeolus, 347
  bilineatus taylori, 347, *348*
  blomhoffi blomhoffi, 349, *349*, 350, *350*
  blomhoffi brevicaudus, 349
  blomhoffi dubitatus, 349
  blomhoffi siniticus, 349
  blomhoffi ussuriensis, 349, *350*
  contortrix contortrix, 352, *352*
  contortrix laticinctus, 353
  contortrix mokasen, 351, *351*, 352, *352*, 353
  contortrix phaeogaster, 353, *353*
  contortrix pictigaster, 353, *353*
  intermedius intermedius, 354
  intermedius caucasicus, 354
  intermedius saxatilis, 354, *354*
  intermedius stejnegeri, 354
  piscivorous piscivorous, 355, *355*, 356,
    356, 357
  piscivorous conanti, 356, *356*, *357*
  piscivorous leucostoma, 356
AHAETULLA
  prasinus, 210, *210*

AIPYSURUS
  duboisi, 287, *287*, *288*
  eydouxi, 287, *289*
  laevis, 287, *288*
ALSOPHIS
  vudii picticeps, 211, *211*
ANILIUS
  scytale scytale, 13, *13*
  scytale phelpsorum, 13
ANOMOCHILUS sp., 14
APARALLACTUS, 242
ARIZONA
  elegans elegans, 113
  elegans arenicola, 113, *113*
  elegans noctivaga, 113
  elegans occidentalis, 113
ASPIDELAPS
  lubricus lubricus, 258, *258*
  lubricus cowlesi, 259
  lubricus infuscatus, 259, *259*
  scutatus scutatus, 259
  scutatus fulafulus, 259
  scutatus intermedius, 259
ASPIDITES
  melanocephalus, 65, *65*
  ramseyi, 65
ASTROTIA
  stokesi, 290, *290*
ATHERIS
  ceratophorus, 303
  chloroechis, 303
  desaixi, 305, *305*
  hindii, 303
  hispidus, 301, *301*, *302*
  nitschei nitschei, 303
  nitschei rungweensis, 303
  squamiger, 303-305, *303*, *304*, *305*
  superciliaris, 303
AZEMIOPS
  feae, 298, 299, *299*, 300, *300*

B

BITIS
arietans arietans, 306, *306,* 307, *307,* 325
arietans somalica, 306
atropos atropos, 308, *308,* 311
atropos unicolor, 308
caudalis, 309, *309, 310*
cornuta cornuta, 311, *311*
cornuta inornata, 311
gabonica gabonica, 242, 312, *312,* 313
gabonica rhinoceros, *297,* 312, *312, 313*
nasicornis, 313, 314, *314,* 315, *315*
peringueyi, 309, 316, *316, 317,* 318
xeropaga, 318, *318*
BOA
constrictor constrictor, *20,* 21
constrictor amarali, 18
constrictor imperator, 18, 20
constrictor melanogaster, 18, 19
constrictor mexicana, 18
constrictor nebulosa, 18, 20, *20*
constrictor occidentalis, 18
constrictor orophias, 18
constrictor ortonii, 18, 19, *19,* 20
constrictor sabogae, 18
constrictor sigma, 18
BOIGA
cyanea, 214, *214*
dendrophila dendrophila, 209, 212
dendrophila annectans, 212
dendrophila gemmicincta, 212
dendrophila divergens, 212
dendrophila latifasciata, 212
dendrophila melanota, 212, *212,* 213, *213*
dendrophila multicincta, 212
irregularis, 213
trigonata, 214, *214*
BOLYERIA
multicarinata, 29
BOTHRIECHIS (BOTHROPS)
aurifer, 378, *378*
bicolor, 378, *378*
lateralis, 376, *376,* 378
marchi, *345,* 377, *377,* 378

BOTHRIECHIS [BOTHROPS] *(Continued)*
nigroviridis, 377
schlegeli, *375, 379, 379, 380*
supraciliaris, 379
BOTHROPS
andianus andianus, 383, 384
andianus asper, 383, *383,* 384
atrox, 346, 383
alternatus, 384, 385, *385*
BOULENGERINA
annulata annulata, 246, 260
annulata stormsi, 260, *260*
christyi, 260
BUNGARUS
caeruleus caeruleus, 266
caeruleus sindanus, 266, *266*
fasciata, 246, 267, *267*
multicinctus multicinctus, 268, *268*
multicinctus wanghoatingi, 268

C

CALABARIA
reinhardtii, 56, *56*
CALLOSELASMA
rhodostoma, 358, *358,* 360
CANDOIA
aspera, 41
bibroni, 40, *41*
(b. australis), 41
carinata, 40, *40*
(c. paulsoni), 40
CARPHOPHIS
amoenus amoenus, 174, *174*
amoenus helenae, 174
amoenus vermis, 174
CASAREA
dussumieri, 29
CAUSUS
bilineatus, 320
defilippii, 320, *320*
lichtensteini, 320
maculatus, 320
resimus, 320, *320*
rhombeatus, 319, *319,* 320

Index of Technical Names (continued)

D

E

Index of Technical Names (continued)

Index of Technical Names (continued)

Index of Technical Names (continued)

Index of Technical Names (continued)

COMMON NAME & SUBJECT INDEX
Page number in italics refers to photograph.

B

Common Name & Subject Index (continued)

Common Name & Subject Index (continued)

C

Common Name & Subject Index (continued)

Common Name & Subject Index (continued)

Common Name & Subject Index (continued)

Common Name & Subject Index (continued)

M

N

Common Name & Subject Index (continued)

Common Name & Subject Index (continued)

Q

R

Racers, 133–151
RACER, BIMINI, Alsophis vudii picticeps, 211, *211*
  BLACK, Coluber constrictor constrictor, 135
  BLACK-MASKED, Coluber constrictor etheridgei, 136
  BLUE, Coluber constrictor foxi, 136, *136*
  BUTTERMILK, Coluber constrictor anthicus, 136
  COPPER-HEADED, Elaphe radiata, 104, *104*
    (*See also:* RADIATED RATSNAKE)
  FOREST, Drymoluber dichrous, 150, *150*
    BRAZILIAN, Drymoluber brazili, 150
  HORSESHOE, Haemorrhois (Coluber) h.
    hippocrepis, 141, *141*
  MEXICAN, Coluber constrictor oaxaca, 135
  RAVERGIER'S, Haemorrhois ravergieri, 133, 142,
    142
  SOUTHERN BLACK, Coluber constrictor priapus,
    135
  SPECKLED, Drymobius m. margaritiferus, 149,
    149
  TURKISH, Haemorrhois ravergieri cernovi, 142
  WEST INDIAN (*See:* BIMINI RACER)
  YELLOW-BELLIED, EASTERN, Coluber constrictor
    flaviventris, 135, *136*
    WESTERN, Coluber c. mormon, 135, *135*
RADIATED RATSNAKE, Elaphe radiata, 104, *104*
Rainbow Boas, 29, 41
RAINBOW BOA, ARGENTINIAN, Epicrates cenchria
    alvarezi, 35, 36, *36*
  BOLIVIAN, Epicrates c. gaigei, 35
  BRAZILIAN, Epicrates c. cenchria, 28, *28*, 29, 35,
    35, 36
  CENTRAL AMERICAN, Epicrates c. maurus, 35
  MARAJO ISLAND, Epicrates c. barbouri, 35
  PARAGUAYAN, Epicrates c. crassus, 35
  RED (*See:* BRAZILIAN RAINBOW BOA)
RAINBOW SNAKE, Farancia erytrogramma
    erytrogramma, 188, *188*
Ratsnakes, 81, 82–105
RATSNAKE, AESCULAPIAN, Elaphe longissima
    longissima, 83, 98, *98*, 99
  AMORGOS ISLAND, Elaphe l. rechingeri, 99
  BAIRD'S, Elaphe obsoleta bairdii, 88, *89*
  BEAUTY, Elaphe taeniurus, 106, *106*
    Elaphe taeniurus friesi, 106
  BLACK, Elaphe obsoleta obsoleta, 86, *86*, 87, *87*
  EVERGLADES, Elaphe obsoleta rossalleni, 90, *91*

RATSNAKE *(Continued)*
  FOUR-LINED, Elaphe quatorlineata, 83
  GRAY, Elaphe obsoleta spiloides, 92, *92*
  GREAT PLAINS, Elaphe guttata emoryi
    (*See:* PRAIRIE RATSNAKE)
  GREEN, Elaphe triaspis intermedia, 95, *95*
    CENTRAL AMERICAN, Elaphe triaspis mutabilis,
      95
    YUCATEC, Elaphe triaspis triaspis, 95
  GULF HAMMOCK, Elaphe obsoleta williamsi, 92,
    92
  ITALIAN, Elaphe longissima romana, 99
  JAPANESE, Elaphe climacophora, 83, 106, *106*
  KEELED, Zaocys dhumnades, 207, *207*
  KEY, Elaphe obsoleta deckerti, 91
  LINDHEIMER'S, Elaphe obsoleta lindheimeri, 88,
    88, 89
  MAHOGANY, Pseutes poecilonotus polylepis, 199,
    199
  MANDARIN, Elaphe mandarina, 106, *106*
  MANGROVE, Gonyosoma sp., 105, *105*
    RED-TAILED, Gonyosoma oxycephala, 105
  MEXICAN, Elaphe flavirufa, 96, *96*
  MOELLENDORFF'S, Elaphe moellendorffi, 101,
    101
  PERSIAN, Elaphe longissima persica, 99
  PRAIRIE, Elaphe guttata emoryi, 85, *85*
  RADIATED, Elaphe radiata, 104, *104*
  RED, Elaphe guttata guttata, *80*, 84, *84*, 85
  ROSY, Elaphe guttata rosacea, *84*, 85
  RUSSIAN, Elaphe schrenckii schrenckii, 100, 102,
    102, 103
    SOUTHERN, Elaphe s. anomala, 102
  TEXAS (*See:* LINDHEIMER'S RATSNAKE)
  TRANS PECOS, Elaphe subocularis, 94, *94*
  TRINKET, Elaphe helena, 106, *106*
  YELLOW, Elaphe obsoleta quadravittata, *82*, 90,
    90, 91
Rattlesnakes, 86, 243, 298, 397–433
RATTLESNAKE, ANGEL DE LA GUARDA RED
    DIAMOND, Crotalus ruber elegans, 421
  ANGEL DE LA GUARDA SPECKLED, Crotalus
    mitchelli angelensis, 415
  ANIMAS RIDGE-NOSED, Crotalus willardi
    obscurus, 429
  ARIZONA BLACK, Crotalus viridis cerberus, 425,
    427
  ARIZONA RIDGE-NOSED, Crotalus willardi
    willardi, 411, 412, 420
  ARUBA, Crotalus unicolor, 424, *424*

Common Name & Subject Index (continued)

Common Name & Subject Index (continued)

T

U

V

Common Name & Subject Index (continued)

Common Name & Subject Index (continued)

X

Y

Z

Grafiche ALMA S.p.A. - Milano   PRINTED IN ITALY